Illustrated **BUYER'S ★ GUIDE**™

HARLEY-DAVIDSON

SINCE 1965

Allan Girdler

MBI Publishing Company

First published in 1998 by MBI Publishing Company, 729 Prospect Avenue, PO Box 1, Osceola, WI 54020-0001 USA

© Allan Girdler, 1998

All rights reserved. With the exception of quoting brief passages for the purpose of review no part of this publication may be reproduced without prior written permission from the Publisher.

The information in this book is true and complete to the best of our knowledge. All recommendations are made without any guarantee on the part of the author or Publisher, who also disclaim any liability incurred in connection with the use of this data or specific details.

We recognize that some words, model names and designations, for example, mentioned herein are the property of the trademark holder. We use them for identification purposes only. This is not an official publication.

MBI Publishing Company books are also available at discounts in bulk quantity for industrial or sales-promotional use. For details write to Special Sales Manager at Motorbooks International Wholesalers & Distributors, 729 Prospect Avenue, PO Box 1, Osceola, WI 54020-0001 USA.

Library of Congress Cataloging-in-Publication Data

Girdler, Allan.
     Illustrated buyer's guide. Harley-Davidson since 1965/ Allan Girdler.
       p. cm. (Illustrated buyers guide series)
     Includes index.
     ISBN 0-7603-0383-5 (pbk. : alk. paper)
     1. Harley-Davidson motorcycle--Purchasing. I. Title.
    TL448.H3G564   1998
    629.227'2--dc21   98-3270
                                           CIP

On the front cover: The Harley-Davidson Road King first appeared in 1994, and it remained as one of the line's flagships ever since. *Jeff Hackett*

On the back cover: The 1983 XR-1000 is one of those collector bikes you'll have to pay top dollar for if you want to bring it home. *Jeff Hackett*

Printed in the United States of America

Contents

Acknowledgments

Luckily for me, every time I write a book I find there are people who know more than I do and are willing to share that knowledge.

On this occasion, special thanks to David Edwards and Robyn Davis at *Cycle World* for letting me ravage the files; to Bill Milburn and Kip Woodring, who know when The Motor Company was right and when they weren't; and to Kal Demitros, who returns my calls despite having earned an office with a view.

Introduction

When I first went to work as a motojournalist I wasted a lot of the company's time and money.

Several times a day, every day, the telephone rang and a reader asked for advice. Should he buy, oh, a Tornado Supersport or would he be better off with a Blitzkrieg Battlestar?

Out came the files and tests. We compared performance times, power ratings, brakes and torque, carrying capacity, trade-in value, and reliability indices. Interesting and valid, all of it, but the calls could take an hour or more, and although I was making the readers happy one at a time, I wasn't doing what I was paid to do, which was make them happy all at once each month. That, I did at home on my own time.

Then one day I realized the callers weren't really asking for advice. They already knew what they wanted, so they called the magazine for endorsement. Permission. Approval. Ratification. All I had to do was deduce what they wanted to hear, and tell them that. Which I did.

Time and money were saved, but I still had an ethical problem because tricking readers wasn't what I was there for either, even in good cause.

So I switched to giving good advice.

You know what you want, I said early on. Get it. Look up all the facts and prepare yourself so you'll know what you're getting into. That we can help with. The other part, the actual choice, is up to you. You know in your heart and gut what you want, so do that.

The problem was solved and the point was made. This is said here and now to make the same point, again. This is a buyer's guide, emphasis on guide. This is not holy writ.

What we've done is collect all the pertinent facts about late-model Harley-Davidsons and their related derivatives, from model year 1957 for Sportsters, 1966 for the Big Twins, on through model year 1998.

The most basic facts came from the factory's own press kits, issued each year and borrowed for this occasion from the files of the magazines to which they were sent. The experienced facts, what the various models did and how well they did it, what worked well and what drew the engineers back to their drawing boards, came from the magazine staffs and from the guys who were there, the service writers, tuners, and dealers, with a huge boost from the owners of the various machines through the years. Some of the data came from public record, as when H-D filed notices of recalls, which also has happened.

Most of the guidance is delivered in the form of how the bike in question actually performed, what is more or less likely to happen next, which electrical connections come loose, how to replace a troublesome generator, and so forth.

Setting the stage here, this pioneer motorcycle isn't the very first Harley-Davidson. That machine was lost decades ago. This one, on display at H-D's Milwaukee headquarters, represents the first version. It's a single cylinder with belt final drive and the clutch, so to speak, is the lever that tightens the belt. There are two major points here. First, note that this is a motorcycle with the engine in the center of the frame and pedals, for starting, added on: Most machines of this era were bicycles with engines added. Second, look at how easy it was to add the second cylinder and make a V-twin simply by filling the space between the first cylinder and the rear frame tube. *Courtesy Harley-Davidson Archives*

The financial advice, in the form of which models are most likely to retain or gain value and which are the turkeys of tomorrow, mirrors the advice given in the stock market: The past doesn't predict the future, but you'd better not ignore it either.

As in the stock market, if you watch it long enough you develop a sense of what's going on, and you can make an educated guess as to what's coming next. Same here.

All of which brings us to the real point, namely that Harley-Davidsons are fun to own and ride.

One of the true contradictions of our sport is that (1) all H-Ds are alike and (2) no two are the same. Every Harley in this book is relatively modern, powered by an air-cooled 45-degree V-twin with overhead valves, two valves per cylinder, and brakes and suspension front and rear. This means every bike in the book can be ridden regularly and maintained at home by an owner of normal mechanical aptitude.

Yet, all this being so, it's hard to imagine four motorcycles more different than, say, a 1958 XLCH, a 1984 FLT, a 1993 Softail, and a Buell Lightning. They are all fun. They are all different. Different people like different kinds of fun, and that means not every Harley fan likes the same Harleys.

This is not always a bad thing. The free market works best when there are buyers and sellers, after all, and the author got two of his three Harleys cheap in large part because at the time of purchase he was the only buyer on the horizon.

Calm, proud, and confident, Walter Davidson, one of the founders and by the record the best and most enthusiast rider in the quartet, poses with his 1908 H-D after winning an endurance run with a better-than-perfect score. You'll see the same spirit on the faces of winning tuners and races in 1998. *Courtesy Harley-Davidson Archives*

There are emotional involvements and issues here, however, and the final and most important part of this introduction is to say that first, every effort has been made to keep prejudice and preference out of the contents, and second, if any is found, ignore it.

As the song says, you can't please everybody so you'd better be sure you please yourself.

Some Moments in Time

Harley-Davidson's history has been described elsewhere, and that's not our subject anyway. But even so, we can't begin to understand modern times unless we have some idea of how we got to where we'll start the discussion in this book.

So, as a reminder, H-D history began in 1903, with the completion of the company's first motorcycle. (The Motor Company, as it's called in-house, wasn't an actual company yet, but never mind that.) Founding partners William Harley and William, Walter, and Arthur Davidson incorporated in 1907 and kept on growing. H-D didn't invent the V-twin; in fact, the company innovated hardly at all. Instead, H-D was known for sound engineering and value for the dollar. There were several hundred motorcycle makers in the United States in the pioneer days, a handful after World War I, and by the end of the Great Depression there were only two brands—Harley and Indian—and Indian wasn't in good shape.

There's a lot to be said for sound engineering and good value.

The history of the Harley-Davidson models that leads directly to our area of interest started in 1936 and 1937. In the first of those model years H-D introduced the Model E, an ohv V-twin displacing 61 cubic inches. The Model E, quickly and affectionately dubbed the Knuckle-

Setting the record straight, yes, these are women, the bike is a Harley V-twin, and the year is 1914. There have been women riding motorcycles for as long as there have been motorcycles, and if you look really close you can see how long some H-D fans have worn their hearts on their blouses. *Courtesy Harley-Davidson Archives*

head, was an up-to-date motorcycle, more so than anything Indian ever built, and it became an instant hit.

In 1937, Harley updated the bread-and-butter 45-cubic-inch side-valve V-twin line, and that series became the W models. (Pause here to note that at this stage of the Motor Company's development some of the letters, *E* and *W*, for instance, stood for the engineering department's I.D. The ohv 61-cubic-inch E engines came after the side-valve 45-cubic-inch D engines, just as the side-valve 45-cubic-inch W engines followed the 74-cubic-inch side-valve V engines. After that, in two senses, the factory used another internal code, with EL and WL being the higher-compression versions of the basic E and W. Mark the margins. This doesn't matter now, but it will later.)

What mattered in 1937 was that the W series joined the Model E in having recirculating oil systems, with an oil tank and a two-stage pump to move oil from tank to engine and back. Earlier Harley engines had a one-way system, like a fuel tank with the oil kept in a tank until it was pumped to the engine and used up.

What matters to us here and now is that first, the Model E grew into the 74-cubic-inch F, and then the iron cylinder head of the Knuckle became the aluminum head nicknamed the Panhead.

Harley-Davidson believed in evolution generations before it adopted the name. The Panhead began as a new top end on the existing Knucklehead's cases and cycle parts. Then it got telescopic forks instead of leading links, and gained the model name Hydra-Glide. (This was the first public use of a name, although in the book this followed the W-series Sport twin of 1919 and the Servi-Car three-wheeler.) With the new engine and front suspension proven, the Hydra-Glide gained foot shift and hand clutch, reversing the earlier controls, and then got rear suspension instead of a rigidly mounted rear wheel and the model name became Duo-Glide.

With the rest of the model brought up to contemporary practice, the lower end was improved and a tuned version offered, designated FLH. This was added to the FL, the *H* being a factory letter usually used to designate some extra feature.

By 1965 the 61 E series was abandoned; the 61 cost as much to make as the 74 but sold for less because it was smaller, thus wasting the factory's time and money. Instead, the factory invested in electric starting for the FL and FLH to keep pace with overseas innovations, and the Big Twin's name became Electra Glide.

In 1966, with the Panhead having done tremendous work as a test bed, all those new parts and systems got another top end. These cylinder heads looked, if you squinted just right, like the business end of a coal shovel, so the new engine was named the Shovelhead and the Big Twin entered the modern era.

The Sportster's Ancestry

Skip back to before World War II , where, as the Great Depression ended, the middle of the Harley line was occupied by the W, WL, WLD (the sports model, *D* for the top-line tune), the WLDR competition model, and the WR, stripped for racing. For the war effort the factory supplied the military with the WLA—*W* for the model, *L* because the engine in street tune (the plain *W* meant low compression, for commercial use), and *A* for army. The WLA had raised suspension for off-road service, reduced power for durability, and the world's biggest oil-bath cleaner so the rings would live through the dust. The Harleys did more errand running than combat duty, but they served with honor.

The Founding Fathers. From left William Davidson, who ran the plant; Walter Davidson, the natural rider and first Motor Company president; Arthur Davidson, the most outgoing of the four, who gravitated to sales manager; and William Harley, the chief engineer and designer. This portrait was taken in the 1920s, by which time Harley-Davidson had passed Indian and become the largest American motorcycle company. *Courtesy Harley-Davidson Archives*

The great-grandfather of the current V2 engine, the Knucklehead, so called because the rockerboxes look like a clenched fist, appeared in 1936 and powered H-D out of the Depression. Like the V2, the Model E Knucklehead was an air-cooled 45-degree V-twin, with one four-lobe camshaft in the gear case below the vee. The early engine's timer, housing the ignition's points and condenser, is the shiny cap to the right of the pushrod covers. The generator mounts on the gear case, to the right below the timer. *Courtesy Harley-Davidson Archives*

The W was a good machine for its day, which came to an end with the war. The guys in Milwaukee knew this. They anticipated the return of peace and prosperity by getting back into the small bike market with a 125-cc two-stroke, and by updating the W's engine and chassis.

This was a major move. The W, like the E and F, was built like a car in that the engine and gearbox both bolted to the frame, but the engine and gearbox were separate structures. The new model had the engine, transmission, clutch, and primary drive all in one assembly, "unit construction" as they said. The new model, carrying the letter *K*, got hand clutch and foot shift (as did the F); but while the big bikes got the gear lever on the left, where Harleys had always shifted (in contrast to the right-side Indian tradition), the Model K had the shifter on the right, where the English rivals did it. And the K had telescopic forks and swingarm rear suspension, again keeping pace with the imports.

Tradition lived on in that while the K was unit construction, it had the W's four one-lobe camshafts at the engine's lower right, in an arc below the valves, and the valves were in the cylinder, not over the piston in the head.

The K was maybe three-quarters new. It looked newer than it was. It was also slow—slower than the smaller ohv bikes from overseas. The factory tried to fix this with a souped-up version, the KK; then a stroker, the 54-cubic-inch KH; and a souped-up stroker, the seldom-seen KHK. The bigger engine was better but not good enough.

So for model year 1957 Harley-Davidson did another major update and came out with the XL, better known then and since as the Sportster.

And the modern era began.

Charting the Stars

Rating systems have been with us since, oh, since Harley met the Davidsons. And the good folks who bring out these buyer's guides have been using one through five stars for nearly as long. This is because the system is fair and it works (that is, it's clear that five stars are better than one).

The implications come because although all the models in this book are the same brand and they all are V-twins and were all produced during the modern era, the 1958 XLR and the 1998 Road King are surely at opposite corners of the envelope—and it's a big envelope.

Further, this guide is supposed to help the enthusiast in the market for a new Harley or maybe one from the previous model year and to provide background and tips for the restorer, who will run the engine only at shows. (And maybe not even then. More than a few restorations would be more accurately described as full-sized models.) There are people in the market for a Harley to ride to work and school and to the other coast, and still another corner is occupied by vintage racers.

All Harley-Davidsons are the same, no two Harleys are alike, and the same can be said for the buyers/owners/riders/collectors.

Adding what threatens to become a fifth dimension, nostalgia is a whole heap better than it used to be. I could buy my first Harley, a 74, for $75 when I was 17 and the bike was 20, because back then an old motorcycle was an outmoded piece of transportation. Against that, several years ago a whole bunch of trusting souls bought $20,000 Ferraris for $100,000 only to see the price drop to $40,000 before their custom license plates arrived.

Some of the bikes in this book have been good investments in the recent past. Some of them, and maybe not the same some, may be good investments in the future. But don't . . . stop. We can't say don't bet on it because that's exactly what we do when we decide an old motorcycle (or any tangible object) will be worth more when we sell than when we bought.

The result of all this jumbling and factoring is that each model will be evaluated first as a motorcycle: How well does it do what it was built to do? As a subclause, what's the expected popularity of that function? Of, say, riding to Daytona or racing there?

Next factor, the intangible merits. For some, certain Harley models are instant objects of affection, while for others they're merely machines to get someplace on. It's as easy to explain as the reasons why someone's smile makes your heart beat faster. What people want matters at least as much as what they do, eh?

Nonetheless, there are predictable trends. Experts in this field have pointed out that the objects of desire change right along with the age and circumstances of those who desire said objects. (An easy way to explain this is to say people buy what they couldn't have when they were younger.) The secondhand machines of now will be treasures tomorrow.

Thus (finally) the rating system, the stars. Five stars are the tip of the top, the best bet. One star is to tip you off to a model to stay away from. And the twos, threes, and fours are what you'd infer: all based on merit, perceived value, and an educated guess as to when and where this market peaks.

Which it will, and that's the surest bet of all.

Because of all this, the circle has been joined. From here on out it's figures and facts, technical history and trends, everything to be known about the modern Harley-Davidson.

All you have to do is find the one you want.

Chapter 1

1957–85 Sportsters

No motorcycle company is an island, the poet might have said, so it's natural that a motorcycle model, like any product or even any idea, fits within its time.

In 1954, when Harley-Davidson was competing against the imports by making an obsolete engine larger, the car companies learned a lesson that helped them for the next 20 years. In 1954 Plymouth came out with a car people said they wanted. It was small on the outside, big on the inside, and it was low in power so it could be low on maintenance and long in life.

Plymouth lost third place in sales to Buick, whose cars were big and flashy. Chrysler Corporation noticed. The thinkers there decided the public didn't exactly lie. What they did (and do) was tell pollsters what they think they should say.

So in 1957 the Plymouth was big, had a V-8 engine, and set the world's record for tailfins. In that same year the Ford was new, ugly, and big, and the Chevrolet was old, lovely, and small. At the end of the model year Ford had beaten Chevy for the first time in a generation, and Plymouth was safely back in third place. New beats old, big beats small, and by so much that good looks don't overcome ugly.

So?

So in 1957 Harley-Davidson introduced a new middleweight. It was, oh, call it seven-eighths modern. In typical H-D fashion it was newer than it looked, and in keeping with the times, the overall design was based on the notion that if bigger wasn't always better, bigger at least sold better.

Shorthand says the new machine, happily named the Sportster and coded XL, was a KH with overhead valves.

Not exactly true. The overall design was the same, with unit construction, chain primary on the left, four one-lobe cams on the right, four speeds with foot shift on the right, drum brakes fore and aft, swingarm rear suspension with coil-over shocks, telescopic forks in front, and, of course, the 45-degree V-twin with fork-and-blade connecting rods.

But the Sportster didn't simply boast overhead valves. It also used a larger bore and shorter stroke to get the (approximately) same displacement, usually rounded off to 54 cubic inches, or 883, and later 900 cc.

The only feature that was not modern, explaining the part about seven-eighths, was that the cylinders and heads were cast iron. There's nothing wrong with the material itself. Cars would use iron for years after this, still do, in fact; but the imports went to lighter and cooler-running aluminum by that time, and the big Harleys, the Panhead 74s, had used alloy heads since 1948.

There's never been an official reason for sticking with cast iron, but the best guesses are first: The early Panheads gave trouble and the factory had had enough of that with the K and KH, and second, iron was cheaper and easier to work with.

Another odd historical note is that the Sportster arrived with two letters, X and L, while every other Harley began with just one, E, K, W, or J. Not only that, but X had been used a few years earlier, for a shaft-drive opposed twin built as a military project. The Motor Company had done the U, V, W, and X. So when the Sportster arrived at the drawing board, why wasn't it the Y?

Because it wasn't, is all. More important to us now, just as General Motors believed all car buyers wanted a Cadillac and made the Buicks and Oldsmobiles as much like Caddys as money allowed, so did Harley's managers assume that imports or not, two-stroke singles or not, what the motorcycling public really wanted was an FLH.

Thus, that first Sportster, introduced for the 1957 model year, was very like a miniature FL. There was an elaborate mounting and shrouding for the headlight and the triple clamps, the fuel tank was large, having a 4.4-gallon official capacity. The fenders were long fore and aft and fully valanced, meaning they wrapped around the tires side to side and protected the rider from slush and spray, which is what they're supposed to do.

The factory expected the Sportster to appeal, and it did. It sold well that first year, and there were very few teething problems, which must have been welcomed by the buyers as well as the sellers.

The real success story though comes because, unlike at some of the car companies, Harley's execs knew they didn't know everything. Headquarters relied heavily on the dealers. The annual production, for

The first Sportster, as introduced in 1957, was supposed to be a smaller version of the top-line Big Twin. The large fuel tank and generous fenders offer range and weather protection, the two pipes into one muffler add quiet and efficiency, the seat is sprung even though there's rear suspension, and the headlight mounts on a nacelle, as on the larger machine. The crash bars, now called case guards because the lawyers got nervous, were an option. *Courtesy Harley-Davidson Archives*

The new model was thoroughly modern. A 45-degree V-twin, of course, but the engine and transmission were in unit. For a spotting tip, all the smaller X-series engines have final drive on the right, while the F-series final drive is on the rider's left. The XL frame began as a combination of steel tubing and cast iron forgings and ended just aft of the seat. *Courtesy Harley-Davidson Archives*

instance, was decided by how many bikes the dealers would order and which models.

The dealers liked the XL, which did increase sales and floor traffic. But, they reported, it wasn't enough. There was a whole new sporting crowd, and there was a lot of amateur racing in the woods and across the deserts. The California dealers in particular asked for a lighter and more versatile version. The factory agreed, with the provision that dealers would have to order at least 60 examples.

The California dealers agreed, so for the 1958 model year there was an XLC, the basic Sportster except that it had no lights, horn, or battery. Ignition was magneto, self-contained, and borrowed from the racing-only KR. The XLC's rear fender was cut short, the exhaust pipes were unbaffled, and (the dominant fashion note for the next 30 years) the large and decorous 4.4-gallon tank was replaced with a 2.2-gallon tank, taken from the KR dirt tracker, which got it from the little two-stroke single.

Parallel to the XLC, there was also new tuning. Research during World War II unveiled lots of knowledge into combustion and compression ratios. The side-valve Harleys and the earliest ohv engines had an upper limit of 6:1 or so. Harley engineering has always been conservative, so it's a good bet that the original Sportster engine ran 6:1, and the production version became the XL because it was 7.5:1. (*L* has meant higher compression at H-D since before the company began keeping official records.)

Pump gas had improved along with postwar engines, and the new XL was as sturdy as the designers had hoped, so as soon as that was established, in time for model year 1958, the factory released an upgrade. Compression ratio was raised to 9:1, the valvetrain was lightened, and the valves were bigger. The official literature said power was boosted 12 percent, which is tidy except it never said what the XL's original power rating was: The best rounded-off estimate was 40 brake horsepower for the XL and 45 for the optional version. The option was coded XLH, *H* having stood for The Next Step since Bill-Harley-knew-when.

There were buyers who went the factory's route plus. This buyer got the optional windshield, saddlebags, turn signals, spotlights, rear crash bars, luggage rack, and even a cover for the kick lever's return spring. The dual seat is sprung. The oil tank is below the seat on the right, and the battery is across from it. *Courtesy Harley-Davidson Archives*

Returning to why the motorcycle guys are smarter than the car guys, the California scrambler was even more successful than the original XL. It happened that the looks of the XLC were a match for what owners were already doing, especially on the West Coast. The chopper movement, by the way, was initially based on off-road racing, known as TT for reasons too involved to detail here—check the competition chapter in this section—and the stripper version looked and sounded at least as fast as it was.

H-D took advantage of this, first by offering a lighting kit for the XLC, so it could be registered and ridden on the street, and for 1959 the XLC became a full all-states model, with lights and such ready to be removed. But it still had the peanut tank, shorter fender, straight pipes, and magneto ignition.

Here's where note-taking comes in handy. By 1959 there were four versions of the Sportster: the plain XL, with big tank and all-weather fenders and stuff added to make the small bike look larger; the XLC, the stripper with straight pipes, small tank, solo seat, short fender, and so forth; the XLH, which was the semi-dresser with boosted engine; and the XLCH, the sports bike with tuned engine.

They were all on sale at the same time and places. Beyond that, where notes give way to the catalog, Harley-Davidson was big on options. Again like the car people, H-D's sales and marketing forces had learned that the buyer wants to be special, to have a vehicle built just as he or she wanted it, so there were optional seats, paint schemes, high or low bars, saddlebags, and windshields.

Plus, you could swap back and forth within the four models, with a solo seat for your XLH, a bigger fuel tank for your XLCH. Some of the options were silly; for example, a chrome-plated cover for the return spring on the kick start. But some of the options, such as special paint for a couple of bucks, or unpainted body metal for do-it-yourself painters, were bargains.

The dealers asked for a sports model, for riding and racing in the deserts and woods. The fenders were trimmed and the lights removed and the fuel tank was the peanut tank, 2.2-gallon, as seen on the 125-cc two-stroke and the KR racer. The XLC had the original tune, but for a few dollars more you could have the hotter camshafts and higher compression of the XLCH. *Courtesy Harley-Davidson Archives*

Within this framework, there was constant change. The 1959 XLCH, for instance, came with a single exhaust pipe, mounted high and on the right. This was presumed to be stylish. The imports also had scramblers, what we now call Dual Sport although the term hadn't been invented yet, and some TT racers had the pipes high to give ground clearance landing off jumps. The Harley planners must have thought they'd done the fashionable thing.

They were wrong.

The sporting crowd went to the races, and they saw that the racing Harleys had two pipes, both low on the right. The straight duals marked the machine as a racer as well as making enough noise to infuriate Mom and Dad and the neighbors, always a plus in youthful circles. So the straight dual option was often added to the XLCH that one year, and to the plain XL or XLH, which had two pipes feeding one low and quiet muffler on the right.

The Sportster line saw changes and improvements in every model year. Some of the changes were useful. For instance, the first XLs had 18-inch wheels, while the XLCs had 19-inch wheels. The Motor Company subsequently switched both models to 19 front and 18 rear. And it seemed as if in every model year, the factory said there was a new seal to keep the dry clutch dry inside the oil-bath primary case, but that problem never did go away.

The overall important part here was that Harley-Davidson had provided the mass market with the Superbike.

That's not quite the same as inventing the Superbike, which we can't say H-D did because guys like Glenn Curtiss built V-8-powered motorcycles in 1907, and Vincent Black Shadows were topping 150 miles per hour in the 1950s.

But those were one-offs, so rare that most bike nuts had never seen one. The XLCH was right there in the showroom on Main Street, and the XLCH was lighter than the XLH, so it went faster, and it would dust off any import in town, as well as all the Corvettes and XK-120 Jags.

There was some simplification in that the more mildly tuned models, the XL and XLC, were quietly phased out of production. There was no reason to buy the lower compression version once all regions had good gasoline.

There was also a hint of things to come. In 1965, Harley-Davidson took another giant step into the present and offered electric starting for the Big Twins.

Not a new idea, obviously. In fact, arch rival Indian invented electric start for motorcycles back in 1914, at a time when Harley had just come out with a reliable method of kick-starting, to which they applied the elegant term step-start. But Indian's batteries and charging system weren't as good as the concept, and the electric-start version failed so dismally that all examples were yanked back into the factory and stripped of their innovation. Electric starting was considered both impossible and

For 1959 the XLCH was a full model, with the tuned engine, smaller tank, skimpy fenders, and with the smallest legal headlight riding below the eyebrow bracket. There was no battery to take up space below the seat so the XLCH had the KR's central oil tank. This factory photo was obviously done for what we'd now call virtual action. Interesting that the model wore a cap, no gloves, slacks, and street shoes. Effective helmets were barely invented by 1958, never mind being mandated by law. *Courtesy Harley-Davidson Archives*

We here begin a period of mix and match. The high pipes and single muffler were offered in 1959 only for the XLCH. This restorer has added a pad and pegs for a passenger while chrome-plating everything in sight and keeping the small tank. *Cycle*

The XLCH's high muffler was supposed to proclaim off-road capability, but the average buyer swapped for louder duals. Now the high pipe is more valuable. The CH's tires were semi-knob, another sign of off-road activity, and the authentic tires are now nearly priceless. *Courtesy Harley-Davidson Archives*

unwanted until the Japanese, who hadn't been making motorcycles in 1914 and therefore didn't know it wouldn't work, made it work. And Harley and the rest of the world dutifully followed. Sort of.

When the FL line got the electric starter, it required bigger and better batteries and that meant 12 volts instead of 6. Following suit, the XL line got 12 volts, and better lights, for 1965.

The next step came in 1966, when the XL line got a new carburetor and the now-classic hamcan air cleaner. The new carb was radical and didn't have a float bowl. Instead, there was a diaphragm control that was supposed to allow just enough fuel to go from tank to inlet tract. There were early problems, followed by dealer bulletins and owner instructions, with the result being that the XLCH earned a reputation for being hard to start.

Then came a divergence. For 1968, the engine cases were revised to allow an electric starter to be bolted to the primary wall behind the rear cylinder. The touring-oriented XLH got electric start. The more sporting XLCH got the revised cases but without the electric starter.

The XLH used points and coil ignition, which makes maximum power at low speeds, while the XLCH had the magneto, which is weak at low rpm and stronger as it revs, which is why it's so good for racing. And the XLCH by this time came with three-quarters of the PB cams done originally for the XLR: The rear exhaust cam had milder timing, so it could give more compression and thus aid starting at kicking speed.

Kick starting is either an art . . . or a curse.

There are few acts in motorcycling more satisfying than being one of the kickers in the crowd, sneering at the push-button wimps, leaping into the air, and having your beast roar into life.

There are few humiliations more, well, humiliating than doing that leap and getting . . . silence. Kick after kick, while the other guys shut their engines off and stand around and give you tips their fathers gave them, secretly pleased all the while that it is you, not them.

This is dwelt on here for several reasons. One, it's valid history. The guys who owned CHs 30 years ago say, "Oh no, starting was easy for me, you just gotta know how."

Tell that to the owner who's kicking his in present time, and you'll get a look that says it's lucky for you he's too tired to teach you the lesson such flippancy deserves.

What this means now is that owning an XLCH can require at least one skill—how to start it—that the owner of a contemporary motorcycle not only doesn't need but may not have even heard of. The XLCH owner learns other skills; for instance, knowing which bolts you can take off without ruining the bike (said skill being acquired because sometimes the most essential bolts simply fall off). Did I mention that XLs vibrate?

What the above also means now is that the owner of an XLCH gets instant respect in any motorcycling crowd worth nodding to. If you don't know what you're about, you couldn't have ridden there on an XLCH.

The 1966 through 1969 XLs were the most different of those in the XLH versus XLCH era. They got a lot closer together in 1970, first because the XLCH lost its magneto. The XLH-style timer by then had automatic spark advance and retard, while the magneto needed operator assistance, as noted. A magazine test of the 1970 XLCH said it was easier to start, and the automatic timing must have been why.

The 1970 models also included an odd option, a fiberglass seat/fender that was called, with logic, a boat-tail. This was a worldwide quirk. Fiberglass was billed as the material of the future and various makers, Ossa in Spain for instance and Norton in England, did much the same thing to their bikes. In our case, H-D acquired a fiberglass factory that made golf carts, and it must have seen the boat-tail as some sort of easy way to make something different.

Not many people ordered the option, and yet the company kept it in the catalog for 1971. (Even more of a surprise, the bodywork was a central part of the new-for-1971 Superglide, of which much more information will be given in a subsequent chapter.)

Big news for 1971 was that the shared ignition was moved into the gear case cover, with the points and advance/retard shielded from the weather.

Equally major was that the original XL clutch, which began life with the 1952 Model K, was replaced. This is a good news/bad news item, in that the original clutch ran dry plates and needed less spring pressure and less hand pressure to hold the engine and gearbox together. The new clutch was wet, running in the gearbox/primary case's lube supply. Since gear lube was, and is, slippery, the clutch springs were stiffer and working them took more muscle. That's the bad news. But the dry clutch used to get wet and stick, and 20 years of re-engineering didn't cure the problem, so they solved it the practical way.

What matters most here was that the world had changed. When the XLCH arrived, it was the baddest bike on the market. Then the English went from 500s to 650s to 750 twins, and then came the Triumph-BSA triples in 1968 and the Honda 750 Four in 1969.

The XLCH wasn't slow, as we'll see, but it wasn't the fastest, either, and it no longer made a lot of sense to offer a stripped and Spartan sports model if it didn't offer performance to make up for the lack of amenities.

Flag aside, just about every shiny object on this early XLCH was an option. Check out the light-colored extension below the passenger peg. That's a ride-off centerstand, useful for tire changing and chain lubing. The factory has never supplied such stands standard, but the accessory people offered one that bolted to the frame's lower rear forging, the fabled twin tomahawks. *Cycle*

This early XLH, identified by the big tank, the timer, and the headlight housing, has been treated to a set of staggered dual pipes and a dual seat with grab rail. *Cycle*

Thus the XLCH got electric start and all the options—the big and little tanks, the boat-tail bodywork, the various exhaust systems, two pipes feeding one muffler, one muffler for each cylinder, and even pipes banned in several cities and states.

Making things even more confusing, sales during this period were not only strong, but the CH outsold the plain H even when there wasn't much difference between them, which must mean that the buyers liked the badge.

The Mechanics

What the buyers of 1957 to 1971 Sportsters actually got is difficult to measure.

For one thing honest reporting didn't arrive in motorcycling in the United States until Joe Parkhurst introduced *Cycle World* in 1962. Until then the reports weren't exactly dishonest, but it was more like the magazine guys borrowed bikes from their pals at the factories, and since they didn't have scales or clocks, they rode them hard, put them away wet, and didn't always return them, and if they ever met a motorcycle they didn't like, they were too polite to say so.

Then, even when *Cycle World* and *Cycle* (under Ziff-Davis ownership) did perform impartial tests, the standards were different. For instance, *Cycle World* would weigh test bikes with half a tank of fuel because you can't ride a motorcycle with the tank truly full or truly

This is a 1966 XLCH, a high point for the model. It's kick start only, which allows a more compact oil tank and battery and less weight. It's also got the now-classic hamcan air cleaner denoting the floatless Tillotson carburetor, the loud dual pipes, the peanut tank, and the short dual seat. It was the fastest bike on the market, as the triples and fours weren't here yet. *Courtesy Harley-Davidson Archives*

empty, while *Cycle* would top the tanks because the weight of the fuel has to have an effect on the performance. It's a question with two different and correct answers.

The prime puzzle, though, is that even when we have some scientific applications, what we got with testing and measuring Sportsters didn't always match what should have been. Even so, just as we have elections mostly to see if the polls were accurate, so can we also look back and note what the facts on the 883 Sportsters seem to have been.

The first 1957 XL unquestionably had a bore and stroke of 3.0 x 3.8 inches. Compression ratio was 7.5:1, estimated power was 40 brake horsepower, wheelbase was 57 inches, and the factory listed a shipping weight of 495 pounds. Pre-Ziff Cycle reported a miles-per-gallon rating of 57, top speed of 101.4 miles per hour, and a standing quarter mile took 15.03 seconds. There were honest clocks at California's dry lakes, and they seem to have been used here.

The XLCH must have been lighter and faster simply because a motorcycle with no lights, battery, or muffler and a chopped fender must weigh less than one with electrics and a long fender. In 1960 there was a published test of an XLCH, and it was reported to weigh 492 pounds with road equipment and a full tank, while removing the road gear stripped away 27 pounds. The factory clearly made its shipping weight as light as it could possibly get away with. Ridden by an experienced hand, the XLCH turned the quarter mile in 14.17 seconds, which was a good time but wasn't quite as quick as the tuned exhaust and pared-down configuration would have predicted.

A 1965 XLH test listed a quarter-mile time of 15.5 seconds, clearly a lot slower. The tested model had a smaller fuel tank, 3.8 gallons versus 4.4 for the first version; but it also had two mufflers instead of one. Claimed power was 55 brake horsepower in 1965, by the way, presumably because the hotter cams were part of the H tuning combination by then.

The confusion begins about 1968, when *Cycle World* tested an XLH. The electric start was supposed to add 40 pounds, which seems like a lot for a larger battery and the actual starter, but the wet test weight was 510 pounds, only 18 pounds more than the earlier XLCH. The 1968 example did the quarter mile in 13.86 seconds, the best so far.

Hey! Just thought of something. First, the magazine guys were getting better at testing and riding; *Cycle*'s Cook Neilson won national drag, salt flat, and road race competitions, for instance. And there was competition between the magazines. It could be that the better times were from better riders trying harder.

Then again, *Cycle World*'s boat-tail XLCH, with a small tank and kick start, weighed 495 pounds with tanks topped. Probably the safest assumption here is that the electric leg added 15 pounds, and that some odd quirk let all the early XLs weigh just about 500 pounds no matter what. They also ran the quarter in less than 14 seconds if the rider showed no mercy.

What to Look For

Major caution here has to be that all the models in this section are 40-something to 25-something years old. The XLs were bought to be used. That is, there weren't many buyers who took the machine home for a daily polish and weekly cruise to the sports bar, unlike some of the larger Harleys we'll meet later.

Sportsters were the sports model, meaning they were ridden hard, and the engine was what racers began with at the drags of the dry lakes. (Fastest ever was an 89-cubic-inch-displacement XL-based, nitromethane-burning grenade the factory built for Dennis Manning's streamliner. Team star Calvin Rayborn rode it 265.492 miles per hour at Bonneville, after

The XLCH was able to retain the compact KR-style oil tank until all the XLs got the cases to mount the electric starter. The beetle-shaped object between the cylinders is the horn. The tractor-style seat was replaced with this short semi-dual perch.
Courtesy Harley-Davidson Archives

The magnifying glass tells us the stamping below the horn is 68XLH 4879, that is, a 1968 XHL. Electric start has dictated new cases, with the starter mounted atop the primary drive. Not as neat or light as it was and the battery fills its place. The peanut tank, meanwhile, has become what everybody orders. *Cycle*

rolling it 35 times as he learned how to control the thing.)

Throw in the availability of all the optional tanks, seats, pipes, and so forth, and it's impossible not to believe the owner when he says his dad bought the bike just like it is now. It could have been.

Even so, the starting point is engine identification. The factory used an easy system back then. There's a flat spot cast into the left case half at the peak between the barrels. Stamped on the plate will be, to make one up, 59XLH0123. That means—pause here for "duh"—that the engine was made for the 1959 model year, and it was for the plain H, as in timer and mufflers and so on.

Frames weren't numbered then, but all the early frames used cast-iron forgings at the steering head, the seat and rear shock mount, and the rear engine and swing arm mount. There are detail differences, for which you'll need a factory parts book or a really good shop manual. Even so, most of the time the frames are so much alike from year to year that it won't matter if the engine is a 1959 and the frame was made in 1961.

Next, damage. The XL engine is very strong. It's also been subjected to enough stress to break it, which in a way is what racing is all about. So look very carefully at every surface, nook, and cranny. If there are scars, as in a bead of welding across the side of the case or perhaps a half-moon of weld at the lower rear of the primary, that's where the engine let go and somebody patched it up. It can be fixed better than new so it's not a reason to turn the bike down, but it's something you should know when you make your bid.

The XL1000 was a major change. The 2-into-1 exhaust mimicked road racing not TT, the ignition was moved to inside the gear case (witness the little cover aft of the second exhaust pipe), and there's a front disc brake. The bike still had the now-classic peanut tank, though, with a stepped dual seat. *Cycle World*

The weakest point on the iron-top XLs was the rear engine mount. Why, nobody knows, but the factory made the mount thin where it should be thick, and vice versa. Given time, the mount will crack, period. Not only that, the thick section means you can't replace the stock mount without splitting the cases. This was so from the first, and the factory didn't fix it for 30 years.

But you can fix it. An outfit named Pingel, dealing mostly in drag racing equipment, makes a rear mount that's thick and thin in the correct locations and proportions. Unbreakable. Not only that, but the mount will slip onto the assembled cases. All you have to do is chop the cracked, stock mount into sections with a hacksaw or grinder and throw away the sections.

An oddity with these engines involves the oiling system. It's a dry sump system with a two-stage pump, and an oil tank behind the engine and under the seat. There's a pair of gears that pushes the oil from tank to engine, and a larger pair that moves the oil from the sump (the bottom of the cases) back to the tank.

The return half has more capacity than the feed half because the engine needs only a couple of ounces of oil at a time. The rest should be in the tank cooling off. And if this doesn't happen, if the engine fills with oil, it will barely run while puking oil from more orifices than the engine is supposed to have.

The tank is above the pump and sump. Gravity is defeated, in theory, by a ball and check valve, so the sump is kept dry while the engine is at rest.

If this doesn't work, which happens, the sump will fill with oil, and when the engine is fired up, the oil spews from the breather. Not much, as a rule, and it's more mess than disaster, but it's also not what one wants on the shop floor or the driveway.

When an engine has this problem, the canny, would-be former owner takes it out early and starts it for a couple of minutes before the would-be buyer shows up, so the surplus has been pumped into the tank.

Not to say this is a big problem, because it's not. Nor is it dishonest, but if you arrive for the test run and the engine's warm to the touch you at least have a clue.

Beyond that all the normal rules of secondhand purchasing apply. The engine shouldn't make odd or extra noise, nor should it smoke, leak, and so forth. In the case of the really old examples, Harleys or anything else, do take care to examine the title. Because these machines are subject to theft, the states have become prudent to the point of intrusion and there are times it's tough to clear the title.

Interesting. In 1970 this fiberglass boat-tail seat and rear fender with integrated taillight, was an option for the Sportster. Not many people ordered the unit, which sort of dwarfs the tank and engine, but we'll see it again. The exhaust system here is over-and-under style duals. *Courtesy Harley-Davidson Archives*

Swaps and Options

What about the options? There were two major variations: the choice of exhaust systems during the first several years and the fiberglass tail section offered in 1970 and 1971.

The only exhaust system with any special value is the high pipe, the TT-style offered with the first XLCH. As mentioned, this was not as popular as the factory expected it to be, and most of the buyers either opted immediately for the low separate pipes, as seen on the KR and XLR racers, or they added them later. Either way, the high pipe was seldom seen; many people now don't know there was such a thing.

What this means at present is value. A stock high pipe in good condition is worth collecting, and even one that's been banged and rusted can be restored. Don't pay any price asked, but if one turns up at a garage sale, get it. (Collector's note: Those who are truly committed, or should be, don't care about money. What moves them is parts they don't have. Thus, anytime you can scoop up a rare part, you get yourself a bargaining chip. Often the only way you can get the part you need is to offer the part the other chap needs.)

The same applies to the fiberglass bodywork, except that the boat-back model never attracted much attention or inspired affection. The section could be ordered with either the XLCH or plain XLH engine, tank, pipes, and so forth, so the fiberglass doesn't identify a special version or extra performance or anything. On a bike, the boat-tail has no extra value in itself.

The exception to that rule is that the same bodywork was used in 1971 to identify the original—and trendsetting—Superglide. This is unique in motorcycling annals, the notion that the factory would take something nobody much wanted and use it secondhand for a radical new model, which established a style that is still with us.

Even so, there were those who bought the FX and pitched the paneling for the FL-style seat and fender. There are those who'd like to take a later Superglide and make a full Night Train as that 1971 was called. Don't let that fiberglass get away if you can help it.

What else? Magnetos. They sell new for several hundred dollars. They have a reputation for disservice that's only partially deserved. They work if they're done right, and they can be serviced and rebuilt infinitely. Just as one example, Joe Hunt makes a bearing carrier/points plate out of billet aluminum that sells for less than the dealer gets for the stock, pot-metal carrier. The XLCH-ready magneto has a long shaft with a skew gear. An XLR or KR magneto uses a shorter shaft and a larger, straight-cut drive gear. The short shaft and large gear have been out of production for years. They're worth 10 times their weight in exhaust pipes or fiberglass.

Model	Utility	Saddletime	Collectibility	Style	Accommodations
1958–59 XLC	★★★☆☆	★★★☆☆	★★★★★	★★★★☆	NA (solo seat)
1957–71 XL, XLH	★★★★★	★★★☆☆	★★★★☆	★★★☆☆	★★★★☆
1958–69 XLCH	★★★★★	★★★★☆	★★★★★	★★★★★	★★★☆☆
1970–71 XLCH	★★★☆☆	★★★☆☆	★★★★☆	★★★☆☆	★★★☆☆

About Those Stars

If this treatise has one major sociological revelation—and it does—this is it: Pre- and Post-Evolution models are to Harley-Davidson what the Civil War was to the United States of America.

The underlying force here is simple human nature, in several guises. One, we find it hard not to prefer times when we were there and the other people weren't, which is why everybody had his or her own Golden Age.

Two, we like to find fault.

And finally, there's what the sociologists call the Scarcity Principle: the fact that I like what I've got better if you don't have one.

In the previous generation, the old-line Harley guys mocked the times when American Machine and Foundry had a controlling interest in H-D. The people who felt this way ranted about how this huge conglomerate had swept down and taken over the Motor Company, milked it dry, and did poor work, all for greed.

In historical fact, the founding families did as much damage as the company could survive, while AMF bought H-D away from another group that would have dismantled the parts and sold them off. Not only that, there's some evidence that AMF bought H-D in part because the head of AMF was a motorcycle enthusiast and didn't want the last surviving American motorcycle company to go under.

In any event, AMF spent a lot of money on the plant, if not on the product or the people, while the people put extra value into bikes that had been built before the dreaded AMF took over.

You don't see much of the anti-AMF sentiment currently, because AMF bought the company in 1968, which is a long time to hold a grudge unless you're Serbo-Croatian, Irish, or a neo-Confederate, and because the AMF episode was eclipsed by the Evo engine just after the company was bought out in 1981.

To be fair here, there were some problems with quality control in 1970, at Harley-Davidson and at most of the car companies as well, due mostly to new rules that took the engineers' attention away from important stuff.

To get back to the point, the Evo engine in XL or FL form is an excellent and up-to-date engine. It is better than the earlier engines by any impartial standard.

Which is good, because what we aren't here is impartial.

The improved engine, quality control, new models, and a talented team of executives all combined to make Harley-Davidson Wall Street's darling in the late 1980s, while also setting sales records and making a whole new class of Harley buyers and fans, people who finally dared buy one they wouldn't have to rebuild before riding. (That's an exaggeration, but that was also the climate at the time.)

So. There are lots and lots of Evos.

There won't be anymore Shovels, XL or FL.

This means, according to the Scarcity Principle, that the Shovelhead models gain in value. At the very least, every early XL rates four stars for collectibility. They were made before the sales boom of the very late 1960s and 1970s, and they came prior to AMF's involvement, which has an intangible (and unjustified, in the author's opinion) effect on the value as well.

Beyond that, some of the early and rare XLs are more, um, early and rare. Thus the high marks for the XLC. Only a handful were produced, only in model years 1958 and 1959. The average new Harley fan won't even know what it is, while those who do know will be mightily impressed. The XLC is a thoroughly outmoded dirt bike. Even if it has the lighting kit it will be more demanding than rewarding in regular use, but it's still fun and impressive in its own way.

(Time for another warning. The official record is quoted here. As will be noted elsewhere, the H-D has several times made models the official record leaves out. If—underline if—you turn up an engine stamped 61XLC001 or the equivalent, stay calm. Don't tell the owner there was no such thing. Buy it.)

We're trying to not have fractions and to stay in group, so the early XLH is collectively rated above average for collectibility. If there was a fraction, the first-year XL would get a B+ rather than a B. There's usually perceived value in being the first of anything, and the XL didn't sell all that well at first, so there weren't that many out there.

Even so, at this writing there are enough recovered and restored first-year Sportsters to make it a tough class to win, while as regular riders they're a lot of work for not that much performance.

Oh. Better say here that all this assumes stock, that the XLC doesn't have bags and windshield, and the XLH isn't stripped with a stroker kit.

The early XLCH gets those extra stars because it's got that classic profile: lean, mean, and instantly recognized. In tune—and these engines can have troubles where ordinary engines don't even have parts—an XLCH is still fast and you can still find the parts once you're plugged into the pipeline.

The caution here is that the semi-pros are already hip. There are restorers who complain that they used to scoop up an XLCH and make a profit on it every year, but now they're harder to find.

Which they are. That doesn't mean they aren't out there. You have to look, you have to learn, and you have to be prepared to bid against the crowd.

1972–78 Sportsters

Because the French philosopher was right and life *is* what happens to us while we're making other plans, this period in the life of the Sportster involves, with some entertaining exceptions, mostly catch-up.

While Harley-Davidson was planning high-performance twins, the rest of the motorcycling world came out with triples (Triumph and BSA), fours (750-cc from Honda and then 900-cc from Kawasaki), and even terrifying two-stroke triples (Suzuki and Kawasaki).

What this meant at the time was that the Sportster wasn't the biggest and baddest machine on the block. Not only that, the federal government became involved in design, under the pretext of safety and the environment. AMF was spending tremendous amounts of money on the new plant and equipment while the engineering department had to concentrate on noise and emissions control.

So first, in 1972 Harley-Davidson took the Sportster down the path of least resistance. Bore was increased, from 3.0 inches to 3.188 inches, which, with the same 3.8-inch stroke, raised displacement to rounded-off 61 cid or 1,000 cc. The factory always referred to the model by cubic centimeters; best guess has always been that H-D didn't want people to talk of the 61 because that was the original size and name of the Big Twin, which was now 74 cid.

We aren't talking slouch here. *Cycle World* reported its 1972 XLCH weighed 492 pounds with the peanut (2.2-gallon) tank half full. The test bike turned the quarter mile in 13.38 seconds, proving the model hadn't lost performance to its restrictive mufflers. The magazine crew said the wet clutch was heavier in operation but gripped well, and they had no trouble starting the CH, which by that time meant mostly that it was kick start only. The XLH had electric starting and a kick lever just in case.

The XL1000 was a popular seller, surely to some degree because there was a boom on and the XL sold for less than the FL or FX. The options ran to items like a chopper-style seat that looked cool and felt like a brick. There were some oddities, however. For instance, the electric start models had different oil tanks and batteries, and the XLH's oil tank could be perforated by the drive chain if it wasn't correctly adjusted.

The annual model years had become an occasion for making mechanical changes, as there was no money for anything actually new. The Sportster got disc front brakes in 1973, and in 1974 a return spring was added to the throttle.

No kidding. Up until then, the practice was to remind newcomers that the throttle works both ways, and because you can slow down by rolling off, there was no need for a spring, and anyway, no spring provided cruise control before there was such a term. (This sounds really foolish, now; kind of like hearing that for decades real motorcyclists didn't use the front brake because to do so would put you on your head. Foolish or not, the above is true.)

The federal government's official intervention hit hard in 1975. Back when motorcycles first got gearboxes and gearshifts, Indian's lever was on the right and Harley-Davidson's was on the left. When Harley went to foot shift, the lever remained on the left for the Big Twins, perhaps

because that was the easiest conversion. The little singles, though, had the gear lever on the right, foot operated, a touch borrowed from the German model from which Harley's design was made. The Model K, which was supposed to meet and defeat the imports, had foot shift on the right, presumably because that's how the English did it.

With some exceptions. Decades after all the car people got together and agreed reverse would be top left of the H pattern, first gear lower left, neutral in the center, and so forth, the motorcycle people were still using hand or foot, left or right, up or down. Neutral mostly was between first and second, but not always. And there were systems that let you move past top gear and click directly into neutral.

Sorry to come to Big Nanny's defense on this (or any) issue, but this variety did make borrowing other folks' motorcycles interesting. Every old-timer has at least one account of what it's like to move the wrong foot in the wrong direction at the worst possible time.

What this means to us is that in 1975 the federal mandate put all motorcycle shifters on the left, by foot, with first gear at the bottom, neutral above it, then second and on up, so to speak.

The first Sportster with this did it via an elaborate double-cross. The actual shaft that controlled the shifter drum came out of the right side of the case; then there was a linkage to carry the action back, down and over, to the shift peg on left. The rear brake, meanwhile, was on the left side of the rear hub, so there was another crossover from the

The XLCR Cafe Racer, introduced for 1977, was different. There was a bikini fairing, a larger fuel tank in road-race style, and the seat and rear fender were sort of like the dirt track XR-750. There were also covers for the battery and oil tank, and what used to be chrome plate or polished alloy was now black. (This example's pipes have been chrome-plated by the owner.) And the frame has been extended back.

In 1979, another major leap. The left-side exhaust carried over (used up the surplus?) from the XLCR, while the extended frame provided a better mounting for the shocks and let the battery and oil tank and electrics be tucked behind covers. The cast wheels make flat tires instead of blow-outs, and the triple disc brakes mean you can stop quickly. *Cycle*

brake pedal on the right.

In 1977, the cases and internals were revised, so the shaft came out of the gearbox on the left and all the mickey-motion was eliminated. (All this history is presented here to, first, let people know how to quickly identify the model's year, and second, to explain all that linkage on the 1975 and 1976 XLs.)

There was more important news in 1977.

Readers who take notes will recall that when the XL appeared, the factory assumed Sportster buyers really wanted a junior FLH. They were partially right. Well, in the mid-1970s the factory assumed Sportster buyers really wanted a junior Superglide.

This time they were a lot closer to being correct. The CH model designation was dropped, along with options like the larger gas tank and comfy seat. The Sportster wasn't a performance bike any more.

Well yes, it performed well, easily as quick as the raucous XLCH had been several years earlier. Thing was, the triples and fours and lighter twins from overseas had taken away the niche. The XLH became sort of a chopper, not really, of course, but it did have the look, and the look sold well.

The XLCR

In 1977 Harley-Davidson made a bold and off-target guess, that the non-Sportster buyer really wanted a sports model.

The model in question was an English fad, that of taking a road machine and replacing the road gear, the bags and windshield and mufflers, and fitting a racing tank, low bars, setback foot pegs, and the loudest viable exhaust. These machines were raced on public roads, from hangout to hangout, and they became known as cafe racers. And it's worth noting that not a few factories were inspired to do versions on the theme. Ducati and BMW in particular offered some nice work.

Harley-Davidson's rendition began with some needed improvement. The original XL frame was based on the K model frame and used cast-iron junctions, with the shocks mounted halfway between the rear hub and the swingarm pivot, feeding into a junction just aft of the seat mount. This gave a direct path into the frame but allowed the force from the wheel to flex the swingarm, which isn't good. In 1972 *Cycle World* said, as politely as possible, that the frame was out of date.

Meanwhile and elsewhere, H-D's racing department and some outside contractors came up with a much better frame.

The general idea came from the frame designed for Norton by two Irish brothers and called the Featherbed, because it rode like one. (This is neither criticism nor accusation. When the Norton Featherbed appeared, all the motorcycle engineers in England, Europe, the United States, and Japan slapped their collective foreheads and said "Of course! That's how to do it!" and they made their versions. There are designers who'll argue the Featherbed is still the best, although it's no longer the most fashionable.)

Back in Milwaukee the new design was used for the road-race KR and adapted for the dirt track XR when dirt racers got suspension, a whole other story for which we have no time now. And there was a version for the XRTT, the last of the all-Harley road racers, which will be detailed in a later chapter.

Well. In the KR days, dirt machines mounted the rear wheel rigidly in the frame, and TT and road racers used shocks and a rear section of frame, which could be bolted onto the swingarm pivot and that infamous cast junction beneath the seat. One machine, one engine, and you could race all five types of national championship events.

Well, again. With the release of the XLCR, obviously an XL with Cafe Racer connections, the factory mentioned the rear frame was from the XR-750. There were reporters, and there are now historians, who didn't quite get this and wrote that there is a front section and a rear section to the XLCR frame.

There isn't. What the engineers did was improve and update the XL frame. It lost the cast-iron junction in the rear and the steel tubes were extended back, so the shocks mount nearly vertically, above the rear hub. That reduced the leverage and the flex and provided room for the battery and oil tank to be less intrusive. The rear section is similar to the XR frame, but it's not something that unbolts from one and bolts into the other.

Stripped 1979 XLS reveals the longer frame rails and the clutter behind those neat covers below the seat. The big and clumsy air cleaner was to let the engine meet newly imposed noise limits. The vehicle ID for this model was stamped on the steering head forging. The magnifying glass lets us see 4E, the XL1000 engine, and H9, model year 1979. The forward mount pegs were for stretching one's legs. *Cycle*

The XLCR retained the XL engine, except that the exhaust was new and different. The two pipes met below the carb, merged, and then branched, with one pipe running forward, around the engine, and back down the left, and another pipe low on the right. This was efficient, if heavy.

Wheels were cast instead of laced, and there was a new tank and seat with vaguely flat-track lines, and a tiny fairing—a "bikini" fairing in the slang of the day—shrouded the headlight. Paint was black, glossy in some places, matte in others. The official word was that the XLCR was Willie G. Davidson's idea, which he'd designed for himself but which the factory allowed the public in on.

That was specious nonsense.

Life has dealt William G. Davidson, grandson of the original partnership's William A. Davidson, an interesting hand of cards. His name is on the factory, as the saying goes, but the title isn't in his safety deposit box.

Willie G. has become the company's personification, and main spokesman as well as chief designer. He does like motorcycles and the people who ride them, and he has influence.

But he isn't in charge. He's an employee, except that for reasons of inheritance he has power he may not have earned and responsibilities for which he didn't ask. Sort of like Prince Charles, except that Willie G. has done a much better job playing the hand he was dealt.

In this instance, the XLCR was an attempt to widen the product line with a minimum of new (and expensive) parts. It was supposed to cash in on a trend, just as the Superglide exploited what was being done by owners.

It didn't work. The noisy intellectual minority that made such a fuss about cafe racers didn't want Harleys. The XLCR came only in black, at a time when motocross ruled fashion and even the stodgy British were abandoning solid black.

Equally, there was nothing wrong with the XLCR. It had the same strong engine and improved frame, the cafe seat was more comfortable than the padded board on the stock XLH, and the larger tank gave a longer cruising range. No matter. The XLCR sold by the handful. An optional passenger seat was offered for 1978, but the outside opinion is the XLCR was kept in the catalog mostly because the company had to use up the ones it had built.

The Useful Others

Striking still another blow on behalf of common sense, 1977 saw the offering of another set of options, labeled the XLT.

The XL frame became all steel—no more cast-iron forgings for the steering head and rear engine mount—in 1982. You could get a larger tank in peanut style, as seen here, and the staggered duals let the brake's master cylinder be tucked away lower than it was during the interim 1979-style frame. *Cycle*

This was mostly the choice of a 3.5-gallon fuel tank, the teardrop shape of which was borrowed from the later Superglides, which in turn got it from the touring version of the Sprint, a lovely little single built by H-D's then-subsidiary, Aermacchi.

(Note here that at this point in time, H-D shut down the import division, which had been making modestly good two-stroke singles for street and motocross. Europe simply couldn't match the Japanese in quality for the cost.)

The XLT had a thicker (and more comfortable) seat, it came with an extra tooth on the front sprocket, and you could order the saddlebags from the FLH. The XLT was clearly designed to be ridden long distances with less strain.

The XLT didn't sell as well as the XLCR, which is saying something.

The Motor Company got the message, but there was no denying the improvements, especially the frame, so there was a phased-in period, meaning they used up all the frames they had stored behind the plant. The 1979 XLs got the better rear frame design; accessory buyers need to know that the 1979 used a different mounting for the rear brake master cylinder, and that's why exhaust systems for before or later, won't fit.

New for 1979 was the XLS with extended forks, a sissy bar with leather pouch, flat bars with risers to put them where the older bars were (but with more style), and with highway pegs so the rider could rest his or her feet out front. The XLCR and XLT were dropped from the lineup, and the XLS sold well. What the buyers wanted was a junior Low Rider.

The concept of making new models with the fewest changes possible carried on in 1980, with additions. H-D, well, the ad agency mostly, had a contest, and the XLS got its own name, Roadster, instead of having new or different lettering following the XL on the Sportster. The mechanicals were the same, but there was extra trim and the fuel tank seen a couple of years earlier on the XLT. The only thing really new was the name, but to this day there are owners who'll insist it's a Roadster, not a Sportster.

The other addition was, you could say, a subtraction. The XLH could be ordered with shorter shocks and a lower, make that thinner, seat. It had a nickname, the Hugger, and it was the factory's amiable way of making it easier for women to buy Harleys. They never said so, not right out loud because they knew the last thing Harley women wanted was a girl's bike, which is what the Big Twin crowd has called Sportsters since the first, by the way.

The all-steel frame was stiffer and more efficient: room for everything and everything in its place. The XL engine still used a generator, in front of the cases, but there's now an oil filter below that. The skimpy seat and small tank proved that fashion still ruled. *Cycle*

33

By 1985, the last model year for the iron-top XL1000, there was one federally certified engine, frame, and major components, with the models varying in trim and extras. This is the XLX, the bare-bones price leader: For $3,995 you got a solo seat, small tank, low bars. and matte black pipes. *Courtesy Harley-Davidson Archives*

The Hugger did so well it became an official model, so it and the XLS added as much to the bottom line, and in difficult times, as the XLCR and XLT took away.

The juggling carried over into 1981. The Roadster had high, curved buckhorn bars and the larger fuel tank. The Sportster had original-length fork tubes, flatter bars, and the peanut tank. Kind of like the earlier XLCH versus plain XLH, especially since you could order either tank with either model, likewise for laced or cast wheels, with the rear wheel either 16 inches or 18 inches in diameter.

AMF may deserve more credit than it has received to date for this, but just after it sold controlling interest in H-D to the executives, some family members, and their banks for the 1982 model year, the Sportster got another major frame improvement. All steel, at last, as the cast-iron junction at the steering head was replaced.

The government and the oil companies get the blame for the 1982's engine change, which was a thicker head gasket to drop the compression ratio from 9:1 to 8:1, because the iron cylinder head and outmoded hemispherical chamber didn't like the horse pi—, um, gasoline being sold at the time. (This can work both directions now, in that earlier 1000 engines can use the same trick if the local fuel is poor quality, or you can raise the compression ratio on your 1982 XL now that the gas is better in some places, which can happen.)

In real life this doesn't matter a whole lot, as the official, nominal compression ratio never was quite 9:1 anyway. But, everything else being equal, compression ratio is the most efficient path to power, if the fuel's up to par.

The Revival Begins

The new frame more than made up for the loss of compression and presumed power. *Cycle World* and *Road Rider* both tested a 1982 XLH, and they both liked the model. The *Cycle World* official weight, taken at the certified scale with the peanut tank half full, was 515 pounds. *Road Rider* published the factory's official dry weight of 460 pounds, which one must note was less than the earlier and surely lighter XL's official dry weight. In test, the 1982 was slower than the 1962, by the way, surely because the newer model was heavier and carried real mufflers and met government specs.

The new owners began to show their talent in 1983. For years, the Sportster was the motorcycle nut's first Harley-Davidson (not counting the little singles, which as noted never did get popular or bring in the business). By happy coincidence, the prices of the other brands were going up faster than their perceived value was.

Harley-Davidson played from strength with the introduction of the XLX.

This wasn't anything new, in several senses. The XLX was a price leader, a bare-bones Sportster with a solo seat, small tank, one front brake disc, and hardly any chrome plating. The full model name was XLX-61, admitting at last that the 1000 engine displaced that classic number of cubic inches.

The XLX was priced several hundred dollars below the other Sportsters, which were continued. And the sticker read $3,995.

OK, that's nearly $4,000, which by no coincidence was what you'd pay for a fancier XLH or a Japanese model of comparable performance. The key here was that the XLX's low price got people into the showroom and offered a way to afford that first Harley. When they'd gotten that far most checked the options box for a dual seat or two-tone paint or whatever. The out-the-door price had gone up, and so what? A lot of happy new owners went out that door.

What to Look For

The usual cautions apply here, but to a lesser degree. With these models, there's not as much chance the cases have been blown apart and rewelded, and there's been less time for a given machine to have been stolen and counterfeited back into circulation. Even so, it won't hurt to look for the scars and grinding marks anyway.

For most of the models during this period, the differences are in the details. There were some special paint schemes for 1976, the United States of America's anniversary, and for 1978, H-D's anniversary, and while the decorations aren't worth money in

The XLH was in the middle, with a dual seat, higher handlebars (never mind that they make your wrists ache), and chrome for the exhaust system. The engineers meanwhile had reduced engine noise to the level that allowed the return of the smaller hamcan air cleaner. *Courtesy Harley-Davidson Archives*

The 1985 XLS was officially labeled Roadster not Sportster and had a thicker dual seat and bigger fuel tank topped by a console: In some ways it was back to 1957, with the top-line Sportster a junior version of the Big Twins. *Courtesy Harley-Davidson Archives*

most cases, it wouldn't hurt to have them. If the example in question is supposed to be a Roadster or a Hugger or an XLT, check the machine against the catalog before signing the check.

The XLCR is a special case.

Human nature pulled a fast one here. As soon as the public didn't want these two models and they died on the showroom's vine, the collectors decided to prove the public wrong. The XLCRs went from dealership to collections.

There's nothing wrong with that, in itself, but reading the club publications turns up people in search of this part or that decal that they need to complete the perfect restoration.

Demand for the XLCR appeared the instant the supply was shut off. Not many were made new or sold quickly (one surmises, since this isn't the sort of thing the PR department tells you), so the factory didn't stock up on spare parts. Thus it's worth paying extra attention to be sure the bits are the real McCoy.

Different models appeal to different people and therefore lead different lives. If the present owner of, say, a 1972 XLCH doesn't know anything more than he wanted a Harley and got it from a guy who'd been transferred to the Seychelles, he's probably telling you all he knows. The standard XLs were big sellers, often to buyers who just wanted a motorcycle. If there have been some changes made, it's okay because the parts are no more than an 800 number away.

Hold on a sec, however; an XLCR is almost certain to be owned by a collector now, even if it wasn't bought by one when new. The present owner should know its history and what's been taken off or put back. If he doesn't, it's fair to wonder why not.

The Rarity Dilemma

This is below the bottom line. The XLCR was collected from Day One, as noted. They didn't offer extra, also as noted.

This sounds snobbish, admittedly, but the Cafe Racer was rejected by the minority and in large degree it was adopted by the minority that loves believing the majority is wrong. (It's the author's secret notion that those who boo Jeff Gordon also root for the Chicago Cubs. Same sort of people as XLCR fans.)

For this reason, and speaking strictly about investments, the XLCR gets two stars for collectibility. I know, for 20 years you've heard otherwise. Forget that. The XLCR has gone as far as it's gonna go. The parts are already subject to bidding wars. So buy 'em if you like 'em, as the drill instructor used to say, but if you do, you are indulging rather than investing.

The silver sliver here is the original XLX. It was unique, it did the job, and it has made a positive sort of history, so if there's a dark horse in the collectibility column, the XLX is it.

Model	Utility	Saddletime	Collectibility	Style	Accommodations
1972–85 XLH and XLCH	★★☆☆	★★★☆	★★★☆	★★☆☆	★★★☆
1979–85 XLT and XLS	★★★☆	★★★★☆	★★★☆	★★☆☆	★★★★☆
1985 XLX	★★★☆	★★☆☆☆*	★★★★☆	★★★☆	★★☆☆
1977–78 XLCR	★★☆☆	★★★☆	★★☆☆	★★★★☆	★★☆☆

*(stock)

About Those Stars

Now comes the crunch. Now comes the true reason behind the part in the introduction where it says, if you want it, get it.

This is a cloud for the silver lining. The midhistory Sportster, considered as a group, didn't make the history the first Sportster did. Nor does this middle group have the technical improvements the current group has. And the middle group carries the stigma of AMF. Unfair, but fairness doesn't matter in the free market.

The plain XLs sold in great numbers, so there are lots of them around. The two models from this era that became famous did so because they were failures, in the market at least.

What we have here, then, is a group of low averages. They can give trouble, which detracts from utility. Most don't have much style, and the one that does has been overrated for other reasons and so forth. As for the group, if you find one you like and buy it, you'll have a used Harley that can be used daily, given maintenance: The iron-top XLs are quirky, but they are strong.

If the author is correct and the Shovel-style Harleys appreciate because they aren't new and improved, this tide will lift all the XLs. But it won't lift them above average.

Chapter 2

1966–84 FLH, FLT, and FLHT

The history of the first true Shovelhead begins with good genes and better timing.

Today's Big Twin, as mentioned earlier, began with the Knuckle-head of 1936. Harley-Davidson's traditional gradualism means that every part, specification, and dimension has changed during the 60-plus years, but *the* H-D engine is still an air-cooled, 45-degree V-twin, with fork and blade connecting rods, one camshaft with four lobes, a separate crankcase and gearbox joined by a primary drive, and so forth.

Folklore holds that parents put most of their effort into the first-born (which is why it's better to arrive later), but in this instance it was the second major version, the Panhead, that got experimented on. As soon as the Panhead's teething troubles were cured, the model got tele-scopic forks, rear suspension, hand clutch and foot shift, and finally, in 1965, electric start. In terms of major modification, nothing comes close to the Panhead's (sorry) evolution.

In 1966, with all the other changes working well, the factory took the next step and replaced the Panhead with an aluminum version of the hemispherical combustion chamber first seen (in cast iron) on the 1957 Sportster.

The major change in the cylinder head was first the shape of the combustion chamber and second the rocker arms, which swivel on a shaft that mounts to the cover, more properly called the rocker box. The Pan heads mounted the rocker shafts to the top of the head and covered the valve gear with that pan.

Oh yeah, the new nickname, Shovelhead, came because to some the right-side top of the rockerbox looked like the back of a coal shovel.

There were two stages of tune in 1966, with the FLH (a title invented when the lower end of the Big Twin was beefed up in 1955) rated at 60 brake horsepower and the FL, with lower compression ratio, at 54.

Reports from the day say that although the new engine did have more power, the Electra Glide, the name that came with the electric starter, was slower than the kick-start Panhead because the starter and larger battery added 75 pounds to the curb weight.

Cycle World tested an FLH in 1967 and reported a weight of 783 pounds, surely as heavy as a motorcycle ought to be allowed to be, with a top speed of 98 miles per hour. The open road was closed by then, and buyers of the big bikes surely weren't as concerned with performance as

they had been, and it's safe to say that the current buyer/owner of these machines won't much care.

More to the point, then as well as now *Cycle World* found the FLH to be an excellent mount, more than capable of covering the highway in comfort and style, once the operator accepted the size and weight as part of the package.

Speaking of packages, the important news from 1969 was the perfection of the dresser.

They didn't call it that. But back in the pioneer days riders in for the long haul threw saddlebags over their rear fenders and devised windshields of canvas and isinglass. Such equipment became available as accessories, and in 1956 H-D offered a package of bags and windshield, said package being called the King of the Highway group.

It was a popular option, but it wasn't enough. In 1969 the new top of the line was the FLH with a fiberglass fairing mounted on the handbars, plus saddlebags and a third luggage case, riding atop the rear fender. (The factory called it a Tour-Pak, their spelling; everybody else called it a top box for the same reason we still use the term saddlebags even though they no longer get flung over the fender and they mostly aren't made of leather.)

There had been accessories for decades, but this combination, sold as a package by the factory through the dealers, was a first. History shows it was a welcome option, for H-D and just about every other factory as well.

Early Electra Glide presents American motorcycling's classic profile, unhampered by the habit of *Cycle* in its Ziff-Davis days, of adding cute girls to the portrait. Equally obvious here is the family resemblance between the equipped FL and the equipped XL. *Cycle*

39

From the rider's shoulder one can see that there are two gas tanks bridged by the panel with speedo and switch, that the FL is wide in most places but narrows usefully in the center, and that the operator has floorboards and the passenger, nestled close on the dual seat, gets foot pegs. *Cycle*

On another grumpy note, the *H* in FLH represents the factory's identification of another stage in the engine, just as the *H* did in the preceding JDH, the VLH, and the KH. The *H* did not then, nor does it now, nor has it ever, stood for Highway or Hot. Period. The FLH appeared in 1955 after the factory was sure the new Panhead was working well. They made some improvements to the lower end, mostly bigger and better bearings and oiling components, and because it was safe, added another stage of tune, with hotter camshaft, higher compression ratio, and even polished intake ports. And as the FLH proved to work as well at low speeds as the FL did, gradually the two merged, kind of like the XLH and XLCH.

The identification system does have its quirks. The official factory code considers that because you could order an FL without kick-start while the bikes with electric start came with the kicker backup, those with the button were designated FLB or FLHB, the *B* presumably for the big battery.

Next, for several years after the mass market shifted, chuckle, from hand shift and foot clutch to the other way around, the big twins could be ordered with the old system, just as reverse gear was an option for the sidecar crowd.

And the police package was good business for H-D during the 1950s and into the 1960s, so there were models designated FLP and FLHP.

This may or may not matter. The *B* for battery, and the *F* for footshift, as in FLHF or even FLHBF, were used on the build sheets, the paperwork that came down the line and went out the door with the motorcycle.

The same goes for the police package and, of course, for the routine customer versions.

But not all the data was stamped on the cases. You may find an FLP parked in a row of FLHs at the show; the *B* and the *F* and the *S* for sidecar were only on paper.

About the actual stampings. In the 1960s the system began with the year, as in perhaps 68FLH0001. In the 1970s the factory swapped ends, and the cases will have FLH0001H0, with the *H* representing the eighth decade, the 1970s, and the zero for the first year; that is, it's a 1970 FLH.

The first three years of the Shovelhead-powered Electra Glide were important.

First, they were the last years before AMF took full control. (See the Sportster section for a full explanation.) As mentioned earlier, AMF was not evil. In fact, the conglomerate probably saved Harley-Davidson's life, but folklore prefers the pre-AMF models.

Second, they were the last of the old style as well as the first of the new style. The 1960s Shovels had ignition timers and exterior housing for the points and condenser driven off the camshaft. They had 12-volt generators mounted to the front of the cases. They had ever-reliable kick levers.

There were major changes in 1970. The ignition was moved inside, into a housing that was part of the gear case cover, driven off the end of the camshaft. The generator was replaced with an alternator inside the primary case.

The new timing case cover had a cone shape, so the early engines are now called generator Shovels and the later ones cone Shovels, less often alternator Shovels.

There were some obvious gains here. An alternator is more powerful at low rpm than a generator, so the battery will be kept charged during stop-and-go duty, and having the points inside is clearly better. As an extra, the oil tank got a dipstick on the side, as opposed to the early versions which tucked the fill cap beneath the seat. But putting the alternator inside the primary drive housing widened that housing, which required moving the floorboards—more on them later—outboard.

Road Rider magazine tested a 1970 FLH and was pleased in general. They experienced some electrical bothers and a handling quirk, a weave at 95 miles per hour that went away if you kept the power on (gulp!), and a valve lifter that lost pressure but cured itself.

What the magazine liked least was the wider stance, which made it too easy to drag the floorboards. Later there would be complaints that the wide and low exhaust pipes dragged on driveways.

Detail notes here should mention two weak points for the Shovels. First, the cylinder heads provide one, only one, mounting bolt for the exhaust pipe flange. This wasn't enough. The engine mounts rigidly in the frame and the exhaust system bolts rigidly to the engine and the frame, so there shouldn't be a problem.

But there is. *If* the muffler, tailpipe, and head pipe aren't aligned with the engine before the head pipe-to-exhaust port flange is tightened, it will work loose. And it's just about impossible to tighten without the right tools. In the short run, have the right tools in your saddlebag. In the long run, there are kits, which require some outside work, to add a second bolt and fix the flaw permanently.

Second, the cone motors, with alternators, have a plug from the case to the regulator. It comes loose. It did it when the plug was a push fit, it did it when a retaining spring was added, it's done it despite all the factory's modifications. If your Shovel begins to crank over slowly, check the plug.

Character

From the viewpoint of the present, the early, make that *true* Electra Glide, generator or cone version, seems to be a motorcycle like no other. It is that. What we don't always appreciate is that even when new, the Electra Glide was a motorcycle like no other.

Switching from hand shift and foot clutch to the modern reverse was more difficult than one might think. The object in front of the front cylinder is a helper spring for the clutch, which was heavy anyway. The shift lever has two pegs, fore and aft, so you always push down to shift. The rear cylinder has split exhaust pipes, with one routed across the bike and then back and down to the second muffler on the left. The chrome thing above the peg is a heat shield. The *H* decal signified the higher state of tune. *Cycle*

Why is this FL posed on the railroad tracks? Same reason as the young lady: art. This Electra Glide is one step shy of the Highway King package because it's got the windshield instead of a fairing and a luggage rack not a top box. *Cycle*

This is a good thing. Well, it's good if you like Electra Glides, and if you don't, why are you here? The big Harley-Davidson grew and changed to fill a specific need, ergo the floorboards, the heel-and-toe rocker shift, the dual saddle suspended on a sprung post.

Sports-fan critics of the day made a kind of sport out of sniggering at the FLH to the point that the magazines—*Road Rider* excepted—didn't pay much heed to the FLH until late in the 1970s, when *Cycle World* took a daring step and assigned a desert racer to tour for a weekend, full fairing and bags included.

He was impressed, and the dam was broken. Even so, at this point in history we need to remember that riding an FLH was and is like being in a foreign country: There's no point in complaining about the differences, since that's part of the deal. Knee-dragging, tire-burning wheelies on the street are not part of the deal.

In mechanical terms, the Shovelhead FLH came first with Tillotson carburetors, was switched to Linkert, and later, when the U.S. firms didn't want to bother with meeting government requirements at low volume, to the Japanese Keihin. All worked; all can have fussy fits.

In mechanical terms, the FLH got a disc front brake in 1972, about which *Road Rider* mentioned the brake was too responsive to rider input, the first and only time anybody said that about a Harley-Davidson brake. *Cycle World*'s test 1973 FLH, which it called, "a remnant from a past era," weighed 738 pounds. It did the standing quarter mile in 15.42 seconds, which was pretty quick for a full dresser that included stuff like spotlights and case guards.

In 1974, the FLH throttle got a return spring, under federal fiat. Until then cruise control was free, hard as that is to believe now.

There were some tentative approaches to special models, which would become an H-D specialty in time, as will be detailed later. There was a Bicentennial insignia offered in 1976, for instance, and in 1977, along with the usual black or silver paint schemes, there was the first official Classic, an FLH with all touring gear plus beige, brown, and cream paint, and even a brown seat.

Next year, 1978 that is, for Harley-Davidson's 75th birthday the observation was the Special Edition 75th Anniversary Electra Glide. (That has to be the longest tag ever hung on a motorcycle.)

What it meant was an FLH done in black and gold, with stripes, with real leather covering the seat and with an anodized eagle on the clutch cover: another styling first seen all over the motorcycle ever since.

Return of the 80

With the trim came major technical news. The breaker points and condenser were replaced with electronic ignition; the good news being that it needn't ever be tuned, the bad news that you can't fix it in the unlikely event it does break.

Most major, the Shovelhead got a larger bore and stroke and a displacement increase from 74 to 80 cid. There was tradition here, in that the side-valve Harley (and Indian) Big Twins of the previous generation had grown from 61 to 74 and then to 80 cid.

That was because bigger holes represented a cheap and easy way to gain power. This time the reason was to retain power. Gasoline lost quality, while government regulation of noise and emissions gained strength. The larger engine had a lower compression ratio and a rated power of 65 brake horsepower, where it had been for the original Shovel 74. And it was softer, quieter power.

The factory put on a brave face and offered the bigger, softer engine as a package: the FLH-80 in Black Cherry paint with cast wheels, the electronic ignition, and a large (and homely) air cleaner.

The air cleaner, plain as the nose on someone else's face, is the quick way to identify the 80. Another is to count the fins on the cylinders: The 74 barrel has 10 fins, but the 80 needed a thicker base, which required more room for the nuts that hold the barrel to the case. As a result, the 80 has only 9 fins.

Cycle World's test 1978 FLH-80 weighed 752 pounds with the dual tanks (total capacity 5 gallons) half full. That's not bad, considering. Not surprisingly, the 80-mile-per-hour top speed was slower than some earlier examples. But more to the point, the FLH-80 was at its best on the open highway, cruising at 65 or 70 miles per hour, which is just what the buyers wanted to do with it.

Somebody at H-D or AMF must have been reading marketing books. In 1979 the special model FLH-80 became the 80-engine option for the basic FLH, while the new top of the line was the Limited Edition Electra Glide in tan and "creme" (the factory's spelling, not the author's). The LEEG (that doesn't initialize well, eh?) had the cast wheels, fairing, top box, and bags, all part of the deal.

Two notes here: Cast wheels were introduced for racing, where they quickly became standard for road courses and were all but abandoned on dirt tracks. Cast wheels can be lighter than laced ones if cast in magnesium, but they are heavier when done in aluminum. They are supposed to work better on pavement because they don't flex, while the

Harley-Davidson's designers have always been strong on symmetry, which is why the chrome dome on the front hub opposite the brake. The semi-bumper/chrome strip on the fender was an option, as were the turn signals. The brake pedal is as awkward to use as it looks. The chromed cap above the pedal is the ignition timer, and the FLs in the late 1960s shared the hamcan air cleaner. *Cycle*

theory is they aren't as good on dirt, because they don't flex.

What matters to us here, though, is that there are traditionalists who insist on the old, laced-up, spoke, wire, whatever-you-wish-to-call-it, wheel. Wire wheels look great, classic, and all that. Thing is, wire wheels require tubes, while cast wheels can have tubeless tires. Cast wheel rims are designed to grip the tire and keep it in place.

This is a sermon, okay? Lets hope the reader never experiences this firsthand, because just as you've never been cold until you've been cold on a motorcycle, so have you never been scared until you're at speed and your rear tire picks up a nail and the bike leaps and lurches and begins to flop side to side while the bars tear themselves out of your hands and you look in the mirror, and yes, the semi is bearing down on you. Fear, we meet again.

Against that, if a tubeless tire gets punctured, the handling gets a little vague. "Oh," you say, "a nail." And you ride to the next exit and either get it plugged, or you pump the tire up, ride a couple of miles, and so on until the dealer can fix it.

That's the choice you make, wire wheel or cast. Sorry for the lecture, and to be painfully honest, your preacher-of-the-day has cast wheels on his daily driver and wire wheels on his collectible racer, so even those who know better can't resist that classic look. Even so, be sure your choice is an informed choice.

The other note concerns the seat. The Harley-Davidson buddy seat, that tractor-style that was cushioned by the sprung mounting post, the one invented before rear suspension became common, is the best seat ever put on a motorcycle.

Alas, fashion overcomes function. The buddy seat, which was so good Indian came to Harley-Davidson at the height of their feud and asked permission to copy it—no kidding, it's all in the history book—had one fatal flaw.

It was too high. It had to be high because it had to travel, but low seat height became *the* advertising claim, and the old high profile became out of fashion, so the sprung and cushioned seat was replaced with one that bolted to the frame. The factory did retain the buddy seat as an option, until frame changes made that impractical. Even so, it was a loss when the tractor seat was abandoned.

Presumably on a calculated whim H-D offered an FLH complete with sidecar in 1979. The code name was CLE. The 80 engine was standard and the CLE's forks have more rake so the steering will be lighter. This is done because the offsetting drag of a sidecar can make the steering difficult, not to say cumbersome.

Only a handful of the rigs, as they're called in side-hack circles, were sold. It was an unusual model. On the classical one hand, there's nothing so charming to the general public except maybe a hot air balloon. Two people on two motorcycles constitutes a gang. Two people with bike and chair become guests for Sunday dinner.

The other hand here is that a sidecar handles like no other vehicle on the surface of this planet. Very much a learning experience and requiring constant vigilance, the sidecar has been limited to the dedicated since the arrival of the cheap-and-easy family car back in the second decade of this century.

It may have been a coincidence, but the FL version of the 74-cid Shovel-head had a lower compression ratio so it would be easier to start and would run cooler at low speeds in, for instance, Memorial Day parades. *Cycle*

The 1980 FLH line was limited for historical reasons. There was the Classic, with all the extras, in black- or tan-based paint schemes, and there was the Electra Glide, with the 74 engine standard, the 80 engine optional, and all touring gear except the top box.

FLT and FLHT Tour Glide, 1980–1984

The biggest news for model year 1980 was the Tour Glide, the first really new Harley in 10 years and to some degree proof that AMF *did*, contrary to folklore, invest in the product.

The designation was FLT, FL for the engine. Why they went from E to F when the displacement grew from 61 to 74, and then kept the F when the engine grew from 74 to 80, nobody at the plant has ever explained. (Might be because G was used for the Servi-Car, H is used for something else, the I-80 sounds like an interstate highway, J was the original Big Twin, K the unit 45 that preceded the Sportster? Sorry, got carried away with guesswork.)

FL here stood for the 80 engine and transmission, which in H-D tradition carried over as used in the FLH.

Just about everything else was new. The frame especially. The most noticeable feature was a three-point mounting system. Engine, gearbox, and swingarm are all together, solidly connected. But the connections between the driveline, seat, forks, and the rest of the machine were cushioned with flexible, compressible mounts. They were synthetic material instead of rubber, although everybody refers to the stuff as rubber and everybody refers to the isolation-mounted Harleys in general as Rubber Glides, but they do that because there's no better name, just as we call tires rubber when they, too, are reconstituted carbon-based synthetics.

The flexible mounts didn't cure or even reduce the vibrations inherent to a narrow-angle V-twin. Instead, they isolated the frame and thus the seat, bars, and floorboards from the vibrations, which achieved the same thing.

The FLT had a completely new frame, extended in front to permanently mount the fairing to the frame, rather than mounting it on the forks in FLH style. And the front suspension placed the fork tubes behind the steering stem, while conventional telescopic forks mounted in front of the stem, so steering at low speed would be lighter than the machine's (considerable) weight would otherwise dictate.

Further, the gearbox contained five forward speeds, and the drive chain was enclosed with a constant oil bath. The engine got a spin-on

Here's the full-pop version of the FLH, carrying the bar-mount fairing, top box, small backrest for the passenger on the long seat, crash bars front and rear, and dual spotlights to supplement the headlight. From here it's possible to see why the guys looked at this side of the rockerboxes and decided they looked like the back of a shovel (if you have a good imagination). The massive battery required to spin the massive engine appeared too large for the space it occupied. This example of an early Electra-Glide has benefited from some attention, because the round air cleaner identifies a Linkert carburetor, used only in 1966 on the first Shovelheads, while the classic fairing didn't appear until 1969. *Cycle*

Stocked with all the options, this is a 1967 FLH with turn signals, added lights, a top box with what looks like provision for still more lights, fishtail mufflers, and bumper bars to shield the fenders and saddlebags. (There used to be contests to see who'd put the most stuff on a scooter.) *Cycle*

oil filter and there were two headlights; in sum, everything was bigger and better.

As proved to be the case. *Cycle World's* test of an FLT virtually exhausted that publication's supply of superlatives. The FLT weighed 781 pounds with half the 5-gallon capacity on board. But it did the quarter mile in 15.86 seconds, had a top speed of 91 miles per hour, and returned 42 miles per gallon: The FLT wasn't quite as fast as the FLH, which was no surprise, but it was ever so much more comfortable, quiet, and easy to ride that it had to be declared a clear, undebatable improvement. And in its way, it was as modern in 1980 as the Model E Knucklehead was in 1936.

The Eagle Flies the Coop

Hardly a man is now alive,
Who remembers that day in '75 . . .

Did I get that right? The poem is included here because history, like news, tends to fade with time. There are hundreds of thousands of Harley-Davidson owners who by now are puzzled when the grizzled vets curse AMF.

As briefly as possible, some recap: The founding families did their best when their turns came, but they lacked financial clout and (some say) the vision and ambition of the original four partners.

By the late 1960s the motorcycle boom had become the property of the imports, and Harley-Davidson was left behind. There were offers and counter-offers, culminating in the takeover and (to some people, including the author) the rescue of H-D by AMF.

This came at a troubled time in world history. There was social unrest and upheaval. AMF management knew more about finance than sports or marketing. AMF invested in the plants and expanded production. The company leapt further than it had known how to look. Quality control was lost in the shuffle, and when sales slumped all the myriad factions in the place blamed all the other factions.

Belts were yanked tighter and costs were cut. For instance, the import division, a project noble in purpose as President Hoover said of Prohibition, was abandoned. The workers were annoyed and resentful, and yes, some of AMF's moves were clumsy. But AMF wasn't evil, nor were its intentions bad.

In any case, AMF wasn't getting the expected return on its investment, while at the same time some of the managers and stockholders felt a smaller top, so to speak, would work better. So there was a buy-out. Guys from H-D, AMF, and the original families leveraged Harley-Davidson away from the conglomerate and into some really big debt, thanks to trusting and optimistic banks. And later they took H-D public again, against the odds and with the help of the financial wizards and, in a success story that became legend, it all worked.

This is a 1967 FLH photographed several years ago. The owner had changed the mufflers, found a neater top box, and put highway pegs on the crash bars.

Back in the product line, the FLT was the new benchmark. Because it was designed as a complete machine, all done at once around a proven drivetrain, it avoided all the compromises the FLH had inherited over the decades.

In 1981, the same year the "Eagle Flew Alone" as the ads proclaimed, the 74 version of the FL engine was dropped, for the same reason the 74 had replaced the 61: It wasn't any cheaper to make smaller holes. And the 80, in the FLH and the FLT, got a reduced compression ratio so it could burn gas with lower octane ratings, which was more of a save than a plus. There was also an oil control package consisting of better seals and some added drain lines so the oil would go where it was supposed to go. The alternator was made stronger as well, because the FLT had lots of lights and radios and such.

Now we come to a branch in the family tree. As further proof that AMF wasn't as neglectful as critics said, the engineering department had been at work on a different way to use the isolated engine mounts. The result was to be the future of Harley-Davidson, but because that model line was lettered FXR and named Super Glide II (a tag later dropped), the machines are described in chapter 9.

The Era Begins to End

Harley's management, new or old, has always been careful to consider the traditional buyers. For 1981 the limited-edition model (lower case here because there was something given extra status every year since) was the Heritage, an FLH-80 with the suspended seat, fringed leather saddlebags, and a windshield instead of the old fork-mount fairing. It had real bags and such from the past, in other words, and the paint was orange and near-olive drab, a combination that looks much better than it sounds.

There was a lot of juggling going on. The FLT was still the flagship, in the sense that it was the largest and most expensive, and the

Fashions change. This is an Alternator Shovel, a.k.a. the Cone Motor because the generator and timer were replaced with alternator and points in the cone-shaped housing outboard of the camshaft below the carb. This photo was taken at Daytona in 1997, and this FLH looks older than it is because the owner has fitted higher handlebars, leather saddlebags, fishtail pipes with no muffling to speak of, and a stepped, a.k.a. King & Queen, seat. The chrome trim has been removed, while silver conchos have been added. These are typical changes, and this is what you'll find in the used FLH market.

FLH still had a following, but the FL line was no longer where the excitement was.

So for 1982 the FLH was a carryover and the FLT, no longer using the 80 designation because there was no more 74, got new bars, seat, floorboards, and better ignition.

Next door, so to speak, one of the new developments was a toothed belt to replace the chain. This was done doubly, at first, on one of the FX models, but the primary drive belt wasn't as happy as the final drive belt was, so after a short run, H-D went with primary chain and toothed belt.

But not at once and not all at once. The FLT's gearbox had five speeds, remember, and it was wider than the four-speed in the FLH. The belt was wider than the chain, and there wasn't enough room, at that time, for the belt on the FLT. There was room on the FLH, however, so that's where it went first, in 1983.

In the same year there was a retro-style model, the FLHT. It had the new frame, front end, and five-speed, but came with the old-style fork-mount fairing.

The options were being reduced. The 1983 line was the FLH Electra Glide Belt Drive (why they spelled it out that far, they didn't say), the FLT and FLHT Tour Glides, and the FLT and FLHT Classics, meaning they had the top box and extra trim.

During calendar year 1983, in time for the 1984 model year, the Motor Company announced the V2 Evolution engine.

This properly belongs in the second section of this book. For the record here, the V2, quickly named Blockhead by Steve Kimball of *Cycle World*, was a much-improved top end on the 80 cases. It was the fourth top end, the fourth or fifth set of cases, and the third displacement since the original ohv Model E of 1936.

In the sense of Shovelhead history, the V2 was introduced but didn't replace the earlier engine, not right away or all at once. The Shovelhead was kept in production until June 1984. Both engines were therefore used during that model year, with the Shovel assigned to the FLH Electra Glide Classic and to three versions of the new FXR.

As the official end to the engine, frame, and suspension, the factory ended the model year with a special run, the final FLH, built as the FLHX (deluxe), and the FLHS (stripped). Both were offered in either black or white paint with gold trim. The factory says there were 1,250 examples of the X, and 500 of the S.

The FLH, with the sprung saddle and bar-mount fairing that gave a profile like no other on two wheels now belonged to the ages.

What to Look For

Part of the search is easy. The FLH buyer from day one until now has been a rider, not a racer. FLH people tend to add things to their machines, as opposed to the XL and FX crowd that strips things off and soups them up and moves them around.

This is a major plus. There will be an occasional example of neglect, perhaps, but there won't be an FLH with a Suzuki front end; such things have been done to Sportsters, alas.

What will be on the market will be lots of mainstream. The Shovelheads were in production for 18 years, and they sold well for many of those years.

What you'll find will be mostly FLHs. The first-stage tuning option became the norm early on, with the FL limited to commercial, as in police, use. And, as mentioned earlier, there were a handful of odd machines, with reverse gear, hand shift, and so forth, but the odds are against any one buyer, you or me for instance, turning up such an example.

Earlier mention was made of the engine code, as in a 1967 FLH being stamped 67FLH. Between 1970 and 1980 the code became more of a code: An FL is stamped 1A, an FLH is 2A, an FLHS is 7E, an FLH-80 is 3G, the 1979 Classic is 3G, and the 1980 Classic is 3H. (Might mention here that the codes are for your identification purposes

Here begins Instant Nostalgia. This is a 1981 FLH Heritage delivered from the factory with the fringed saddle-bags, the windshield, and the extra lights, just like the optioned FL shown earlier. The luggage is equally authentic because this was a *Cycle World* test bike, and Peter and Barbara Egan took it on a tour of the West, where it acquitted itself admirably: Nostalgic or not, the later Shovelhead FLHs make great highway machines. *Cycle World*

The FLH Heritage was more modern than it looked. The brakes were disc, the ignition electronic and the electrics reliable, for three instances, and the old parts, the sprung dual seat and the floorboards, were retained because they worked well. The only flaw revealed by *Cycle World*'s trip, visible here if you look really close, was the loss to vibration of the passenger's left-side foot peg rubber. *Cycle World*

only. Our sport hasn't yet gotten to the point where you lose the contest if your numbers don't all add up, if you have 1969 cases in a 1966 frame. It's okay for us, even though the Corvette and Porsche crowd will ban you from the clubhouse if the rubber stop on the door was made in the wrong year.)

From 1981, the coding was FLH-80, AA; FLH police, AB; FLH Classic and Sidecar, AG; FLH Heritage, AJ, and FLHS-80, AK.

A cynical comment here is that the code could come in handy for one of the low-production models. It's possible that some strange person could forge one of the precollector bikes, as in the paint and emblems on a machine that began as one of many. It wouldn't be worth it in money or prestige to most of us, but it's possible, so it's fair to check that the Heritage in the paper does carry the correct letters.

Speaking of time well spent, the Shovelheads began life when all engines used oil. They continued that tradition. Some of the dribbles are on purpose—a chain oiler, for instance—and some are simply leaks. But be ready to clean your FLH often and to be amazed at the number and complexity of the nooks and crannies where the grunge hides and breeds.

The better magazines, *Road Rider* in particular, used to track the problems, high points, and trouble spots of the Big Twins. Using that data shows first, the generator Shovels did have trouble with the regulators and generators, while at the same time, the electrical output wasn't always enough to keep the battery up unless the rides were long ones.

That's why the kick lever was retained until the alternator Shovels arrived. That also means the battery had *better* be kept charged. Driveway bump-starting a dressed FLH isn't something you'd like to do every day, or even once.

Also note the fact that the drum brakes didn't always stop the FLH as quickly as some riders would have liked. The disc brakes are better, even though they require arms like Popeye's.

The first-generation Shovelheads, 1966 through 1973, did have some serious mechanical failures, blown crankcases, flywheels, bearings, and such. This is where some of the anti-AMF talk comes from, even though it's not something that came from the change in ownership. And the best news here is that all such disasters will have happened and will have been repaired by now.

The *Road Rider* surveys are the best evidence of what did or will happen in real life. Their readers reported a life of 24,000 miles for the generator, for instance, versus 42,000 for the alternator. An Electra Guide would get 40 miles per gallon of gas and 870 miles per quart of oil. Five years later FLT owners said they got 47 miles per gallon and 700 miles per quart, to which the factory said the oil-control kit would make things better, which seems to have happened.

There were valve gear concerns in 1978 through 1980, a time when fuel quality was poor and quality control was worse. The weak parts surely will have been replaced by now, but if not, the engine can be fitted with low-compression pistons and improved guides and gaskets.

Has the point been made that almost all the parts for any FLH can be swapped and retro-fitted in both directions, all through the 18 years of Shovelhead production? True, and it does come in handy.

One system with potential problems is the ignition. The early electronic systems from Prestolite did have some random failures. There are those who plain don't like black boxes. Points and coils can be used; heck you can even fit a magneto if you're determined enough. In a more practical mode, black boxes fail early when they fail. The best move is to do nothing.

In strictly mechanical terms, for the FLH and the FLT, newer is better. The alternator works better than the generator, the softer tuning is less stress on the lower end and gives the same performance, disc brakes stop better than drum brakes, and so forth.

What we're looking at here is, first, the mechanical condition of the motorcycle in question. The youngest will be 15 years old, so there will have been wear and tear and perhaps even some rebuilding of the top end, the electrics, or whatever.

The last of the Shovelhead FLH series also came in semi-modern dress. This example carries the classic bar-mount fairing but has improved fiberglass boxes. The seat here was transitional, in that it was extra thick but bolted solidly to the frame. It worked in its time but lacks the traditional appeal of the sprung seat. *Cycle World*

The FLT was really different and as big as it looks here. The 80-cid version of the Shovelhead engine was retained, but the frame and front suspension and frame-mount fairing were all new.

The standard *caveats* apply. The papers should be in order, and there shouldn't be any leaks or groans or clanks, well, with the one exception: The early electric starters will sometimes have to heave on the oars, so to speak, for the first spin.

The exceptional *caveat* must be that the FLH was the perfect example of its type at its time, the big road machine. It was different then, and it's different now.

If the cliché ever fit—if there ever was a motorcycle about which one could say, "They don't make them like that anymore"— the FLH is that motorcycle.

Across the Great Divide

In the ordinary course of events, this would be the place where the evaluations are presented, the place for the presentation of the stars. But this isn't the ordinary event. We have recently passed, and can just now begin to understand, a major milestone in Harley-Davidson history.

This is the third such event. The first came in 1930, when the Motor Company replaced the intake-over-exhaust engines that formed the basis of H-D production since the beginning. The new engines were side valve, a lot like rival Indian's engines. The new Harleys gave trouble at first.

This led to a division. As the side-valve engines were improved, some, make that most, Harley fans accepted the new stuff. And some, a hardy minority and often the most enthusiastic in the crowd, liked the old JD engines better and rode them for the next 60 years. No kidding. At this writing there are still riders who'll swear the JDH is the best Harley ever.

The second division was the AMF, um, experience. There's some exaggeration here, in that one, there wasn't much difference between the pre-AMF days and the days when AMF was in control, and two, it wasn't something AMF did just to tick off the customers. No matter. There are still large numbers of enthusiasts who swear at and won't have any Harley-Davidson made during the AMF era.

The third division, our division in that it's happening in our time, is the Shovel versus the Evolution. This division at least makes some sense. The Evo is a lot different. It's also a lot better engine in terms of daily riding and repair.

Part of our division comes from this. We are a quirky lot, we motorcycle nuts, and there's always a notion that a motorcycle that needs us is more fun and has more character than one we can simply ride hard, put away wet, and ride again the next day without so much as a glance at the toolbox.

There are now shops that won't let a pre-Evo in the door. Too much trouble, they say. There are shops that won't let the Evo in and won't speak to the guys who ride them. Changing oil and installing chromed-plated gewgaws, this crowd says, isn't Harley-Davidson repair, and if you can't align flywheels or shim the camshafts into perfect clearance, you haven't earned your *Ride to Live* T-shirt.

There's more, and because it's the foolish, irrational, and human part, it's more important.

The FLT had a miniature car-style instrument panel, under glass on the bars, with the fuel cap and filler under cover and key. The panel looks skewed here because it swivels with the bars and forks while the fairing stays in place on the frame. The fairing also offered storage bins.

When the V2 Blockhead arrived, it made it practical for anybody who wanted a Harley to have one. No tools or mechanical experience required. The timing mattered too, as there had been so much attention paid to various foreign goods that all at once it was fashionable to buy American.

Right. Up there on the red-white-and-blue stand, matched only by the soft drink in that distinctively curved bottle and Disney's little rodent in the three-fingered gloves, is . . . Harley Davidson.

The Eagle's flight looked like the Dow-Jones average, as in, up, up, and up. When you have a better mousetrap and you know how to show people the path to your door, which the new owners of H-D surely did, you are solidly in the black.

Everybody wins.

This is a tremendous and true success story. It would be presented in the Evolution section of this book, except that there's a downside, and an upside.

Downside first: You kids out there will be hard put to believe this, but there was a time, starting about 1911, when motorcycles were socially suspect. Only daredevils rode them. (Some of the daredevils were daredevilettes, but that's another story.) Then the bikers were considered hooligans or worse and the movies exploited the shock and horror. Then you did in fact have to fix your Harley more often than you would if you were a nicer person on a Honda.

There was a sizable contingent of Harley-Davidson owners, riders, and fans who, to put it in the vernacular, had Paid Their Dues. So the arrival of the new management, engine, customers, reliability, and social acceptance was not greeted like, say, the arrival of the cavalry?

Indeed not.

Remember the kid's book about the hen who baked? All the other barnyard creatures sniggered when she sowed, weeded, watered, reaped, ground, mixed, and baked, right? But just about the time the frosting was slathered on the cake, she had oh so many pals, eh?

That's how a lot of old Harley types feel about the new Harley types.

It doesn't matter if that's unfair, because we aren't talking fairness here. We're talking human behavior, and we're using that behavior to forecast what will happen tomorrow. In as short and punchy a message as possible, what will happen is the Shovelhead will appreciate.

Skip ahead a couple of chapters. Check out the Softails. What do they look like? Allowing for the new rules and such, what are they trying to be? The answer is the old FLH. The Softails are more honest a replica than the imported cruisers are, simply because at least they are really Harley-Davidsons. Even so, their appeal is largely based on what used to be.

Put more bluntly, they are pretending to be what the FLH really was.

The upside here is the majority's side. The actual product is an excellent product. The people who buy, sell, and manufacture the Evolution Harleys, of all sizes and types, are doing well as well as doing good.

They are doing so well that the company is in the middle of an expansion. During the past several years there have been more buyers than there have been bikes. (More details on that in the next section.)

But back to human nature. For every Harley-Davidson fan who wants an Evo-based machine, there will be such a machine. But they aren't making Shovelheads anymore.

Which brings us to the law of supply and demand and to what philosophers call the Scarcity Principle.

Model	Utility	Saddletime	Collectibility	Style	Accommodations
1966—69 FLH	★★★☆☆	★★★★☆	★★★★★	★★★★★	★★★★☆
1970—84 FLH	★★★☆☆	★★★★☆	★★★☆☆	★★★☆☆	★★★★☆
1980–84 FLT	★★★☆☆	★★★★☆	★★★☆☆	★★★☆☆	★★★★☆

About Those Stars

There are a couple of principles at work here.

One is that new and classic have different values. The 1957 Ford out-sold the 1957 Chevrolet, for instance, while 40 years later the Chevy is an icon and the Ford is a big old lump. There were as many four-seat, big Thunderbirds sold in that model's first year as in the smaller, two-seater 'Bird's three-year production run; but the smaller, slicker original is the one folks remember and pay big money for.

Which means for us here that the Shovelhead is going to be in demand.

This applies most strongly to the early Shovels, the FLHs, and (rare) FLs of the pre-AMF era. They have all the classic components, as in the bar-mount fairing, the sprung seat, and the generator. They have electric start and conventional components, and if they don't, if you want an early Shovel and a throttle return spring or even front disc brakes, that can be easily done.

At this writing, we are leading the curve, but not by much. The older Harley Big Twins, the Knuckle and Panheads, have become collected classics.

Early Shovelheads will be next. They therefore rate five stars as investments and for style, while they beat the average for actually being used as motorcycles: They rate only average for actual use, simply because they do need to be checked and serviced frequently.

The Middle Ground

The later FLH (and the occasional FL), 1970 through the final versions, in either 74 or 80 displacements, are less of a buy. This isn't to say they aren't worth buying, because they are.

Most of what was mentioned already—the coming scarcity of the Shovelhead engine, the view that real Harley types don't let their friends ride Evos, and the predictable day when everybody who wants an Evo has one and so the enthusiast needs something else to want—all apply here. Except that there are more of the later FLHs than there are early ones. And they already have the improvements, and in the later examples, they don't have the sprung saddle.

Nor do the limited editions matter much now. There is some distinction to be gained from having a well-preserved example of one of the early limited-edition FLHs; and a couple of those, the tan-and-cream Classic comes to mind, are in fact attractive as well as useful motorcycles.

As an odd sort of closing note for this model and time, the final two versions of the FLH, the dresser and the cruiser, seem to have disappeared. One seldom sees one for sale.

Guessing at a negative is as tough as proving a negative. The likely reason, though, is that the limited final run went to people who bought them for the future. That is, when they decide to sell, it will be with an eye on putting the grandkids through college. They will be counting on appreciation. Which is fine, for them. If it works. If they find somebody willing to pay extra.

Those who want a piece of history can have one, but the price will be no better than fair.

The FLT: A Job Too Well Done

Strange-but-true story: Ten years after the FLT was introduced and did so well it hauled H-D out of the dumps, your author went looking for a good, stock, early example, to be used in a history book.

There aren't any out there. Wait, better make that, there weren't any FLTs in the hands of people who read the enthusiast press. There were several thousand FLTs sold that first year or two. They can't have been junked or abandoned. Instead, they are parked, owned by people who aren't members of the club. (As an even odder ending to this story, the FLT used in the book turned up parked in the back of the H-D museum, found by the author's wife. Not even the museum guys knew they had an FLT back there.)

Once more, the reminder that an early FLT, with Shovelhead 80 engine and enclosed chain drive, was and is a good motorcycle. It will do the job and can be fitted with some later parts to do an even better job, but the FLT was carefully designed and was intended to do its job, carrying two people in comfort for long distances. It did that, and still will.

However, the machine lacks, sorry to say, character. It's like the dull husband who's a good provider, the homely wife who's better in the kitchen than—not gonna catch me here!—in the ballroom. The FLT has faded from the enthusiast framework.

Extending this with some guesswork, the people who bought the Shovelhead FLTs often still have them. It's no surprise that untrendy people buy untrendy motorcycles. They don't come on the market, and when they do the sellers aren't in a hurry, so it's tough getting an early FLT that's a bargain.

The price won't go down, no worry there. The Shovelhead mystique of tomorrow will take care of that. And there's no reason not to buy one, assuming the sheer bulk isn't a deterrent.

Do remember, though, that when you buy an FLT, all you get is a motorcycle.

Chapter 3

1971–81 Superglides

Late in 1970, in time for the 1971 model year, Harley-Davidson unveiled as nifty a marketing move as the Motor Company ever made. It was part of a careful plan, one mothered by necessity, as the saying goes.

AMF bought H-D, the motorcycle market was expanding, and the company was finding it tough to compete, in the sports and off-road markets especially. Even with AMF's bankroll there wasn't money for engines to match, oh, Honda's four-cylinder 750 or two-stroke motocrossers.

But there were enthusiasts out there building some interesting machines at home. The term was chopper, the term applied when things like fenders were chopped off. Oddly enough, and we'll discuss this in more detail later, the choppers began as street versions of TT racers, stripped and raised for racing on rough ground.

The fashion hit the streets and became famous in the movies. The most obvious feature was a front end kicked out and lightened while the rear of the bike was bulky and packed with coiled muscle like a grizzly bear or a drag racer.

H-D needed something (1) new, (2) positioned so the other motorcycle makers couldn't or wouldn't leap right in, and most of all (3) something the company could afford to make.

The solution came from Willie G. Davidson, who to continue the flow of logic, was (1) grandson of one of the founders, (2) in charge of styling for the company, one of two Davidsons who'd stayed with the firm during and after the takeover, and (3) a guy who knew and cared about motorcycles.

What Willie G. did was lead the team into a combination. They began with the frame of the FL, the conventional Big Twin, and with the Shovelhead 74 engine and gearbox, stripped of the electric start and big battery. The large, short, and fat front end of the FL was replaced by the lighter and longer Sportster forks, complete with the small, eyebrow-mounted headlight that had become the signature of the raucous XLCH.

The new model kept the 3.5-gallon double fuel tanks of the FLH, but the seat and rear fender were the fiberglass combination offered on the Sportster as an option in 1970. The new model was called the Super-glide, coded FX, the *F* for the 74 engine and the *X* for the Sportster parts.

Nothing quite like the FX had ever been offered for mass sale before. They came in black, or in sort of a cherry burgundy, but most

The original Superglide was a performance bike, even though the kicked-out front end and laid-back seating didn't lend themselves to drag racing. This is Cook Neilson, former editor of *Cycle*, at the drag strip in 1970. *Cycle*

The Superglide was a lot more sporting than its father, the FLH, and could tolerate high cornering speed (witness *Cycle*'s Cook Neilson dragging the pegs). The idea was new and obviously struck a responsive chord. *Cycle*

often the paint was white with red and blue.

The name was Super Glide. (Note here that the factory's never been quite sure about this, so sometimes it's Super or Electra Glide, sometimes there's a hyphen, as in Duo-Glide, and sometimes it's plain one word Superglide.)

However, the Superglide was instantly nicknamed Night Train, after a jazz work of the period, and it made a great impression. All the magazines had a good time with the new model, even though they generally had to relearn the kick start technique, and even then there were reports that it wasn't as convenient as it could have been.

The FX was lighter and quicker: *Road Rider* said its example was stable at 120 miles per hour, which must have been a speedo reading. *Cycle World* had a better set of clocks and it reported 108 miles per hour, along with 47 miles per gallon and a quarter mile in 14.43 seconds. *Cycle World*'s scales said 559 pounds with the two tanks and claimed capacity at 3.5 gallons, half full. The FX was, as you'd expect, lighter than the FLH, heavier than the XLCH.

That first model sold several thousand, which meant it did more in keeping the public's attention than in getting into their wallets. Perhaps it was the odd bodywork, which didn't sell on the XL frame in 1970 or 1971. So for 1972 the FX reverted to a conventional steel fender and separate seat.

The 1973 Superglide hit a modest sort of high, in that it got a single fuel tank, 3.5-gallon capacity and styled on the lovely tank, an aesthetic touch first seen on the Italian-built Sprints, the little four-stroke singles with which H-D battled the imports.

The 1974 FX kept the trim tank and conventional seat and fender but made another canny move, the option of electric start. This had to have added weight. None of the magazines actually did a comparison, but judging from the histories of the FLH and XLH, the black button adds 30 or 40 pounds. It didn't matter, at least not to the buyers.

What did matter was convenience. In 1973 the FX, with its lovely tank, conventional bodywork, firmer suspension, and effective disc front brake, had total sales of 7,625. In 1974, with the FXE added to the line, sales were 3,034 for the kicker version, 6,199 for the electric.

If the concept was inspired, the ancestry was familiar: An FLH frame and cone-style Shovelhead engine and gearbox got the optional fiberglass seat and fender offered for the XL. The FX retained the FLH's dual tanks and console but acquired the XL's lighter forks and front wheel and the small headlight suspended from the eyebrow mount. Start was kick only, and there was just the one small muffler. *Courtesy Harley-Davidson Archives*

The moral here was that people liked the looks and the added performance of the Superglide and were willing to accept the added weight (and presumed lack of motorcycling skill) to be sure the engine would fire up on demand.

The factory did the logical thing and let the kick-only model fade out of the catalog, while the label was sometimes FX and sometimes FX1200 (that being the centimetric way to say 74). The Superglide sold well and wasn't messed with at the factory level for the next few years. There was a Liberty Edition in 1976, done with red-white-and-blue decorations over black metalflake. There were some other options in trim and a couple of versions of exhaust systems: The original Night Train had two low pipes on the right feeding one muffler, then there were two separate pipes, then a Siamesed style with the rear pipe curved forward and then down, and then the staggered mufflers were used with a balance tube below the air cleaner, surely as a way to get the machine past the federal inspectors.

Hard to say which came first here, but the factory didn't do a lot of juggling of parts for the early Superglides, as the FX was the model chosen by those who wanted to do radical things to their engines.

The Sportster was the sports/racer, the Electra Glide got covered with extra lights and equipment, and the Superglide was bored, stroked, and reworked.

Then the factory got into the act and the Superglide became the model on which things were tried out, where fashions were tested, and, almost in so many words, where the future came from.

The Low Rider

In 1977, beginning with the 1978 model year, H-D unveiled a major model change. The name was Low Rider, the initials were FXS (the jokers say the *S* stands for short), and what it was was the factory doing what the customers had begun.

The rear shocks were lower, the seat was scooped out, and the forks were set at more of an angle, moving the front wheel farther from the frame and lowering the front of the bike, just as the shorter shocks had dropped the back. Static ride height, measured at the lowest part of the seat, was 27.4 inches.

The FXS had cast wheels—a cast rear wheel had been an option in 1977—triple disc brakes and dual FLH tanks. The actual handlebars were short and flat, but they mounted on uprights, risers in chopper-crowd parlance, so they were as high as conventional bars would have been, but with style.

The Low Rider came in one paint scheme: silver. Cases, heads, and barrels were done in black crackle; the fins were polished.

The new model was a puzzle to the enthusiast press. The members of that group tended to be sports-minded, as in road racing, and they were as puzzled by the Low Rider's popularity as they were by the Cafe Racer's lack of same.

Cycle World tested a Low Rider and reported miles per gallon of 47, top speed of 98 miles per hour, the quarter mile in 15 seconds, and curb weight of 623 pounds. Handling was stable and predictable, the magazine said, while to keep from bottoming out, the lowered suspension was stiffened and the ride was rougher than the testers enjoyed.

Form had forced function's knuckles down on the tabletop, so to speak, beginning a trend that's with us to this day.

Radically styled or not, the Night Train was a viable motorcycle. This one, about as stock as a motorcycle can be after 26 years of service, came to Daytona Beach from the Frozen North in 1997, and your observant author got the photo just as the owner prepared to hose off the grime.

The fiberglass tail section attracted attention but didn't lure buyers, many of whom swapped for conventional seats and fenders. So for 1972 the Superglide did the same thing, still with the dual tanks and still with kick only. *Courtesy Harley-Davidson Archives*

What Harley-Davidson did was, (1), appeal to the public's tastes and, (2), invent the factory chopper. Perhaps in reaction to meeting all those nice people, there was an appeal in the Low Rider's crouched, muscular profile: Wearing velvet gloves isn't so bad if you have an iron fist.

Think not? The Superglide section was the best selling of the factory's three lines that year, and nearly half the FXs were the Low Rider version.

Playing to strength, in 1979 the FXE carried over, still with kick lever although electric start was now standard for all Harleys. The Low Rider's new equipment was a sissy bar, the metal framework that keeps passengers (sissies or otherwise) safe in the knowledge they can't fall off the back. And with the sissy bar there was a leather pouch—a "stash pouch," they said with a wink and nudge. (In those days drugs were supposed to be cool. One hopes they'd do it differently now.)

The Fat Bob

The big news for 1979 was another extension, literally, of the factory chopper.

Some history: TT racing was invented in the United States by American fans of English motorcycles; TT stands for Tourist Trophy, as awarded on the Isle of Man. An executive with the Indian Motorcycle Company went to a TT meet and was impressed with the fun the guys had riding their street mounts over hill and dale. He passed the specs

on to the AMA, and TT became a popular Sunday sport.

Riding big bikes off road required raising the engines and extending the front suspensions and swapping big tanks and long wrap-around fenders for short and skinny ones. Open exhaust pipes were mounted higher, also useful in the enduros of the time.

TT mods became what the sharp dudes rode on the street, which is where the chopper, originally known as a bob-job, came from. (That term was used because earlier in the century when women went from long and elaborate hair styles to short and basic ones, they were said to have bobbed their hair.)

Long after TT racing became something you needed a racing machine to do, the extended forks, high pipes, peanut tanks, and so forth were the mark of the movie outlaw, which meant they were in style.

One of the terms that emerged from this foolishness was bobbed, as in bobbed fenders. When you cut back on the fenders, kicked out the front, cut off the mufflers, and so forth but kept the Big Twin's big tanks, you had a fat bob.

The Superglide was proving to be far more popular than the factory dared hope. The execs obviously made the decision to play to strength, to see how far they could take the motorcycling public in this direction.

Thus, the Fat Bob, initialed FXEF. It was the Low Rider plus the larger (5 gallons total) dual tanks, and with higher bars, buckhorns in the vernacular, instead of the low bars on high risers. The Fat Bob could be ordered with cast or wire wheels, still 16 inches in the rear and 19

Suspecting the public would appreciate convenience, H-D offered the FXE, a Superglide with electric leg added. The FXE also had that lovely fuel tank, staggered dual exhausts, and disc brakes. The FXE sold well and still looks good. *Courtesy Harley-Davidson Archives*

Superglides went back to radical with the 1978 FXS, the first Low Rider. Kick and electric both came standard, while the exhaust was two pipes into one muffler that looked like a megaphone. The seat was more sculpted, and the dual tanks returned. Seat and bars were both lower, which justified the name. The front end got extra rake. Steering slowed. Sales didn't. Cycle World

inches in the front, the Superglide (and Sportster) combo since 1971.

With this, still in 1979, the Superglides got electronic ignition and all the other mechanical improvements given to the Big Twins that year; and as with the FL line, the 80 engine was an option.

The Wide Glide

More history: In 1940 Harley-Davidson's big twins were introduced with 16-inch wheels and 5.00x16 tires, replacing the 18-inch wheels and 4.00x16 tires used during the 1930s. Fashion was supposed to have made this change, but it's just as fair to guess it was a response to Indian's sprung rear hub, because the larger, fatter tire absorbed more bumps, and you could pretend your bike had rear suspension. Sort of.

That first year the buyers squawked loud enough to keep the 18-inch combo as an option. The taller wheel and narrow tire worked better for sport, as in TT.

The Hydra-Glide's telescopic forks arrived in 1949. The fork legs were set apart enough to clear the fatter tire, so, when the sporting FL guys went back to the 18-inch wheel or even used a 19-inch wheel from a Sportster, the forks looked . . . Wide.

So? So for an early 1980 model and for that model year's new model (or so it was thought, hint, hint) there came the Wide Glide.

Again the factory did what the backyard guys had done, with good effect. The Wide Glide was another extension, literally and figuratively. It was a Fat Bob with wider triple clamps, wider front axle, extended forks, and a 21-inch front wheel, as tall and thin as the motocross wheels of 1980 were, and as tall and thin as even the furthest-out custom builders had dared to go.

The Wide Glide, lettered FXWG—the factory began initializing instead of simply assigning a letter out of the box—came standard with the 80 engine, the Fat Bob twin tanks, a skimpy little front fender, and a rear fender with a ducktail, for all the world likes an old-style front fender swapped to the back.

The Low Rider had cast wheels and disc brakes, while the swingarm was less than massive, and the frame, while sturdy, lagged behind the state of the art. And what doesn't show here is that the giant opening of the slash-cut muffler has an actual outlet about the diameter of a quarter. *Cycle World*

The dual seat had a rest for the passenger, the bars were the highest ever sold on a stock bike, the foot controls were moved forward—highway pegs, is what they're called—and the paint was black with flames. Yes! From the factory!

Each giant step worked. The buyers liked the new models and they sold well. Not before time, as the English phrase has it, because H-D was about to buy itself back from AMF.

The Wide Glide made another sort of history, in that while the magazines didn't understand why people liked factory-made choppers, the other factories did.

Well, that's not quite right. The Big Four didn't need to understand the appeal of the Wide Glide, Fat Bob, and peers. What they needed to know was what the public wanted. As soon as Harley's production version of the chopper was a proven winner, the Big Four made cheerfully frank copies, to the point that H-D ran an ad, with a new Superglide described in Japanese. "Here," the headline read, "is your next model."

And it was. The trade name was custom, then cruiser, but the theme and idea was the chopper, born in the 1930s, taken public by H-D and used by the others ever since.

The Sturgis

Nor was that all.

For the late-breaking 1980 news, we go back to ancient history. Those first Harley singles and twins used drive belts, leather-strapped copies of the industrial equipment of the day. Belts were cheap and

The magazine guys were bemused by the Low Rider, as they were by the Night Train, because they weren't used to style overruling performance, as in the extended front end and thin seat. But the FXS did, and still will, perform. *Cycle World*

effective and could be used as clutches simply by making them tighter or looser.

Then came drive chains. In fact, legend says H-D used belts until William Harley, the engineer member of the founding partnership, designed a clutch and gearbox that was as good as the simpler belt. (The clutch and chains arrived in 1912, by the way.)

But by the late 1970s, a time when H-D was generally considered outmoded anyway, there was lots of talk about newer ideas, drive shafts for instance. BMW used drive shafts for generations, and Yamaha for one did well with the system. Furthermore, the old-fashioned chain was thought of as messy, sloppy, and maintenance-intensive, and of course there were the new requirements for noise control.

Harley engineers began working with Gates Rubber Company and developed a new belt system that incorporated toothed belts on pulleys.

The actual material wasn't rubber, any more than tires are made of rubber, although that's what we say in both examples. The project took lots of thought to get the correct material and do all the testing. For one thing, a belt is wider than a chain of equal strength and that meant finding space next to the engine, gearbox, swingarm, and rear hub. And the belt doesn't unsnap the way a chain does. There's no clicking off the master link and sliding in the replacement.

In the end, H-D got the job done. It also did the marketing right, in that the primary and final belt drive system was introduced in the 1980 new-this-year model.

The name was Sturgis, after the South Dakota rally that was on its way to being Where To Go for the faithful.

The Sturgis, lettered FXB with *B* for belts, was a Low Rider plus the belt drive with the 80 engine as standard. The Sturgis had its own paint, black with black chrome plating so the informed spectator would know what it was. (A technique H-D sometimes forgets to use, as we'll see later.)

A lot of homework was done. The final drive belt was seamless and jointless, so replacement meant removing the swingarm, not the project one wishes to tackle at roadside. The factory guys knew there'd be concern here, so part of the deal at first was a spare belt, with clip-together

Still another variation in controls, the FX got pegs instead of the FL's floorboards. The pegs were semi-forward, and the shifter was a trailing lever instead of the rocker used on the bigger machine. The actual gears were as large as ever, though, and lifting the short lever takes more muscle than stepping down on the rocker does. That's the horn on the left and voltage regulator in front of the oil tank on the right. *Cycle*

ends. It was to be used only as a spare, to limp into town, like the dinky spare tires that now come on cars.

Nobody really knew how it would work, though. The expected belt life was 20,000 miles, while the rear tire on a Big Twin was rated at 14,000 miles. Because replacing the tire meant taking off the rear wheel anyway, the suggestion was to take the bike into the dealership every time you needed a rear tire and have the belt replaced at the same time.

Which wasn't a bad idea. In actual practice, of course, people aren't nearly that sensible. At the same time, the belt was much sturdier than predicted.

By now, a generation later, only the prudent few carry the spare belt. Most riders simply keep an eye open for fraying and have the belt replaced when it begins to wear visibly, or just before the year's major tour.

Meanwhile, the primary belt didn't work out as well. It ran inside the primary case, while the final drive belt was outside. Heat did more damage than rocks and rain did, so the primary belt was abandoned and the secondary belt is now standard equipment on all Harleys.

That's all to the good. The belt drive is quieter, cleaner, and much less fuss. And if anybody claims that people are sensible and practical, remind them that the other makes have shamelessly copied Harley's old ducktail fenders and chrome-plated everything, but the belt drive, the best technical change of its day, has been ignored.

The Superglide evolved into a line of H-D products. This is a 1980 FXE. The kick-start option has disappeared and the cumbersome air cleaner has been imposed, but the clean lines and lovely tank remain. *Cycle World*

Back to radical with the FXB Sturgis. All black and chrome, with the twin tanks and extra padding for the seat and forward-mount pegs, the FXB had lots of show. *Courtesy Harley-Davidson Archives*

The Sturgis was a large motorcycle. *Cycle World*'s scales registered 610 pounds with the 3.5-gallon tanks half full. Top speed for the bare Sturgis was 106 miles per hour. The fully faired FLT, same engine, did 91 miles per hour for *Cycle World*, proving the fairing was better at weather protection than streamlining. The Sturgis covered the quarter-mile in 14.32 seconds and returned 48 miles per gallon.

Fuel used was premium, which ultimately wasn't good enough. The Sturgis was lighter (!) than the FLT, so it was geared higher. That meant less revs when you pulled the bike up a steep grade, so the Sturgis pinged under load.

Cycle World and *Road Rider* said the Sturgis' operator seat was good for a full day on the road, same as the FLT, while the Sturgis' passenger seat, more of a perch than a place to enjoy the ride, wasn't up to touring demands.

What with being a sports-derived model, the FXB Sturgis was delivered with electric and kick starts. One 150-pound test rider, the writer as it happens, experimented and could not fire up the 80 engine on the kicker. (Of course, I wasn't desperate. Even so . . .)

For still another benefit, the Big Twins were given a new clutch with diaphragm spring. The primary case was also closed, with permanent lube and no drips in or leaks out. The belt final drive was, of course, also run dry. To sum it up, the late Shovelheads of all description run a lot cleaner than the early ones did.

The Final Versions

The record should show here that first, the executives within H-D and some gutsy banks enlisted for the project bought Harley-Davidson from AMF and then went public, which proved to be a good move for all parties, from employees to investors.

Also noted elsewhere, AMF was derided as the villain during that conglomerate's tenure.

Unfair. They were clumsy, but the AMF guys weren't evil, and this record shows there was a lot of money spent on engineering and improvements, along with new factories and production equipment. That the engineering department had the talent and energy to justify the spending will be shown in the second part of this book.

For here, some hints. The factory reps knew the 80 wasn't happy with the fuel available, so for 1981 the 80's compression ratio was reduced to a nominal 7.4:1. The hope was the 80 would run well on unleaded, 87-octane. Sometimes it will; sometimes it'll demand 89 or 92.

Also in 1981, the FX line was joined by what was at the time called Superglide II, the FXR, which is detailed in the next chapter.

For here, there was parallel production. The 1981 Superglide Ones, so to speak, were the standard FXE Superglide, the FXS Low Rider, the FXWG Wide Glide, and the FXB Sturgis. (Helpful of the factory not to use all the letters they could have, eh?) All had electric start and four speeds forward, and the engines were mounted rigidly in the frame, a distinction to be explained in the next section.

The 1983 models, the last for the original-style Superglides, were merged some. The Low Rider got belt drives, extended forks, and some trim, and it was lettered the FXSB. There was no separate Sturgis. You had to pay extra to get the flamed tank for your Wide Glide, and if you didn't want any extras you got the FXE Super Glide.

What to Look For

There's a temptation here to label this part, What to Look *Out* For.

This is because the Superglide appealed to enthusiasts who wanted to go beyond the factory's limits. The Superglides received— notice the words "benefited from" are not applied—stroker kits, big-bore kits, aftermarket exhaust, and carbs. The list is endless.

Being overly fair here, there are people who know what to order and how to build it. There are some really excellent products on the market. As the sign in my boyhood hero's shop said, "All You Need Is the Money."

If at this moment you wished to do it, you could build or acquire a powertrain with twice the power and at least as much durability as the stock version. Thing here is, just about every such project is badly done. The performance isn't there and the rig blows up daily. Those who measure six times and cut once, as the saying goes, enjoy the results.

Those who listen to the guys at the drugstore and substitute money for knowledge don't enjoy the results.

They sell the results.

What you don't want to do is buy such a project. The best way to not acquire somebody else's troubles is stick with stock.

The FXB's distinctive paint-and-chrome scheme, the low bars on dog-bone risers, and other touches made the new model instantly identifiable, while the engineering innovations gave buyers a rational excuse for just having to have one. *Cycle*

And then, something even more different! The 1980 Wide Glide gave kick start one last shot, while the stanchion tubes and triple crowns were wider, as if they'd been built to hold a lower, wider wheel and tire. But the Wide Glide got the skinny 21-incher seen here, with extended forks, higher bars, and that tank! From the factory! Again more style than substance, and again, nobody except the purist magazines much minded. *Courtesy Harley-Davidson Archives*

Next, steer clear of a second kind of modification, as in the various accessory seats, tanks, controls, and suspension work, including frame modifications. They don't work as well as stock, as a rule, and there are few things less in fashion now than the fad of yesterday.

The third set of changes could, repeat here *could*, involve fraud.

As noted, the original Superglide was different and later in the model series. Indeed until now, in theme at least, the factory did one special version for a given model year and then eased it into mass production or dropped it.

If you are supposed to be looking at a first-year Night Train the cases had better have H1 at the end of the ID numbers. Same idea for a Sturgis or a Wide Glide. There have been no accounts of forgery in this model range, unlike in the competition department, but because the Shovel-Glides are appreciating the risk is there.

After that, straight stuff. The Superglide arrives after the alternator was fitted to the 74 engines, so there's no bother there. Just be careful to keep an eye on the plug that connects the alternator to the regulator.

The troubles during the bad times, 1971 through 1974, surely will have been corrected by now. The 1978 through 1980 engines can be fitted with the lower-compression kit, if they haven't been yet, and the same goes for the 1982 oil-control kit. And if you installed disc brakes to replace the drums on the early 'Glides, nobody, not even the judge at the show, will hold it against you.

It's probably worth repeating several times, as Yogi Berra should have said, that at this writing virtually every mechanical bit in a Shovelhead powertrain can be replaced with good or better bits, from the factory or from outside.

Model	Utility	Saddletime	Collectibility	Style	Accommodations
1971 Night Train, Low Rider, Wide Glide, and Sturgis	★★★☆☆	★★★☆☆	★★★★★	★★★★★	★★☆☆☆
1972–84 FXs	★★★☆☆	★★★☆☆	★★★☆☆	★★★☆☆	★★☆☆☆

About Those Stars

To repeat ourselves, the Shovel-Glides are at the top of the rising edge of the Shovel-Evo divide. The factory is preparing to produce as many Evos of all styles as the public wants, while at the same time the public is going to have all the new Harleys it is willing to buy.

We will have an unlimited supply on this hand, a limited supply on the other hand. The Evo is what the new people are buying; the Shovel will become the dues-payer's badge. Not only that, the Superglide was the model, literally, of the direction in which Harley-Davidson would lead the rest of the world. Therefore the Night Train, the Low Rider, the Wide Glide, and the Sturgis all rate five full stars for collectibility and for style.

In their original form, it must be emphasized here. One hates to use the word fraud, but the FX didn't sell all that well at first and many that were sold were quickly stripped of their fiberglass. Now, of course, the seat/fender is rare and valuable, but it wouldn't be difficult to put Night Train bodywork on, say, a 1974 FXE.

It would look and act the same; it just wouldn't be authentic. The same goes for the others, the Low Riders and Wide Glides. Check the numbers and codes first.

Probably the biggest challenge here will be finding that first-year FX or FXB. They sold in limited numbers at first because of the market but later by intent. One seldom sees a first-year FXWG or FXB in the paper.

If you do, move on it.

Less for the Rest

We're still talking some extra value here. Just as with the contemporary FLs and XLs, the Shovel-powered Superglides will appreciate in the near future, placed as they are between the already-appreciated Knuckle and Panheads and the everywhere-you-look V2s.

The difference between the first-years and the laters is mostly style. A first-year FXE is just as good and unique and even more useful, due to the electric start, as the first FX. It's just not as different or as rare. Ditto for all the normal FXEs sold alongside the Wide Glide, Low Rider, and Sturgis. They're more common, so they will acquire extra value more slowly.

A possible exception here could be the limited-edition models, the special paint, for example, offered in 1976 and 1978. It's a safe bet that the owner, make that the first buyer, bought it because he hoped the paint scheme would up the bike's value. It hasn't. There aren't buyers bidding up the price. Instead, there are owners asking for more than they'll get, while the buyers treat the special paint like the new tires or battery: It may be a reason to buy this one instead of the other one in the *Pennysaver*, but it's no reason to pay a premium.

Oh, and don't pay extra for kick start unless you really know what you're doing.

Chapter 4

1982–83 FXR Series/ Superglide II

Harley-Davidson's official version is that the engineers first did the FLT, the Big Twin with the permanent fairing, the odd front suspension, and the three-point isolation mounting for the engine and drivetrain. Then, the press releases said, because there was a need for a smaller machine and the FLT looked strange minus clothes, they did another version, which became the FXR series.

This account goes against logic. The rule in design has always been that if it works right it will look right. (This doesn't work in reverse, as some thought will reveal.)

The FXR was simply too good right from the start to have been an offshoot or even the happiest of accidents.

Instead, a better bet would be parallel development, with the high-buck FLT coming out first and establishing value, just as Cadillac and Oldsmobile beat Pontiac and Chevrolet to the V-8.

In either case, late in 1981 and in time for the 1982 model year, H-D announced what was known at the time as the Superglide II. The letters were FXR, with *F* meaning the 80-cid engine and 5-speed gearbox from the big twin; *X* representing the one-piece fuel tank, lighter front suspension, and wheel and small headlight from the Sportster; and *R* for the new frame and a version of the isolation-mounting system pioneered by the FLT.

This is a casebook example of Harley-Davidson at its best. Way back in the late 1960s, as we'll see in the next chapter, the H-D racing department led the company's frames into modern practice. The racing bikes inspired the Sportster's new frame, proving for one of the few times in history that racing really can improve the breed.

The principle applied to the FXR, as the engineers laid out a larger version of the fabled Featherbed, all steel and with the rear tubes extended to allow room for the oil tank and the battery and for triangulation and bracing around the engine bay.

This is how it was done for the racing XRs and then the all-steel XLs, plus for the FXR they specified the isolation mounts, and then they measured and found the FXR frame was five times stiffer in torsion, which is where it counts, than the old FX/FL frame had been.

The First Year

No sooner had the factory told us the new model was the Superglide II than they dropped the name and went to initials.

There were two models in 1982, the FXR and the FXRS.

The FXR came with black paint, restrained trim, laced-up wire wheels, and tubed tires. The FXRS had contrasting paint panels on the sides of the tank and came with cast wheels, tubeless Dunlop Sport Elite tires, a small sissy bar at the rear of the seat, and highway pegs for resting one's feet while leaning back against the passenger who is leaning back against the bar.

The only engine choice was the low-compression 80, used that year because gas quality had declined. The 80 was fitted with the oil-control package: extra drain lines, better valve guides, and better seals.

The new Superglide looked a lot like the last versions of the first version, as in a light front and beefy back. *Cycle*

The timing was as good as the engineering. AMF's buy-out of H-D was a popular move, and the FLT generated interest in the company's products. The press in general was attracted and collectively impressed by what had happened since it wrote the old firm off.

Cycle World, which as noted had gone to some trouble to *not* write the company off, recorded a half-tanked curb weight of 605 pounds, lighter than the previous FX despite the new frame and mounts.

The magazine's quarter-mile time was 14.26 seconds. Top speed testing was revised, so the speed given was 99 miles per hour at the end of a flying half mile. The rationale here was that most motorcycles are geared to deliver virtually all their speed within that distance.

The new frame provided extra space for the battery and tank and let the machine be effectively narrower where it counted, below the seat and the rider. Feet more easily reached the ground, legs were straddled, and *CW* said the seat—make that the occupant—was more comfortable at the end of the day than before. The attention paid to oil usage prompted the magazine crew to measure it, which wasn't ordinarily part of the test. They reported 1,500 miles per quart of oil, right on the factory's claim.

The FXRT

The 1983 model line reverted to names, with the FXR and FXRS being the Low Glide. Odd, eh? It was done because there was a third model, lettered FXRT. The *T* stood for Touring except there was already the FLT for Touring, so the FXRT was named the Sport Glide and the *S* was just for the extra trim and cast wheels.

The FXRT, though, went where no Harley-Davidson had gone for, oh, call it 20 years.

The FXRT was aimed at the mainstream.

This made a convoluted sort of sense. The original FLH was the mainstream, a large road bike when that's what big bikes were. Then

Classic H-D here, as the 1982 FXRS got the 80-cid Shovelhead engine, complete with cone cover for the camshaft and heatshield for the exhaust's balance tube and that massive air cleaner, all in a new and completely modern frame. *Cycle*

came the fours and the imports, and the FLH was replaced at the top of the line by the FLT, which was a bigger bike and very much in its own niche.

The FLT and the FLH both were different, each in its own way. The other factories, meanwhile, got into the big bike market without copying Harley-Davidson, and a strong aftermarket came into being. Guys like Craig Vetter, inventor of the Windjammer fairing, began making and selling the equipment they'd designed for themselves because they weren't satisfied with what was already on the market (read here the FLH and FLT). The Eagle's new keepers wanted to expand along with and into this market.

The Sport Glide was their vehicle, as it were. The basic package was the FXR frame and 80 engine. There was some compromise, in that the five-speed gearbox and the toothed belt were too wide to fit the frame side by side. The Sport Glide got the five speeds and an enclosed chain, like the FLT.

The FXRT's shocks could be adjusted to compensate for load. The medium was air, which makes a fine spring. Not only does air pressure resist load, the more load put on it, the more it resists. Progressive is the word here. You load the bike, see how it sits, and apply the compressor until the bike is level. Neat stuff.

The forks used air pressure for another improvement, antidive. This was proof the Motor Company was still creative. The forks have a pressurized air chamber, and when the front brake is applied and the front of the bike would normally dive as weight transfer compresses the forks, a valve is activated and the air pressure firms the forks and the front doesn't dip. Under normal riding, the forks' effective spring rate is as it would be with no extra stiffness. Again, neat. And it worked.

The FXRT came with conventional saddlebags, meaning plastic boxes outboard and below the passenger seat. Inside the boxes were lin-

Several important details: First, the linkage between the engine and the frame isolates the former from the latter, so vibration exists but isn't felt. The linkage must be tuned for best effect. Second, to the right of the turnbuckles and Heim joints, that shiny cover with the wires is the dreaded connection between the alternator and the regulator. That's the connection that comes loose, so it's good to know where it is. *Cycle*

ers, in case it rained (or for use as laundry bags). The fairing mounted on the frame rather than on the forks, and it looked like, well, like a Windjammer. Not exactly, but the same basic idea.

The FXRT was H-D's return to the mainstream. It was as modern as any motorcycle on the market and had all the features plus at least one, antidive, that the others didn't have.

The magazines were impressed. *Cycle World*'s scales showed 668 pounds half topped up, which was more than the FXRS because of the fairing and bags. The FXRT topped out at 101 miles per hour, which is faster than the bare FXR did, proving that the fairing was an aerodynamic aid, along with sheltering the occupants from rain and cold.

The protection meant you could ride for more hours and miles per day. Meanwhile, the scooped dual seat, with the passenger slightly higher than the operator, went along with the improved comfort. *CW* said it didn't use any measurable oil during the test. Total test mileage was 4,000, which proves as much about how good the FXRT was as anything the magazine said. *Road Rider* computed oil usage at 1,500 miles per quart, the factory's acceptable result.

A good motorcycle, in sum. The magazines were impressed and the factory surely was heartened.

Then the sales figures came in. The mainstream had narrowed since the FLH was the flagship, if one can be allowed a mingled metaphor. H-D dealers and traditional customers thought the FXRT looked too much like the imports, especially the fairing, while the enthusiasts who were buying the Kawasakis and Suzukis with the Windjammers attached looked on Harleys as still being not what nice people were seen on.

The original FXR had its own, very different, frame, using the principles developed for the FLT but with Superglide style. This is the S version, with two-tone paint, cast wheels, a console atop the fuel tank, high pegs, and a small backrest for the passenger. *Cycle*

What to Look For

Step One here is going to be finding one to look at. This is a scissors, in that the supply is trimmed between two edges.

The first is that the FXR series was slow off the mark. Sales were respectable, and the motorcycle market was strong at the time the model came out, but the demand didn't exactly empty the showroom floor instantly, not yet and not for the FXR series.

The second cutting edge is that the people who did buy the FXRs have kept them. Or so it seems, because they appear in the classifieds only rarely.

These two model years, 1982 and 1983, were the final runs of the Shovelhead engine and in some ways they were the best runs. The last 80s did deliver adequate, unstressed power and used less oil than before. True, the earlier engines were more efficient in terms of higher compression ratio, but the tests showed more gain than loss at the close of the year.

The low-compression 80 did have a weak point. Mention was made earlier of the complications that arise from the extreme pressure variations inside a narrow-angle V-twin. Such engines need breathers and timed openings and closings, along with effective pumps for delivering oil to and from the separate tank. But the government also had a say in how the engines were built. That is, we got The Environment and rules that made the designers seal up the engine's ventilation.

What this means for the last Shovelheads is that the crankcase vent is supposed to feed vapor to the air cleaner, but sometimes it feeds oil, which coats the filter and drips out of the box. It's a quirk, not amenable to quick fixes, and when it happens the newly clean engine gets as messy as the old ones did.

It also helps to check the fitness of the air-tuned front and rear suspensions. The adjustable systems are more complicated than the old ones, while suspension isn't something the average owner has on his or her maintenance list. The valves, fittings, and hoses are replaceable and not that complicated, but they could need attention; call it a bargaining chip.

Model	Utility	Saddletime	Collectibility	Style	Accommodations
1982–84 FXR, FXRS	★★★☆☆	★★★★☆	★★★★★	★★★★☆	★★★☆☆
1983–84 FXRT	★★★★☆	★★★★★	★★★★★	★★★☆☆	★★★★☆

About Those Stars

These bikes are highly rated, and with good reason. The FXR frame and suspension were the best H-D had made to date, while the engine was, um, tested by time and perhaps the best of its line.

At the same time there are factors here that will keep the final Shovel/first Rubber Glide from being the best of all possible investments.

Think of this as a conflict: common sense versus the free market. Well, make that the part of the free market that's influenced by people's notions.

Thus, going through the ratings, the FXR and FXRS, the basic and the sport, will deliver good service. They have good, strong components and designs are sound, with the mitigation coming from the need to service and observe (and sometimes clean up after) the engine. The FXRT, with the touring gear, will do a bit better.

All three models are really good on the road, all day. It surely helps to have some experience with rigid-mount FXs, because when you click into top gear and that big engine is pulling and the ride is as smooth as your dad's Oldsmobile, it's impossible not to marvel, and it's nearly as difficult not to just keep going till the tank runs dry. Again, the T-model has more protection and with the right seat, it provides the perfect posture.

The above leads to collectibility, of which the first FXRs have a lot. The supply was limited because they were new and radical, and they didn't sell all that well, the T especially, which means they'll take some time and digging to locate, assuming the present owners wish to sell, which they may not.

What they have going against them first is style. No, no, they look fine, to the impartial eye. But they didn't appeal to the crowd already riding Harleys.

As a clincher, these early Rubber Glides are an obscure chapter in H-D history. They didn't warm the heart the way the old FLHs did and still do; they didn't inspire the buying frenzy occasioned by the Softails. The men and women in cars and the crowd at the biker bar are going to react the same—yawn—at the sight of an FXRT.

This could change, and we the human race could learn to live within our incomes, too. Could happen, but don't bet on it.

Instead, for those who prefer to take their profits in dividends rather than price per share, or for those who are in it for fun but need to tell the spouse or accountant that the profits will come in time, these models are true value.

Chapter 5

1958–71 Racers

Off at the other end of the shelf where this book was displayed in the bookstore, there will be other histories of other makes. The authors of these books, when writing about makes that were imported to the United States, wax indignant over the rules for national championships in this country. They were slanted, these diatribes claim, to favor the domestic product.

Not true. What such partisan historians don't understand is that first, when the rules were made the domestic product was all there was, and second, at that time professional racing was as good as dead.

Proof? In the early 1930s the Great Depression brought motorcycle sales to a standstill. There were only two surviving makers. There was one racing team, Harley-Davidson's. That team consisted of one man, Joe Petrali. In 1935 Petrali won every national event. Yes, every one. How's that for a record that will never be broken?

Something obviously had to be done, so the AMA drew up new rules. The entries had to be production motorcycles, made with road gear that had to be removed later. Harley-Davidson and Indian were the two factories still in business. Both offered 45-cid V-twins, with the valves in the cylinders, side valves or flatheads as they were known then. Because they were the motorcycles people could buy, they were the motorcycles that qualified for the races.

One of the unsung causes of the Depression, which was worldwide, was that most countries erected trade barriers against other countries. The United States couldn't sell overseas, and it was tough for other countries to sell stuff here.

There was one outfit in the United States selling English motorcycles. Its sporting model was a 500-cc (30.50-cid) single with overhead valves. That was the specification allowed to compete with the 750-cc side valves. It seemed fair, and it was fair, and the rules provided good racing for the next 30 years, never mind that the production classes revived the sport at its worst moment.

Why the XLR

There was a branch to this mainstream. That sole importer devised a super field meet in which his customers and anybody else who wanted to compete raced on a closed course laid out in the country. On a dirt surface. They had turns and jumps, and because the Americans believed they'd mimicked the original races on the Isle of Man, they called the event TT, as in the Tourist Trophy.

Motorcycle racing was a small, family sport. A man from Indian who also held a post in the AMA was a guest at an early TT, and he realized

The XLR was a basic package: same frame, suspension, brakes, and so forth as the XLC, while the engine's internals were derived from the full-race KR. *Courtesy Harley-Davidson Archives*

this would be fun for all riders. He wrote up the rules and drew a map, and the AMA reported the new event, and presto! we had another way to have fun on bikes on Sunday.

Still more history: When the TT class was created, it was open to anybody who rode in, so there was provision for the big sidevalve V-twins as well as the intake-over-exhaust 61s and 74s that had just gone out of production but were still in use.

As racing evolved, the national championship included short tracks, half miles, miles, road courses (sometimes paved but more often not), and TT. Because TT had allowed big bikes from the beginning, there was an open class most often won in the late 1930s through early 1950s by hopped-up Knuckleheads.

This matters because after World War II the world moved to overhead valves for almost all engines. Harley-Davidson evolved the sidevalve W series into the side-valve K and KH and transformed that into the ohv Sportster, as seen in chapter 1.

But H-D kept on making racers to meet the rules: the rules for side-valve 750s. The guys at Milwaukee headquarters didn't see a market for 500-cc singles on the street, and they were winning with the side-valve KR so they left that program alone for as long, make that too long, as they could.

But again, there was that TT class, and there were dealers and buyers who wanted to be involved. So right along with the program designing and producing the XL Sportster, there was a program for the XLR, which as any H-D student needn't be told, was a blending of the XL and the KR.

The XLR's internal differences made it faster and more fragile. The shared parts and profile are obvious, but you'll have to check the engine's numbers, stamped on the left-side case half below the vee, to know what it really is. *Courtesy Harley-Davidson Archives*

Some of this is tricky. The KR was a side-valve 750, used mostly on dirt tracks and sold to the public with no brakes and with a rigidly mounted rear wheel. For road races and TT, the KR could be fitted with brakes and with a swingarm and shocks that bolted to the rear of the frame, replacing a triangulated rear section. In that form and when it was fitted with optional larger or smaller fuel or oil tanks, and even with low bars and a fairing, the KR was known as the KRTT.

The parts book says the new TT racer, which appeared right after the first XL and parallel with the XLC, the stripped off-roader, was the XLRTT, no hyphen. The factory's records show they did build some XLRs with no brakes and with the rigid rear section, presumably for some form of run-what-ya-brung dirt track. By the book, these would have been designated XLR.

Making things even more complicated, later in the model run, when the XLR was accepted as a TT bike, the parts books simply list the XLR. The XLR, which we'll call it here to save ink, was a lot more different than it looked.

What it looked like was the stripper XLC of 1958: The XLR was introduced several months prior to the XLC because the XLR was built at the request of the racing department, which knew about the XL before it appeared. The XLC was done for California dealers, who didn't know about the XL until the project went public.

The XLR used the frame, tanks, wheels, brakes, and suspension from the XL (some of the parts were shared with the KRTT as well). The XLR's exterior differences are limited. First, of course, the left side of the cases will be stamped XLR instead of XLC, XLH, or XLCH.

Most often, the XLR will have its magneto ignition mounted at the front of the cases, instead of atop the gear case beneath the carb.

Less visibly, the XLR uses special cylinder heads with larger valves. Spark plugs are shared with the other competition engines. The joke now is H-D had too many and wanted to get rid of the surplus. However—and this requires looking closely—the spark plug boss on an XLR head is raised because the plug's reach is 3/4 inch and an XL plug's is 1/2 inch. An XL head's plug boss is slightly recessed. (Swap meet hint: This can also matter because the XLR heads, especially the rear ones, are rare and worth hundreds of dollars. Sportster heads are worth a tenth as much, and there are piles of them in the used-parts bins at every H-D agency. Rooting through those bins, armed with the knowledge most Harley fans don't have, can literally pay off.)

The XLR's major differences are internal. The XLR engine is mostly KR, as in low-friction and short-lived ball bearings for the flywheels and camshafts, instead of the roller bearings and bushings in the X-series street engines. Camshaft timing, valves, and ignition are also different, and the oil pump runs at one-quarter of the engine's rpm, instead of one-half.

There were several major changes made for model year 1963. The AMA loosened its grip and approved a new frame for the KR and KRTT and XLR. The new frame used more steel and less cast iron and put the rear shocks back where they were more efficient. This frame was

An XLR in action. This is Mark Brelsford, who went on to become a national champion, and his XLR is special. Witness the disc brakes. The best professional TT bikes were 100 pounds lighter and 20 brake horsepower stronger than the production machines. Naturally the team XLRs are now rare and expensive. *Courtesy Harley-Davidson Archives*

The original XR-750 was clearly based on the XL engine. The frame is new and modern, though, and the fiberglass seat/fender and tank are works of art. Forks were from Ceriani and the shocks were Girling, the best on the market at the time. Notice there are no brakes. In 1970 they were not required for dirt track.

stronger and lighter and was, in many ways, the first really modern H-D frame in nearly 25 years.

Fairings were allowed for road racing in the same year, and the factory's team took advantage. Road-racing rules virtually banned the larger engines, but there were some machines built privately or with covert help from the team.

The official version says the XLR was built—well, better make that offered—from 1958 until 1969, when the KR also went out of production and when the rules for national racing were changed.

In fact, as documented by racing historian Bill Milburn, Harley-Davidson assembled and delivered six XLRs in 1970 and two in 1971. They had to have been special orders, done for people with influence, and done because the parts were there and the money came in handy.

They haven't been seen since. And they won't be that tough to identify because between 1969 and 1970, the factory changed the engine identification code. Instead of having the case stamped XLR, a 1970 or 1971 XLR will be stamped 9B (an XLH will have 3L and an XLCH will be 4A followed by H0 for 1970 or H1 for 1971).

The First XR-750

This story has a typically Harley-Davidson beginning; that is, it's sad, perhaps even tragic.

When the AMA's Grand National series was inaugurated in 1954, the Number One plate, i.e. *the* national championship, went to the rider who'd gained the most points in a series comprised of short track, half mile, mile, TT, and road-course races. The short tracks were contested with 250-cc singles, TT allowed 900-cc twins and the other events (the miles, half miles, and road races) used the 750 sidevalve/500 ohv equivalency formula.

In 1968 the AMA changed the rules. The equivalency formula was replaced with rules that allowed any and all 750-cc engines, no limit on the number of cylinders or location of valves. The only rule was the maker had to have produced at least 200 examples and had to offer them for public sale. The new rules were supposed to take effect on the dirt in 1969 and on the road courses in 1970; the delay provided time for the factories to make the new bikes.

The Motor Company was deep in one of its periodic rough patches at that point in time, and the racing department hadn't been authorized to prepare for the day, never mind that everybody knew the day would come.

The team and shop did their best.

It wasn't all that good.

Okay, it was a disaster.

There was no money for a new engine, so the designers shortened the stroke of the XLR by 0.60 inch, reducing displacement from 900 to 750 cc. One fin was lopped off the XL/XLR cylinder, which was cast iron, so the piston would reach the top of the barrel despite the shorter stroke. The change in displacement required new camshafts, stamped A instead of PB in case you need to look closely. But the rest, as in the ball bearings, dry clutch, quarter-speed oil pump, front-mount magneto, straight pipes, and an engine sprocket using a tapered key instead of splines, was shared with the XLR. The initial power claim was 62 brake horsepower, which the reporters of the day suspected was overly modest but proved to be optimistic.

Back when the AMA began accepting optional frames, the H-D race shop devised some truly excellent designs, smaller and more tightly shaped to the engine and stiffer. The new dirt racer, designated XR-750 for the X-series competition version and the displacement, got

The XR-750's magneto mounts in front of the front cylinder, as it did for the XLR and KR. Rear frame section is a preview for the XL and the FXR, while the little springs holding the strap for the oil tank below the seat date back to 1930, no kidding. Left foot peg mounts on a plate bolted to the frame's left-side tomahawk. And look carefully at the steering head. *Courtesy Harley-Davidson Archives*

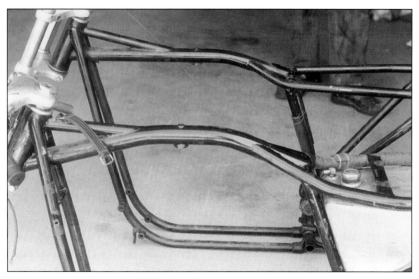

Here's why research is required. The rear frame is a stock, 1970 XR-750 unit, with a horizontal backbone and a brace that slopes from steering head to backbone. The front frame is an ex-team Lowboy frame, with a backbone that slopes down toward the steering head and a brace that's horizontal. These frames were built for the team and not sold to the general public, but some of the 20-odd such may still be out there. Looks sharp.

a modification of this new frame (which was called the Lowboy in road-race mode, by the way).

The frame was designed by the team's engineer—yes, just one—and was produced for the factory by the Widman family in St. Louis, then as now a Harley-Davidson dealership with resources. They could make the 200 required examples cheaper and quicker than the factory could, which tells something about the Widmans and probably something more about the state of the factory in 1969.

The fuel tank and seat/fender were fiberglass and were easily the best-looking use of that material ever put on a motorcycle. The XR-750 got full suspension, Ceriani forks in front, Girling shocks and springs in back.

The XR-750 was for flat track and came with no brakes. There was a Road Race Group, as the parts book calls it, offering the four-shoe drum brake, as seen on the earlier KRTT and XLRTT, for the front. A stock XL brake could be put on the back, and there was a fairing and a 6-gallon fuel tank, which were also shared parts.

Oh, speaking of that, you could also get the dirt track tank and seat for your XLR, and there's a listing for a Sportster decal. There must have been a notion somewhere in the marketing department to use the XR and XLR as a sales tool. There was one factory photo of the XR with this decal, but it was never seen in public again.

The Waffle Iron

The XR-750 in its original form was shown to the public at the Houston show, held with the opening of the racing season, in February 1970. It was a beautiful motorcycle.

That was darned near its high point.

As was made too clear too quickly, the iron-topped engine produced more power than it could withstand. The iron didn't shed the heat fast enough, a flaw that had been concealed with the XLR because TT racing is on the power, off the power, and that allowed the engine to cool.

But at Daytona and on the miles, the power is on most of the time and the engines melted, leading first to the rude nickname Waffle Iron and second to as bad a racing season—make that two seasons, 1970 and 1971—as H-D ever had. (Oh okay: Indian won all the nationals in 1928 and 1929, but H-D's team had been disbanded, so that's not quite the same.)

In 1972 H-D introduced the alloy-top XR-750, which as we'll see in the second part of this book, made up for all the failures.

Meanwhile, the iron XR's history is as murky as it was tragic. The official AMA requirement was 200 examples, built, assembled, and inspected by the AMA. That was done, and pictures taken, so the record always says there were 200 XR-750s, cases stamped 1C1 then the four numbers for each engine, as in 0036 or 0194 (which are the author's engines), then H0, for the last year of the eighth decade of this century, 1970.

More contrast. This is Mert Lawwill, H-D team leader and defending national champion in 1970, aboard a team XR. It's got two carburetors, with the one for the rear barrel jutting forward on the left, and it has a rear disc brake. *Courtesy Harley-Davidson Archives*

As they say in court, however, engine 1C10194H0 also had on it #228 when it arrived, and there was a separate run of XR-750s, true XR-750TTs, done by an outside contractor for the factory's road-racing effort. (The AMA's national championship was, as mentioned, based on all five types of events, but presumably because Daytona and Louden and, in time, Laguna Seca were publicized in the national press, the factory exerted much more influence and effort on road racing than flat track during this period. The work was done outside because management was locked in combat with the union.)

The team-prepped XRs had numbers beginning in the 500 series, as in 1C10501. Exactly how many such engines were built can be debated. These engines used special cylinder heads, with two carbs facing the rear on the right and the rear exhaust moved to the left and all sorts of other tricks that did incredible damage to the spirit of those 1934 rules.

None of it quite worked. Well, there was one high point in the Waffle Iron's history. In 1972, before the alloy XR was ready, legendary road racer Cal Rayborn went to England for the match races. H-D management didn't want him to go, so he rode an XR owned and prepped by Walt Faulk, who worked for the Motor Company, but not in the race shop, and who raced his own stuff on his own time.

Faulk kept the underdesigned and overstressed beast in health just long enough, and Rayborn got three wins and three seconds in the series' six races. The English fans still talk about it.

That XR-750 is in the AMA's Motorcycle Heritage Museum at Westerville, Ohio, and don't even think about making an offer.

And then, not before time, the alloy engine arrived and made a much more comfortable sort of racing history.

What to Look For

Best beginning here is something along the lines of, "Kids, don't try this without adult supervision." Vintage racing lore, skill, and enthusiasm are as deep as they are narrow.

It's a tremendously concentrated hobby. Where hundreds of thousands of motorcycle nuts buy, sell, own, and enjoy the hundreds of thousands of F-series Shovelheads and iron-top XLs, there were perhaps 500 XLRs made between 1958 and 1970. There were officially 200 original XR-750s, and former team manager Dick O'Brien said years later that

only 100 or so of that batch was actually sold. The public learned of the debacle in time to buy Triumphs or BSAs—the team guys even dragged out the old KRs when things were at their worst—and the second half of that 200 was parted out, so the accountants could write off the cost of the machines against income.

Next, there are no stock racing bikes. They've all had something done back when they were new or later, when the owner had a notion or couldn't find the right parts. And it takes a trained eye to distinguish the former from the latter. Even chaps as smart as you or me need to look at these machines over and over before we can spot, oh, a short-rod engine, a replica frame, or an engine that's been moved to a better spot than the factory had in mind.

Lawwill again, still trying to defend his title in 1970, but this time aboard a team XRTT, the iron XR-750 in road-race trim. The fairing, tank, and seat are derived from the earlier KRTT, and the XR has a disc rear brake and a huge four-shoe drum brake for the front. The rules required the parts to be offered to the public, so the 1970 catalog offered a road race group, an 18-inch front wheel (with brake), fairing, shield, and 6-gallon fuel tank. Few bought them, and the iron XRTT is the rarest model on our list. *Courtesy Harley-Davidson Archives*

Plus, there is potential for deceit. Mind, I said potential. If a greedy person found the left half of some XLR cases, with the XLR stamp, he or she could take an XL right case half, a reproduction XLRTT frame, glass, front brakes, and so forth, and presto, the world would have one more historic racer than the factory ever saw.

It could be done. This isn't to say it has been done, or that the builder of an out-front replica would or could ever forget to tell the new owner exactly where his historic treasure came from. But in the world of vintage cars, such fraud isn't even news.

Caveat Emptor, as the banner above the used chariots used to say. (That's Latin for read the books, take notes, and spend a year or so learning the territory before putting down the money.)

After all that comes the actual search and research. Both are also specialized. XLRs and XRs almost never appear in the usual places, like the classifieds or the swap meets where you can't count the road machines lined up and ready to go.

It's almost all word of mouth. The best way is simply to find out where the vintage races and meets are—refer to the Appendix for details. Go there and talk with people and the day will come that presto II, a friend will call to say he knows a guy who has an XLR in his barn.

The good news is that this is still happening. It defies logic and experience, but the fact is there were 100 or so XR-750s sold in 1970 and 1971 and the collectors' club—again, refer to the Appendix—has located nearly 40 survivors.

This has to be the highest survival rate ever recorded for a racing machine sold to the public, and they are still turning up. The most recent at this writing wasn't just an XR-750, it was one in factory trim, complete with a set of twin-carb heads made only for the team and not sold to the general public. The guy who found the bike paid less than half that day's going rate.

The key points here? Know the subject, insist on verification, and be prepared to take yes for an answer. That is, if you find one like the ex-team example mentioned above, get it. Anything that can happen can happen again.

Models	Utility	Saddletime	Collectibility	Style	Accommodations
1970 XR-750	★★★☆☆	★★★★☆	★★★★★	★★★★★	NA
1970 XRTT	★★★★☆	★★★★☆	★★★★☆	★★★★★	NA
1958—69 XLR, XLRTT	★★★☆☆	★★★☆☆	★★★★☆	★★★☆☆	NA

About Those Stars

One of the several reasons the stock market in Serbia is a bit more risky than the exchanges in England or Japan is that there are fewer players and less to play with. Each part is more of the sum.

So it is here. The XLR gets the lowest ratings. At the vintage end of the scale, the XLR was ignored by the factory and wasn't raced in major events, so we aren't talking legend here.

At the modern end of the scale some of the vintage clubs have classes for 900-cc twins, but most don't. Some events are open to 900-cc road racers, but most aren't. The XLRs didn't have much to do in the past, so when we relive (or rewrite) the past, there's not much for the XLRs to do.

Fair? Nope. Nor does that matter. An XLR is fun to have and ride. You can get the parts, albeit with some effort and at some cost. An XLR is an honest look at history. It's rare and attractive, and one can be a good buy assuming it still has the right parts and price. But it's not a sure thing.

An iron XR-750, in dirt or road-race trim, is a sure thing.

We're back in the free market here. There's a finite—well nearly finite—number of iron-top XRs that went out into the world. Some are still to be found. Some of those already found are restored works of art, and some, less perfect as a rule, are still being raced.

All the vintage clubs provide for the iron XRs. Not only can you get the parts—see qualifying clause above—but an XR can be updated and improved. You can race on dirt and on road courses, and on occasions such as Daytona Beach's cycle week you can race the same XR in two road races and two dirt-track meets in the same week, which is about as much fun as you can have with your goggles on.

In terms of style, there's kind of a dividing line. The lay public hasn't a clue. In fact you can win root beer betting that your iron XR is really an XR, but there is now an XR mystique and the folks who know will be dazzled. Call it a test of character.

The accommodations factor doesn't apply here; however, the other factor, its actual riding, is pretty good, limited only by the rider's physical size (an XR is a small motorcycle).

In terms of investment, a dirt XR outranks the XRTT not because the dirt bike is more valuable, but because the XRTTs are more scarce and have already moved into the treasure class while the XR-750s haven't. Yet.

Topping it all, an XR-750 is a work of art. Just to see it glowing all warm orange and iron in your garage is to justify all the time and effort.

If that doesn't earn five stars, nothing does.

Chapter 6

Evolution Era

1986–98 Sportsters

Remember the joke about Abe Lincoln's axe? Seems this museum had the very axe Honest Abe used to split those rails. Of course, since then the axe had been through two new heads and three new handles.

The same idea tells as much about history and continuity when applied to the XL engine from 1957 until it evolved—make that, was magically transformed—in model year 1986.

Outwardly this was classic H-D. The new-for-1986 Sportster was identified as the XLH-883. This made sense in that the previous models used XLH and there was an 883. At the same time, it didn't make sense because there wasn't anything else, as in XLC, XLCR, or plain XL.

The new 883 returned to the original XL's displacement and the same dimensions of 3.00-inch bore and 3.812-inch stroke. The configuration was the same, with 45-degree vee, fore-and-aft cylinders, and four one-lobe camshafts.

However, pause for emphasis, this 883 was much less like the older one or the ones in between than it looked.

Most important, the cylinders and heads were aluminum alloy—cries of At Last!—and the combustion chamber was revised and updated to allow a higher compression ratio, 9:1 with no-lead horse pi—, um, gasoline. Hydraulic valve lifters freed the owner from adjusting valve clearances and made the engine quieter, which in these days of federal scrutiny didn't hurt. The rocker boxes were in layers so the top of the engine could be dismantled and serviced in the frame. The flywheels were forged in one piece; no longer were they bolted together with that risk of misalignment. The new engine carried over the alternator, electronic ignition, diaphragm clutch, and oil filter from the final versions of the iron XL. There was a new engine mount, and the frame rails were revised because the size and shape of the new heads required it.

The new engine looked like the old, on purpose, but the major components no longer interchanged. The old and new engines wouldn't fit in each other's frames, and where the old engine needed 455 parts, the new engine used only 426 (and of those, 206 parts were new).

Which is why it was like the same axe with different head and handle.

The Evolution 883, the XL engine with alloy top end, first appeared as the Evo XL in XLX trim, with solo seat, small tank, one-tone paint, low bars, one disc front brake, . . . and the list price of $3,995 that had done so well for the XLX.

They didn't use that designation, in fact the XLH-883 tag probably was there to distinguish the new model from the iron-top XLX.

Beyond that, the XLH-883 was available with different paint, dual seat, and so forth, without a designation change. The XLX was its own

model. But those are side issues.

The new engine with the old price worked just as well the second time, that is, H-D sold all the bikes they could make.

Nor was that all. No sooner had all the budget-minded Sportster fans lined up to get a bargain than the factory announced a second XLH, New and Improved.

The "new" was the alloy engine in the revised frame. The "improved" was a larger bore and a displacement increase to 1,100 cc. The larger bore allowed larger valves, but all the other parts were the same.

The factory called it the XLH-1100, a name H-D wisely figured would emphasize what was different. The 1100 came with a stepped, two-person seat, higher bars, and a choice of paint schemes, *and* you could order any of the parts and bits in combination. That is, you could have the seat, bars, and paint with the 883 engine, or an 1100 with low bars, solo seat, and so forth.

In two strokes, Harley-Davidson created a model line of Sportsters, all with the new engine.

And it was improved. There was only one glitch: early in the production run it was discovered that there was a flaw in the shifter mechanism and the gearbox could—in fact would—lock itself into gear. There was a recall for that and for the cast wheels (which came from Aus-

The Basic Evolution Sportster was . . . basic: an XLX with solo seat, small tank, one front brake, low bars, and a low sticker price. *Courtesy Harley-Davidson Archives*

The revised XL engine was a lot more changed than it looked: aluminum heads and cylinders, with improved breathing to give the same performance with less displacement, and a major improvement in engine life. That's an oil filter in front of the cylinders, where the generator used to go. *Courtesy Harley-Davidson Archives*

tralia, of all places), but beyond that the new XLH was as trouble-free as a motorcycle can be.

The 1100 option was more than a marketing move. The 883 was rated at 54 brake horsepower, which translated into 42 brake horsepower at the rear wheel. That meant the new 883 in XLX trim was marginally slower than the XLX with the iron 1,000-cc engine. The opposition, read Honda, had just entered the V-twin wars and the 883 Harley was slower than the 1,100-cc Honda.

But the 1100 was rated at 63 brake horsepower, delivered close to 50 at the rear wheel, and made the XLH faster than the old model and the Honda.

The XLH-1100 listed at $5,199, which was quite a jump for larger holes in the cylinders and ports, except that it delivered the extra parts, trim, and paint as well as performance. The XLH-1100 was also $2,000 less than the next Harley on the floor, the basic FXR, which gave the buyer a clear choice and the salesman a clear target.

Model Year 1987

The advice on timing being everything has already been given, but it's worth repeating here because in 1987 H-D made news with an idea that wasn't as new as people thought.

It was the Hugger, which in 1987 was a model all its own, with lower suspension and a thinner seat, and thus a low static height so certain people could put their boots on the ground. The certain people were women, just as they had been in 1980 when H-D introduced the name and the option the first time.

Fudge No. 1 was that H-D never actually referred to the target market by gender.

Fudge No. 2 was the assumption that women, suddenly freed from eons of oppression, had just this instant discovered motorcycles.

History, complete with pictures, proves that the gentler gender has been riding since an engine was strapped to a bicycle. But heck, if you can sell somebody something by telling them they're new and daring and they fall for it, why not?

Fudge No. 3, shabby in a more factual way, was that the claimed seat height, 26.75 inches, was measured with the seat compressed by a 185-pound occupant, somebody who was not, you may be assured, used when the ads were photographed.

Never mind. The Hugger's time had come and the ad campaign got new people into the sport and that's good.

Mechanically, the Hugger was standard for the year. All the XLH engines got revised combustion chambers, the 1100 heads were given smaller ports and valves to increase velocity, and the changes were credited with a 5 percent boost in power. The gearbox's four speeds were juggled, with first, second, and third all taller; this gave higher speeds in the lower gears and helped in passing traffic.

Model Year 1988

The Motor Company had major news, as the optional 1100 engine became the optional 1200 engine. This was easily done, with the bore increased to 3.50 inches from the 3.35 of the 1100 or the 3.0 of the 883. The compression chamber for the 1200 was larger, so the compression ratio would be the same despite the increased displacement, about which you'll hear more in due course.

Low bars, small tank, and centered speedometer make for a clean, uncluttered view. A second mirror is easily added, while the addition of a tachometer is less important because vibration when you rev to redline makes a tach redundant. *Courtesy Harley-Davidson Archives*

Perhaps by coincidence, the XL engine had grown from the 883-cc size it began with, to the 1,000-cc size the Big Twin was at first, and then to 1,200 cc or 74 cid, which the FL engine had been until recently. Perhaps because it made the smaller bike seem too close to the big one, H-D has always referred to the XL-1200 as that, never the 74.

The larger bore was a major improvement. The magazines in general have always (well in recent years anyway) liked the Sportster and done lots of tests.

For comparative purposes, here are some results from the tests performed by *Cycle* and/or *Cycle World*:

Model	Weight	1/4 mile	0–60 mph per hour
1988 XL883	478 lbs	14.24 sec	4.96 sec
1987 XL1100	475 lbs	13.15 sec	not given
1991 XL1200	494 lbs	13.00 sec	4.0 sec

As a long-term note, it's interesting that no matter what's done to a Sportster, what's bolted on or taken off, it always weighs just less than 500 pounds.

It follows that when you add power, you gain performance. Checking all the files, the best Sportster performances recorded by a legitimate test procedure were 13.08 seconds for the XLCR and 12.88 seconds for the XR-1000 (chapter 12 has the details of that one).

That clean 13-second run will whip any car you'll ever meet and all but a handful of the larger multis.

Coming right after the XL-883 was the XL-1100, with a larger bore and heads revised to match the increase. The 1100 came stock with the extra instrument, dual seat, higher bars, and second mirror, although the dealer would often delete some of the extras on request. Right after the XLH-1100 came the XLH-1200, with yet another bore increase. Laced-up wheels were an option, as was the dual seat and so forth. *Courtesy Harley-Davidson Archives*

The important part, though, is part of our family's feud. The V2-powered FXR was arguably the best motorcycle Harley-Davidson ever made: not the best buy, best investment, or best shrine to old-fashioned virtue, but it was the best motorcycle.

And Cycle's test gave a quarter-mile time of 13.5 seconds. Yes indeed. If you want the quickest Harley in town, you gotta buy the paper boy's bike or the girl's bike.

Wasn't there some writer who claimed riding faster is the best revenge?

Model Years 1989–1990

Saving some time and space here, the two years are combined because what happened mostly was refinement and shuffling of the parts so there'd be maximum choice at minimum bother to the plant.

There were four versions. The basic XLH-883 had a solo seat, small tank, cast wheels, and a speedometer plus warning lights. The Deluxe XLH-883 had a choice of paint colors, a dual seat with passenger pegs, laced-up wheels, and a tachometer. The Hugger came with the basic parts plus buckhorn bars, higher so the (presumably) smaller person could reach the levers. And the XLH-1200—the 1100 was dropped after 1987—had the dual seat and pegs, two-tone paint, buckhorn bars, and both speedo and tach.

Oh yes—and there were other options: the touring gear, a larger fuel tank, and various items of trim. You could add this, subtract that, and pretty much tailor your XL to your own ideas, and a lot of people did; which is why it's okay to find a 1200 engine in basic black with solo seat or the Hugger suspension or any of the myriad combinations offered.

Model Year 1991

Back to major changes, with first, the addition of a fifth speed for the venerable XL gearbox.

This took some doing. In effect, it's five pairs of gears packaged in a cavity where four pairs used to fit. The clutch and shift mechanism had to be changed, but the five speeds only added half an inch to the drivetrain's width, which was an achievement.

Why'd they do it? Partially for marketing reasons. The semi-skilled public always assumes the more speeds, the more sporting. It's not always so, but setting the public straight isn't in the sales department's job description.

In this case, though, what the five speeds did was allow a lower low, for crawling around the parking lot without fuss, and a higher high, to drop revs and thus vibrations at interstate speeds.

The other major modification for 1991 was more clearly an improvement: Belt drive, seen first on the FX Sturgis and then made standard for the FLT series, was fitted to the XLH-1200 and the 883 Deluxe.

This was a win-win move. Belt drive proved itself on the larger bikes. There was no question the belt gave longer, quieter, and cleaner service. The top XLs got the belt first for marketing reasons; fashion expands best when it works its way down. At the same time, for manufacturing reasons, all the XLs from 1991 on have been five speeds because it's easier to make them all the same.

Throughout the years, Sportsters were offered in a number of different versions. The bike above is the Deluxe XLH-883, which offered the buyer a choice of paint colors, a dual seat with passenger pegs, laced-up wheels and a tachometer. *Courtesy Harley-Davidson Archives*

Nor did the factory miss another opportunity. As part of the belt drive project there was a kit, with which one could retrofit an earlier Evo XL. (In common with thousands of other such owners, I waited until the chain on my 1986 XLH got worn and replaced it with the belt kit, at the same time going to a new rear tire so I'd get two jobs for the labor of one.)

Consolidation

Yet another H-D habit has been followed with the Sportster's most recent history. For the 1992 model year the chain-drive XLs got O-ring chains. There were revisions to items such as brake pad material, and the Hugger was lowered another 1.5 inches, making the girl's—oops, small person—Sportster the Super Hugger, a name to which nobody outside the ad agency paid any attention.

In 1993 all the XLs got belt drive, another logical move once the status of the system was established. The main reason it was logical was that 1993 was the 90th anniversary of the Motor Company (the company didn't incorporate until 1907, but the first Harley-Davidson motorcycle was made in 1903). Anniversary models had by this time become a tradition in themselves, so in 1993 there was a special run of Sportsters.

In fact, each of H-D's model lines, six in all, got a 90th anniversary model. In the XL's case, plans for the model year called for 1,993 XL-1200s to be built with serialized nameplates, jeweled cloisonné (an enamel decoration where the enamel is fired on a metal background), fuel tank emblems, and two-tone silver and charcoal satin paint. Everything else about the 90th Anniversary XL-1200 was stock and standard. (The factory never says how many of such special examples are actually sold.)

For 1994 the XL frame was beefed in the rear and the covers for the rear struts were made straighter. The clutch cable got a quick-release feature; previously you had to remove the primary cover to replace the clutch cable. The 883s got the stiffer top triple clamp that was used on

The Hugger's only difference is that the suspension is slighter shorter and the seat's padding is slightly less dense, so the calculated static ride height with a person of a given weight aboard, is fractionally lower. But the option is useful for short people, and it makes the opposite sex feel welcome, so it's been a good deal. *Courtesy Harley-Davidson Archives*

the 1200s—they didn't tell us the 883s had wimpy clamps until then, by the way. Ditto for an improved ignition switch and wiring loom.

In 1995 the 1200 got a larger fuel tank, 3.2 gallons from 2.2 for the venerable peanut, and styled as a mix between the peanut and the teardrop of the older Superglides and Sprints. All the XLs got electronic speedometers, as in no more cable routed across the front of the headlight.

As a keeper of the records, note here that the basic 883's list price, in solid color, solo seat, and so forth had (pick one) risen/been held down to $4,995. The choices of paint options were wonderfully bright and modern.

Names and letters returned for 1996. There were two new models, the XLH1200C Custom and the XLH1200S Sport.

The Custom featured, quoting the factory here, chrome on the standalone headlight, the handlebar clamp and riser, and the covers for the top triple clamp, and there were chrome and black accents for the engine.

There were low-rise bars for the high-rise mounts and a stepped seat and—most radical of all—a 21-inch front wheel, as seen first on choppers and then the factory's FX customs. The 1200C used Hugger tricks and had a seat height in Hugger territory.

Out in the world, here's what you'll find. The guy on the left has added a kit to tip the license plate forward, a passenger pad and a Fat Bob tank and console. The guy on the right has lowered the speedo and fitted a solid rear wheel. Both have left the stock pipes, which is rare.

The 1200S was clearly aimed at a different enthusiast. The Sport came with adjustable suspension, tunable for compression, and rebound damping and ride height. Tires were Dunlop Sport Elites on 13-spoke cast wheels, and there were a low seat, bars, and even a checkered-flag motif for the fuel tank.

The press release added that all the XLs got "high-contact-ratio transmission gears," which

translates into better quality control, with the gear teeth matching each other better, fitting better, and running quieter.

H-D missed a historical marker in 1997, as all five XLs got the 3.3-gallon tank: Yes, it was listed as 3.2 at first, but actual capacity of the tanks on all brands has always been more variable than the spec sheets admit. The old tank, nicknamed peanut, simply didn't have enough capacity for modern times. Because the tank first appeared on the Model S—the DKW-copy two-stroke single introduced in 1947—this ended a 50-year run.

Beyond that for 1997, 13-spoke cast wheels, 19- and 16-inch, became standard for all the XLs, replacing the 7- and 9-spokers. Laced-up wheels of the same size were still offered as options. And all the Sportsters received smaller and more powerful sealed batteries, another of those features you don't notice when new but appreciate later.

Remember back in 1957, when the factory assumed the XL buyer wanted to get as close to the FLH as he or she could? The owner of the XLH-1200 has done just that.

The most predictable news for model year 1998 has to be that H-D came up with a set of 95th anniversary models. There were six in total and each, quoting the factory brochure here, "flaunts special graphics and paint."

The paint for each is two tones, Midnight Red and Champagne Pearl. The tanks get a special emblem and each model, including the 95th Anniversary Sportster XL1200C (the Custom), has a serialized nameplate.

The Sportster news, though, came with a model that should have been called the Super Sport. (Note that the plain models were XLH883, XLH883 Hugger, or XLH 1200, while the two flagships, Sport and Custom, drop the H and use XL1200.)

The 1998 1200S got what in the old days would have been the CH treatment: raised compression ratio, hotter cams, dual plug-single fire ignition, and a tailored spark curve. There was an option, sure to be popular, of a race-style muffler from famed tuners Vance & Hines.

This is good stuff. One, the souped engine proves the H-D engineers can improve performance and meet the rules. Two, although no tests have been published for the 1998s at this writing, impromptu comparisons on press day showed the Super Sport will in fact dust the normal 1200S or any other H-D currently on offer.

Details aside, the other Sportsters carried over for the year.

What to Look For

Opportunity is the word here.

The Evolution XL engine, sometimes called the XLV because the factory calls the F-series Evo engine the V-2, is simply a better engine than the original XL engine was. Period.

At the same place and time, this 1200's owner has gone in a different direction, with wire wheels, sculpted seat, low bars, and open pipes minus that ugly balance tube. This XL, like the one in the preceding photo, was in Daytona Beach in 1997 and represents the bikes you'll find in your paper's classified ads.

The new engine, though, has been artificially restricted, in that the factory was free to tune the old XLCH to its practical limit, with no emissions rules and not much noise limit to worry about. Now there are world-wide requirements to be met.

But because the rules change when an owner makes improvements (and because the engineers know more about improving engines within the rules) the XLV engine can run longer and with less stress than the older engine ever hoped to do.

As one could predict, because it can be done, it is being done. The factory and the aftermarket both provide a complete line of camshafts, exhausts, carburetors, gearsets, larger bores and strokes, all the good stuff for the new XL engines.

There's a whole other set of upgrades, in that the 883 owner can convert to a full 1200, the chain can be replaced by a belt, and so on, up the line. (Adding that fifth speed is beyond this scope, but don't worry, the extra speed isn't all that useful in daily life.)

There are still more upgrades because the Sportster is featured in racing classes, sort of like the original box-stock Class C racing of 1934, with a series on dirt and a series on road courses. You can get kits to convert your XL into a dirt tracker or style it like an XRTT circa 1972. Or if your taste runs the other direction, there are kits to make a Little Big Bike, as in a scaled-down FLH circa 1962.

There's not enough room here for the details but there are lots of books and magazines on the subject.

Some of the equipment is also made for the V-2 engines,

Current (at this writing) models are moving in different directions. The XL 1200C (for Custom) got a King Peanut tank, enlarged from 2.2 gallons to 3.3 without changing the look or the lines, and a 21-inch front wheel, as seen in the Superglide line. Note also the new riser and bars, and how the bike adopts the lower suspension from the Hugger. *Courtesy Harley-Davidson Archives*

which in their own way are even more of an improvement over the old Shovelhead. But it's not as common to see a modified FLT or FLST; mostly they are chrome.

The Sportster, though, was made to become *your* motorcycle. As the sign from the shop of my youth put it, All You Need Is the Money.

What to Avoid

There are some of the usual cautions.

The Evo XLs are too new and too well designed to be subject to the risks of any earlier model, so there's no need to worry much about the machine not being what the advertiser says it is. Well, perhaps a swindler could put a 1200 badge and emblems on an 883, but that's about it.

There have been some recalls of the Evo XL line. The gear lock-up and the possibly flawed cast wheels have been mentioned already. These recalls were 10 years ago at least and should have been fixed by now, or perhaps the bike locked in gear and was fixed for that reason. There was also a risk of a bad bolt holding the front brake caliper, and that's worth checking. And there were three—yes three—recalls to fix the positive battery cable. Why three? Because the first two didn't work, why else?

This can be fixed at roadside—my son did just that—but it's easier to make sure early that the cable is intact and is long enough to reach without the stress that breaks it.

The XL 1200S (for Sport), meanwhile, has tunable suspension, sticky tires (stock), triple disc brakes, and cast wheels. Beginning in model year 1996, the 1200C, 1200S, and the 1200 plain got the larger tank standard. *Courtesy Harley-Davidson Archives*

Fashion rules: For 1998 the Sportster got a Supersport model, with the power boosted via heads and cams ala Buell. The XL's top engine isn't as powerful as the Buell, though, in some part because the Buell gets a big and efficient air cleaner, and the XL keeps the traditional hamcan. But wait! Look at this optional muffler, which does boost power and can be offered as an option now because the racing Superbikes use mufflers like that, which makes them cool, which makes them something a Sportster buyer will like. Note also the reservoirs on the rear shocks, the lack of license plate and mirrors, and the grandstand in the background. Sport is what this is about. *Courtesy Harley-Davidson Archives*

Now we come to the quirks, of which there are at least three.

One, the valve lifters are hydraulically damped. This means you don't have to adjust them. It also means one lifter may lose pressure and set up a clatter you won't believe. Sometimes when you pull the lifter down (which isn't too tough, but it's not a roadside operation), part of the lifter will be in upside down and that's why it got blocked.

The next time, it won't be upside down and it will still lose pressure.

What to do? If the clatter arises, shut off the engine, coast to a stop, count to the first number that comes to mind, start the engine, and odds are, the pressure will be back. In some cases, a sticky lifter simply quits sticking and is fine for the life of the engine. I've never found a logical reason for these things to happen, even from engineers, but some Evo XL engines stick and unstick lifters for no better reason other than they just do.

The second quirk involves the oil pump and breather. Recall that the pistons gallop up and down in tandem and create tremendous variations of plus and minus pressure inside the cases. Harley twins have pumps and breathers designed to cope with this; they even use the pressure to deliver the oil.

Current engines aren't allowed to vent to the atmosphere. Their breathers route to the air cleaner, where oil fumes in theory are put back inside the engine and consumed.

This doesn't always happen. When the system doesn't work, fumes and oil in liquid form get fed into the air box and all over the air filter and the engine runs like heck.

There is an elaborate fix for this, involving replacing and rerouting. It's too complicated to explain here. If this happens to your engine all the time, it's worth checking with your favorite dealership or shop. If it happens once, clean up the mess and put everything back. If it happens again, negotiate: The 1998 XL engines have revised oil passages for the pump, and that improves drainage so the mess won't happen anymore, or so the factory tells us. The 1998 pump can be retro-fitted back to the 1991 XLs. Whether it's worth it depends on how much the mess bothers you or how much the dealership will charge for the work.

Quirk number three is that the intake manifold's gaskets will fatigue with time. The manifold assembly is a tight and complicated fit, which makes for good use of space but requires ball-ended Allen wrenches and so forth to get the manifold off and back on. It also requires removing lots of stuff, so you can remember all the words you learned in the Navy before the gaskets are replaced. And oh, yeah, you can tell when it's time because the idle goes to hell.

The Evo XL engine is an excellent piece of engineering, and each version has been better than the one before it; but it does have some odd habits, so expect the occasional frustration.

Models	Utility	Saddletime	Collectibility	Style	Accommodations
1986–98 XLX, XLH-883	★★★☆☆	★★★☆☆	★★★☆☆	★★★☆☆	★★★☆☆
1986–98 XLH1100/1200	★★★☆☆	★★★★☆	★★★☆☆	★★★☆☆	★★★☆☆
1996–98 XL1200C/S	★★★★☆	★★★★☆	★★★★☆	★★★★☆	★★★☆☆

About Those Stars

Fair and impartial application of the rating system makes the Evo Sportsters look worse than they are.

How and why? First because there have been lots of XLs sold. They have given good service and there's a good supply, so there's a slight chance of scooping up a bargain. The investment value for the early ones and the standard later XLs is average. Like the grade C in school, average doesn't sound very good.

Second, the rating rules specify stock and some of the Evo XL's parts, namely the seat and tank, are simply not adequate stock. The solo seat is a pain in the butt, literally, and the tiny tank is the second wrong that doesn't make a right; that is, the seat's so bad you'll be glad you have to stop for fuel every 80 or so miles.

In real life what people do is fit a larger tank and better seat right away, which is easy and not that expensive and makes the bike useful instantly. But that's not part of the rating.

The later XLs, the five-speeds from 1991 on and then the XL1200s in sport or custom trim, cure most of this, as the bigger tank and better seats are now part of the deal, so the ratings improve.

The larger XL engine, the five speeds, and the several anniversary models aren't worth extra money. Haggle, in other words.

And don't be deterred by the lack of charisma or investment potential. The older models can be picked up at budget prices, and they can be tuned and improved into as powerful a version of your personal best as ever wore the H-D badge.

Chapter 7

1984–98 FLT and FLHT

Exactly how this happened hasn't been made public yet, but along about the time Harley-Davidson's Big Twins began to look and act really old, while the inline fours from the other and bigger firms got better and calmer and more suited to doing what the Big Twins had been best at, the press learned that H-D was planning a new engine.

The project involved a four, except it was in vee. It was supposed to be water cooled and shaft drive, and the design was being done by Porsche, the car maker which also did (and still does) industrial design work for clients worldwide.

There were prototypes and some testing, and even a couple of really blurry photos sneaked by reporters who'd burrowed or weaseled their way into the test track at Talladega.

And then, while the audience's eyes were on the magic wand at stage left, Harley-Davidson unveiled the new engine.

It was the V2, the Evolution engine. It was a V-twin, air-cooled, 80-cubic-inch powerplant with the same bore and stroke as the Shovelhead Big Twin; and it was a lineal descendant of the 1936 Knucklehead, never mind that all the parts had been changed one at a time.

The engine was made public in 1983, not long after the leveraged buyout of H-D from AMF, making the V2 project still another example of the work paid for and approved by the much-abused conglomerate.

The V2 made excellent sense on all counts. Sticking with the original format, the V-twin and so forth, kept the tradition going and allowed use of the components already in production and up to contemporary standards, as in the FLT's chassis, suspension, and electrics.

(Note that in roughly the same time frame BMW introduced a line of really new and different engines, a triple and a four. They were excellent jobs of engineering, but they were and are perceived as kind of like the multis from the larger makers. BMW took a long look and one step back and has had much more sales and marketing success with updated and upgraded boxer twins, which of course are to BMW what the narrow V-twin is to Harley-Davidson.)

The V2 engine used aluminum cylinders with iron liners, while the earlier Big Twins were iron. The V2 heads were new, alloy of course, just as the Shovelhead and Panhead before them, but with new combustion chambers, porting, and valve placement. All the changes were made with the knowledge acquired by the research done under the federal

gun. Sorry to say something nice about those guys, but that's the facts.

The electronic ignition allowed the engine to tailor advance to load and other conditions, and allowed a higher nominal compression ratio to coexist with the lower octane ratings of the gas on the market.

All this and a host of other changes and improvements added up to an engine that was lighter, stronger, cheaper, cleaner, and more reliable, all at the same time. In every way except for one minor quibble (see box later in this chapter), the V2 was a better engine and was fully up to the standards and expectations of the day.

What of the V4 project? One set of cases is rumored to have escaped the factory's confines, but because the official history doesn't admit the project existed nobody at H-D will say if the project will ever become reality. Mark it as another evolutionary dead end like those other Germans, the Neanderthals.

Harley-Davidson did another sensible and traditional thing and introduced the V2 Evolution engine at the top, in the FLT. It wasn't quite the bolt-in job it looked like—it couldn't have been—but it was

The Evolution FLT was nearly identical to the original FLT, as in big and solid with frame-mount fairing and all extras, except the engine was the V2.

The Evolution 80 was clearly part of the original F-series family (witness the skewed pushrods allowing one central camshaft to work the four valves), while at the same time the V2 was very different from the Shovelhead. *Courtesy Harley-Davidson Archives*

the vastly improved engine in the still-new frame and running gear.

The new engine was first seen in *Cycle World*, which tested the V2 engine in the November 1983 issue. The bike under test was a 1984 FLHTC. By that time FL stood for the 80 engine and five-speed gearbox, the *H* meant the bike was fitted with the bar-mount fairing from the old-style Shovel FLH, the *T* meant the new chassis and isolation-mounted engine, and the *C* was presumably for classic, represented by a larger top box and some extra trim.

The magazine staff waxed almost poetic in their praise. The FLHTC was a big bike, 762 pounds at the curb with a wheelbase of 63 inches. The 1984 was improved with the adjustable suspension first seen on the FXRS the previous year, and it retained the enclosed drive chain of the earlier FLT.

The ride and handling were as sure, if stately, as ever; same for the accommodations. At the same time, the V2 provided a standing quarter mile of 14.9 seconds, did 96 miles per hour after a half-mile run, and returned 47 miles per gallon on the mixed city/highway loop. The testers were involved with earlier FLTs and with the older engine, so they measured oil usage, but there wasn't any. The stick showed oil as high at the end of the test as at the beginning. The factory's way of showing the improvements, by the way, was to seal the engines of two stock bikes and ride them coast to coast untouched.

The only complaints, make that criticisms, were that the FLT tended to pitch some on broken surfaces and that the testers didn't get used to the H-D practice of having turn signals that had to be held down to be kept on. The factory guys, in turn, said that was so you couldn't forget to turn the signals off. With that, they offered a kit that kept the signals on until turned off, and later they went to the standard system, with automated self-canceling.

There was a midyear change in 1984. The Big Twins for their first several incarnations used a dry clutch adjacent to the lubricated primary chain. This didn't always work well. There was some hope back when the belt drive was introduced that the primary drive could work with a toothed belt, but it happened that while the final drive worked better than predicted, the life of the primary belt was short and unhappy. So they reverted to chain and solved the problem in 1984 by fitting a diaphragm spring, sort of like an inverted flower petal, to the clutch.

This type of spring uses leverage. That is, pushing the petals in the center is easier than the force they exert on the clutch plates at the perimeter. The new clutch not only lasted longer, but it was easier to work and made shifting the gears a pleasure. There was a time when clunking the FL engines through the gears was work.

Because some potential buyers didn't like the newer and bigger FLT fairing, the V2 engine also came in the FLHT, *H* here representing the bar-mount fairing from 1969, which is still with us. *Courtesy Harley-Davidson Archives*

The Evolution engines, the official factory term that came into being about this time, were ongoing projects. The 1985 FLs, which came in T and HT fittings (with either the frame or the bar-mount fairing, and with the variations in top box and trim), got the toothed-belt final drive as the engineers figured how to fit the wider belt and the five-speed gearbox.

Some of the revisions were fixes. There'd been some bother with the starter electrics, as the starter didn't always back off when the engine fired, so there were changes to the relays and such.

Then, in 1986, the designers scored (to most of us) a major win, as they managed to meet the federal noise and emissions rules with a smaller, rounder, more classic air cleaner. The previous one, known as the Bread Box, was an odd shape and interfered with the operator's leg.

A special model in 1986 was the Liberty edition, honoring the anniversary of the statue of that name. The changes were in the bike's graphics only, as you'd guess. All Harleys that model year were given front turn signals that stayed on all the time. The headlights had done that for several years, the reason being added visibility. (Just to gripe here, the studies of daylight lights have never shown a provable gain in safety. This lights-on policy seems to be one of those ideas that's imposed on us because it sounds right, even if there's no proof it is right.)

The 1987 addition was the FLHS, the *S* being for sport and the sport coming from the use of an old-style windshield rather than either of the fairings. It was sporting, in a way, in that it was the lightest and the lowest priced of the FLs, but the appeal had to have been the looks and the price; and not incidentally, the windshield is an effective windbreaker, nearly as good in rain and cold as the larger fairings.

There were some minor improvements but no major changes for the FLs in 1988, and in 1989 the factory moved the top of the line up several clicks. The new tops, in both T and HT guise, were called Tour Glide Ultra Classic for the *T* and Electra Glide Ultra Classic.

This seems something of a stretch. What Ultra meant was the addition of cruise control, a sound system, CB radio, fairing lowers with stowage, and special paint, all along with the bags, boxes, fairings, and lights.

The 1984 and 1985 FLHTs and FLTs retained the split exhaust system and the massive air cleaner used on the earlier Shovelheads. This is an FLHT Classic, meaning a large top box and extra trim. *Courtesy Harley-Davidson Archives*

Oh okay, on reflection ultra means the extreme, which to a large extent these were.

The 1990 press releases spend most of their pages telling us how the 1989 improvements, the cruise control and the intercom in particular, have now been fixed. Same for 1991, except that the fixes were the intercom and the foot pegs. (One of the secret entertainments for the press has always been learning this year what turned out to be wrong with last year's wonders. We aren't cynical without reason, y'know.)

To make up for that, the real 1991 news was the return of the sidecar, with two models for the FLs. Sidecars are odd vehicles, demanding to operate and not especially practical; but they have an undeniable charm, as mentioned, second perhaps only to hot air balloons. Once you learn to steer the rig, you can go anywhere with a sidecar and even the security guards will smile you past. Charm is one thing, but sales are another thing entirely; and only a handful of sidecar-equipped FLs sold, then or since.

There were more minor changes in 1992. The Motor Company's 90th anniversary arrived in 1993 and there was a whole set of commemorative models.

This was really more of a wholesale uniqueness, so to speak. Each of the anniversary models came with a serialized nameplate, two-tone silver/charcoal paint and cloisonné fuel tank emblems.

Pause here for a detail. We have been referring to the Big Twins as the FLs. That's how they began. We saw the FL become the FLT, with

the isolation-mounts, the different front end, the big fairing, and so forth. We and most of the motorcycling public refer to the FLT and its descendants as touring models because that's what they are.

But it's time to note that in 1984 H-D introduced a very different model, the Softail. The details are in chapter 10, but for here we need to know that one of the later Softails, in 1990, was called the Fat Boy. That bike had a 16-inch front wheel and a big tire, like the old FLH and not like the FX Superglides, so they lettered the Fat Boy and its descendants FLST instead of FXST.

Is this clear? It surely takes some thinking and notes.

Adding to the confusion H-D then began calling the fat-front Softails members of the touring family, along with the T-framed touring models.

In the real world this isn't so. Softails have rigid engines, stiff suspensions, and limited luggage capacity. They are the slowest members of Milwaukee's family. They are not touring motorcycles despite the lettering that could lead one to believe otherwise.

There's a chart in the Appendix detailing this. For here, because it's easy to get confused with the strings of letters, know simply that some FLs are touring bikes, and some aren't.

The news for model year 1994 didn't arrive until the spring of that year, but it was major news and carried an impressive name, Road King.

For 1986 the H-D engineers managed to control the gear and mechanical noise so they could refit the smaller, round air cleaner for the FLT series. *Courtesy Harley-Davidson Archives*

The third basic model for the touring family was the FLHS Sport, introduced in 1987. (The example shown is a 1988.) Sport here meant a windshield instead of a fairing and saddlebags but no top box, and yes, the Sport was lighter and more agile because of that. *Courtesy Harley-Davidson Archives*

The Road King was a good move. To understand how and why, begin with fashion. When people began restoring the older Pans and Shovels, they either did so with all the extras—the saddlebags, boxes, and fairings, called baggers by the in-crowd—or they trimmed back to basics, which became known as cruisers.

With the Road King you could be either one. The Road King was a real FL: five speeds, isolated mounts, and real suspension with a windshield on quick-detach mounts. The passenger portion of the seat could be removed easily for the sporting and solo look. There was a cover for the headlight, called a nacelle (French for housing, I think), modeled after the component that held the headlight in the early days of the FLH. And the Road King had the twin-cap fuel tank introduced on the Fat Bob, a Softail-based FL described in chapter 10.

The Road King, with the windshield that came off on demand, replaced the Sport, which had the windshield mounted more permanently. The Road King also removed, or raised, the price of the cheapest FL in the line-up.

The other T-based FLs, the Electra Glides and Tour Glides, carried over in 1995. They all came stock with air-tuned suspension, floorboards fore and aft, saddlebags, the V2 80 engine, five-speed gearbox, and belt final drive.

For 1995, the factory moved big and in both directions. The engineering and top-line news was the FLHTCI, named the Ultra Classic Electra Glide-Fuel Injection.

Yes. The V2 in the Ultra Injection got sequential port fuel injection, meaning there was a pump and timer and the usual black box for such applications. The carburetor was gone. Instead electronics controlled the mixture and delivery. Torque was up by 10 percent, even though the rated power, which had been at 65 brake horsepower for several years and about which nobody much cared, didn't change.

Cycle World's test of the Ultra Injection reflected the model and the world. The technology was impressive and it worked, they said, and while the Ultra Injection wasn't especially quick or fast—standing quarter miles in 14.85 seconds, top speed timed at 91 miles per hour, average fuel economy 42 miles per gallon—it was smoother and out-pulled the carbed FLHT in a top-gear drag race. What's more, the EFI fired the engine right up and you could ride off instantly, no popping or bucking—WAIT!

Later in this chapter, in the section about what to look for, there is a detailed explanation of how to treat a V2 engine and why.

The details would be out of sequence here. Sure, if you can't stand the suspense skip ahead, but either way, do not miss the advice in that section because with no modesty at all I can say it's the most important advice about motorcycle treatment you'll ever get.

Where were we? Oh yeah, the Ultra with EFI, which worked and did add to the model's utility.

At the other end of the FLT scale for 1995 was a basic FLT. It was the Electra Glide Standard and went back to the FLHT letters. Dual seat, frame-mount fairing, bags but no top box, and plug for accessories but no

Owners like to go beyond the factory's version. This FLT has been stripped of any weather protection and has an aftermarket carburetor and straight pipes, and if two people can fit on that seat, they're gonna be close friends.

The Ultra Classics' trim, in T or HT, as seen here, include CB radio, floorboards for the passenger, and protection for the rider's legs ("lowers" in the vernacular).

sound system or radio. The FLHT had returned to the touring basics.

Big Twin tested an FLHT in 1995, and although that magazine doesn't report numbers or do actual timing and measuring, they did find the handling, seating, and controls as good as any on the market, provided you didn't need to go so fast the floorboards dragged, which they do in the high-speed sequence. More to the model's point, the seat was the best on an H-D since the sprung Buddy seat went away with the old FLH frame.

Plus, speaking of items magazines often don't talk about because they don't pay for the bikes they test, the FLHT's list price was $11,995, versus $17,500 for the EFI Ultra.

So, *Big Twin* concluded, the FLHT has everything that matters, even if there's no sound system (and there are those who believe that anyone who needs to play music while riding motorcycles is the sort of person who'd take a book of crossword puzzles on a honeymoon).

Year and model	1995 FLHT
Engine	ohv 45-degree V-twin
Bore and stroke	3.50 x 4.25 inches
Displacement	80 cubic inches
Brake horsepower	64.8 (at rear wheel, observed)
Gearbox	five speeds
Shift	left foot
Wheelbase	62.9 inches
Wheels	16F/16R
Suspension	telescopic forks, swingarm rear
Weight	800 pounds with tank half full
Seat height	28.2 inches
Fuel economy	42 miles per gallon, observed
Top speed	91 miles per hour, observed

The T Gets Dropped

For model year 1996, H-D played to strength in a cautious way.

The strong part was the expansion of the electronic fuel injection program. Having proved that the fuel injection system worked and improved the engine and appealed to the buying public, and having benefited from introducing the latest electronic marvel on the biggest and most expensive model in the fleet, the factory for 1996 offered EFI

with the Electra Glide Ultra Classic *and* the plain FLHT Classic and on the Road King. EFI remained standard on the Tour Glide Ultra Classic.

The cautious part was that just about everything else remained as it had been the previous year. The only major modification was the revision of the inner portions of the bar-mount fairing, the one that lets you tell an Electra Glide from a Tour Glide. The panels looked better, the factory said, and the various switches were relocated and the gauges and such could be more easily read. It was also easier now to get at the various bits hidden inside the fairing, because the attaching hardware had been reduced from 42, yes 42 pieces, to only 14. (The previous section in the announcement mentions that the EFI came with on-board reporting and diagnostic equipment, the better to understand what's wrong if the EFI acts up. One can safely guess the added gear and the improved access were directly connected.)

A more subtle reason for adding EFI to the Electra Glides came clear for 1997.

There was no more Tour Glide.

That wasn't a problem or even a mistake. Instead, by 1997 the only difference between the Tour Glides and the Electra Glides, the FLT and the FLHT, was the frame-mount fairing.

The original Tour Glide, the pioneer with the isolated mounts and improved steering and the fairing that mounted where the rivals mounted theirs, had done its job. It had given Harley-Davidson a new

The Sport option evolved into the Road King, seen here in 1998 trim, with fuel injection. It's clearly the original FLT frame, suspension, and V2 engine, but the Road King has less bulk and fewer things on it. *Courtesy Harley-Davidson Archives*

107

Which doesn't mean you can't add options, like the dual backrests, luggage rack, and duffel bag, even fishtail exhausts, seen here. *Courtesy Harley-Davidson Archives*

and modern look and put H-D's flagship on a par, in size and style, with its peers and rivals.

The buyers, those who moved up from earlier Harleys and those converted from other brands, appreciated the improved suspension and so forth. But tastes change and the sales figures showed that even those who liked the lack of vibration and the ease of handling also liked the home-style fairing better than the contemporary version.

So, when the factory could sell as many machines as it could make, and when they weren't selling all the Tour Glides they were making, they naturally shut down the Tour Glide section and used the space to build more Electra Glides, Softails, and so forth.

As another possible link to that, in the major change for 1997 in what H-D now called the Touring Models, the FLHT line got major revisions to the frame. The most noticeable thing was the lowered seat, now calculated at a loaded height of 27.2 inches, compared with 28.2 inches for the Road King and 28 inches for the Electra Glides that year.

This was done by moving and modifying frame tubes rather than changing the suspension. Less obviously, the relocated frame members gave room for a larger battery, which was needed for all the electronics, while the bike's midsection was narrower and the rider's legs were less splayed.

All useful stuff. We might note here that the above changes made the post-1997 FLT frames different from the pre-1997s, so some parts

from the early models won't fit the later ones and vice versa. This will matter in the mid-future, just as restorers now need to allow for the different versions of the Panhead's frames from 40 years ago. And remember, you read it here first.

The T Returns

Speaking of reading it here first, a couple of pages back, for the 1997 model year, we bid farewell to the FLT.

For model year 1998, the T came back. With a difference. Same engine, revised frame, and all the extras, but the reborn FLT was now the FLTRI, with the *R* for the name, Road Glide, and the *I* for fuel injection.

The obvious change was that the frame-mount fairing was new, lower, and tougher than before. The Motor Company is expanding production, and the public—well, some segments of the public—liked the frame-mount fairing.

The Road Glide's windshield is low enough to look over, which the sporting crowd likes, and high enough to tuck behind in bad weather, which we all like. The frame mount has less effect on the steering than the now-classic bar-mount fairing has, while the Road Glide has less trim and filigree and clearly is designed for higher road speeds. Kind of like a Dodge Viper or the old-line big-block Corvettes; that is, powerful if not agile.

Surprise of the 1998 model show was the revised FLT, shown here in basic 1998 trim. The frame-mount fairing is lower and trimmer, likewise the windshield. The rider can look over the windshield and overlook, in a sense, headwinds and bad weather. The returned FLT is more sporting and as comfortable as the original Tour Glide ever was. *Courtesy Harley-Davidson Archives*

Also for 1998

The other semi-new model for 1998 went in the other direction. The FLHR was a new top to the Road King line, with removable windshield, fuel injection, and trim added where the Road Glide's was subtracted.

And there were 95th anniversary packages for the Road Glide, Road King, and both Electra Glides, which mostly carried over. To make room, as it were, the carbureted Ultra Classic and the EFI-fed Road King versions were dropped.

What to Look For

Because this is important, note here that the V2 engine has proven itself. Best engine H-D ever made, period. There have been several recalls, mostly for the electrics, electronics, and other accessories; but the V2 itself is sound.

Except, begin with one of the author's ex-wives, who gave me standing orders to not fix everything on her car at once. She believed and could prove that if the dome light went out and I fixed it, that would allow the radiator to fall into the fan or the differential to lock up, causing more trouble than the burned-out bulb caused. So I wasn't allowed to fix the bulb, and by Thomas A. Edison, the differential worked fine.

Funny, huh? Except that just about the time H-D figured out how the plug from alternator to regulator could be kept from falling out (which H-D did, by the way), something else became chronic.

Shorthand calls it the V2's base gaskets, but that's like blaming the boy for not being able to do the man's job you sent him to do.

Instead, all Harley engines pump oil to the valve gear in the cylinder head. The oil then drains back to the crankcase. The Shovelhead engines, for one example, drain into the cylinder and the oil then routes directly to the crankcase out of the cylinder below the piston.

The V2 engine's return route is inside the cylinder, from the head down to where the cylinder mounts on the case halves. The oil passage doesn't have a guide tube, as many similar designs do, and there's a vertical bolt and a horizontal bolt close to where the oil passes between the cylinder and the case top.

There's not a lot of flat, uncluttered space in which the base gasket, the gasket between barrel and case, can do its job. That's why it's fair to say the gasket leaks, while not saying its the gasket's fault.

What happens is that it leaks and seeps, from between the cases and the barrels. It didn't happen every time to every V2 engine, but it was common and it became The Flaw just about the time the alternator plug flaw was fixed.

The gasket took the blame, surely because it was less costly to experiment with different gaskets than to redo the oil passage. There was a white gasket, a black gasket, and every model year or so there'd be a little note saying, in Bullwinkle Moose terms, this time for sure.

My spies—perhaps when the Motor Company forbade me to eat lunch in the factory cafeteria unless accompanied by someone from management, they had their reasons—tell me that the worst years were 1991 and 1992, when something between 40 and 80 percent of the V2 engines displayed this problem.

Since then, from 1995 on, there has been a gasket featuring a ring of silicone seal, which works almost every time, and there's an aftermarket kit with a guide dowel and gasket that works when the factory fix fails. At this writing, 1998, the seeps occur maybe 3 percent of the time.

(There are two other major hints, one practical and one philosophical, involving the V2 engine. For space and topical reasons they are in, respectively, the Softail and the Dyna Glide chapters, 10 and 11).

So, the touring FLs are almost always owned by conscientious and knowledgeable people. The buyer of a used FLT-family bike will be mainly concerned with obvious flaws, crash damage perhaps, and with the electronics, albeit because most of the cruise control, starter, and relay problems will have been fixed already.

The choices here will be, how much extra gear do you need or want? Sound systems, intercoms, fairing lowers, and top boxes are more useful to some folks than to others. You'll have to pay extra for the extras, so you'd better want the extras you get.

Models	Utility	Saddletime	Collectibility	Style	Accommodations
1995 FLHTCI	★★★☆☆	★★★★★	★★★☆☆	★★★★☆	★★★★★
1995 FLHT	★★★★☆	★★★★☆	★★★☆☆	★★★☆☆	★★★★☆
1994 FLHR	★★★★☆	★★★★★	★★★★☆	★★★★☆	★★★★☆
1996 FLTRI	★★★★☆	★★★★★	★★★★☆	★★★★☆	★★★★★
1984–98 Other FLTs, FLHTs	★★★☆☆	★★★☆☆	★★★☆☆	★★★☆☆	★★★★☆

About Those Stars

The touring FL story is as tidy as history gets. The FLT was radical when it appeared, it grew and matured, served its market, was retired when the market waned and was re-introduced when demand returned.

These are specialized motorcycles, which should be kept in mind when examining the ratings: Average saddle time for a plain FLT is average for an FLT, not an XLX, and so forth.

Because these are big touring machines for a mature market, the only factors that raise an FLT-series example to better than average are the extras. A Road King and Road Glide have more style and more appeal on that basis. The 1995 fuel-injected Ultra Glide was a first and will hold its value, and so forth.

There may be a hedge here. For as long as there have been loaded touring bikes, dressers as we say, there has been an appeal and even a competition as to who has the most stuff bolted onto the bike. Lights, racks, bars, boxes, trim—the list is nearly endless. As a visit to any rally will prove, the factories have engaged in a competition of their own to see which can collect the most accessory and option money before the dresser rolls out the door.

At this writing, the loaded FLT is the better buy, simply because you can get the extras for less than the first owner paid.

It's possible, the human race being the odd species it is, that the plainer models will appreciate when the dressers are so common as to not draw attention.

That's possible, and that's where the bobbers and choppers came from, the trend-setters taking stuff off because the average rider had bolted stuff on. The plain FLT may become valued for its simplicity, again relatively speaking. If not, or until then, the buyer who doesn't want the extras can find bargains with the basics.

Chapter 8

1984–94 FXR Series

Beginning with hindsight, and forgetting that the format calls for evaluation last in the chapter, we start with the claim that the V2-engined Rubber Glides were the best street motorcycles Harley-Davidson ever made. Not the most popular, not the most profitable or radical or stylish, but the best machines.

There's evidence the guys at Juneau Avenue were surprised at the FXR's success.

The saga begins in the normal H-D manner. Soon after the introduction of the FLT, with its new frame and frame-mount fairing, radical steering, and isolation engine mounts, H-D introduced the SuperGlide II. It was lighter, slicker, and more sporting, with a revised version of the new frame but with more conventional steering and with the isolated mounts, all done with the Sportster-style front end that did so well in the original Superglide.

The official version was that this was a stripped FLT. In fact, it was a vastly improved FXE, the style and performance minus the shakes, vibrations, and occasionally vague handling.

In keeping with how it's done in Milwaukee, as soon as the frame and running gear proved themselves, the FXR series for model year 1984 got the V2, a.k.a. the Blockhead, engine. (The V2 was introduced in the previous chapter. Repeating here, it was a nearly new version of Harley's Big Twin, first seen in 1936 but changed and revised and modified over the years until no two parts interchanged.)

The V2 was (and is) all alloy top and bottom, with up-to-date combustion chambers, porting, and electronic ignition. Displacement was 80 cubic inches and rated power, delivered to the rear wheel, was 44 brake horsepower.

The V2-powered FXRs were exactly that. There was some confusion, though, because the factory's name and letters systems had backed them into several corners.

There was the FXRS, and you'd think the *S* stood for sport, except that the name was Low Glide. There was the FXRT, the FXR with un-Harley full fairing and saddlebags, but it was called the Sport Glide because H-D was trying to establish the FL series as the touring line. And there was the FXRDG, named the Disc Glide because it was a limited edition with an alloy disc, rather than spoked, rear wheel and with some nifty paint and a tank emblem that said "Genuine Harley-Davidson."

The excuse for the basic FXRS model being called the Low Glide was that to get the static ride height down for the ads, a practice as foolish as it was prevalent, the FXRS needed shorter suspension. This made the seat lower, the ride rougher, and the handling less sporting.

The press—this is one of *Cycle*'s crew—was delighted with the V2 version of the FXR: no talk of style or sales campaigns or nostalgia, just ride the bike and enjoy it. *Cycle*

One of the genuine benefits we've taken from racing is that the more time the wheels spend on the ground, the better. Doing that means making the suspension optimally soft, to coin a phrase, instead of overly stiff, which was the old way. As genius engineer Maurice Olley wrote, "Any suspension will work, if you don't let it."

As another minor drawback, lowering the chassis and not changing anything else meant the pipes dragged on corners, which didn't help handling or sport riding, either.

The magazines, purist as always, reported and snorted at this, but the Low Glide's sales went up, teaching a lesson we critics have never been willing to learn.

Meanwhile, the differences between the Sport Glide and the Disc Glide were minimal. We last met the Sport Glide, the one with the touring equipment, when it had Shovelhead power. The Disc Glide's changes were mostly cosmetic. That is, it had the same suspension, engine, controls, and so on as the Sport Glide had. I kept one on, um, test for as long as I could get away with it. There was no technical reason for the disc wheel and paint, but they surely did look good and the factory noticed that, too.

During the 1984 model year, as a running change, the FXRs got the diaphragm spring clutch and sealed primary case described in the FLT

chapter. This improvement—and it was, just compare the clutch action and shifting on a prediaphragm versus the current clutch—allowed even better things.

For 1985, the FXR line got the belt final drive, as good for the sports bikes as it was for the touring family.

Sports? Yup. There were two and a half FXRs that year.

There was the FXRT, the tourer, which got a second front disc brake, a larger passenger seat and a higher backrest. There was the FXRS, the basic model. There was the FXRS option, which (at that time) didn't get its own letter or name. But it was, in fact, the real sport version. It had raised suspension and the second front disc, all for an extra $150.

The FXR was fast, smooth, predictable, and reliable, just as it looks to be here, albeit, as one can also see, the original version's low ride height limited cornering clearance for sport riding. *Cycle*

Surely the engineers had the V2 engine in mind, if not on the drawing board, when they designed the frames for the FLT and FXR. The FXR frame in particular follows the layout of the XR, which is to say, efficient and effective. *Cycle World*

That was the bargain of the year. *Cycle* weighed one at 612 pounds with the 4.2-gallon tank full. The quarter-mile mark came up in 14.2 seconds, the top speed was 92.6 miles per hour, and miles per gallon for the test was 49.6. Everything worked just as it was supposed to, the magazine said. And there wasn't enough oil consumption to measure (we must remember that back then, the magazine guys and other critics weren't quite sure yet about the new Harleys).

Cycle raved. Everything about the FXRS, with its extra brake and a suspension that worked because you let it, was top notch. "The most competent and truly versatile Harley we've ever ridden," they wrote. And there's no doubt they got it right.

The second half model for 1985 was the FXRC Low Glide, the

C standing for Custom, the term then coming into vogue to describe stock motorcycles with chopper features like stepped seats and high bars. The Custom also featured chrome plating for things like the rocker boxes, gear case cover, and the top and side of the gearbox. The front fender was short and sporting, borrowed from the XR-1000 (see chapter 12), and the paint was candy orange with root beer trim, which probably sounds strange but it looked sharp.

The factory said the plan was to only make 1,075 examples of the Custom, while offering the

chrome-plating package as an option for the FLT and FLHT. (There's something of a puzzle here, because the Custom was reported as a good seller, while years later the package, as in the chrome plating and paint scheme, turned up on some 1986 FXRC Customs. The model wasn't in the 1986 catalog, so we can guess that selling the scheduled number of Customs took longer than expected.)

The Evo FXRT was called the Sport Glide because there already was a Tour Glide, okay? Excellent package, no matter what the name, with luggage capacity, weather protection, and the new engine in a proven chassis. *Cycle World*

The Police Package

Speaking of completely different, one of the original traditions, right along with feuding with Indian, was the Harley-Davidson ridden by the motor officer, as in police department, as in speed traps. Police business was one of the major factors in keeping H-D (and Indian) solvent during the 1930s. But when everybody else was doing well, Harley and the police became less than perfect partners. (Indian, of course, went out of business, but that's another story. Check the publisher's catalog.)

Part of the problem has to have been that police departments became less fond of motorcycles. They required skill and training for the officers, for one thing, while the advent of radar reduced the departments' reliance on bikes for pursuit.

There was also competition from other makes. Honda and even Moto Guzzi picked up police business, and Kawasaki, with an American plant and the wish to be (and be known as) an American company, designed a police model and worked hard and well to offer their machine for police use.

The hard bags are quickly detachable and came with inner liners, to keep clothes dust and rain-free; plus, you can use them for laundry bags (the liners that is, not the cases themselves). *Cycle World*

The FXR frame and the V2 engine put H-D back into the police business after a lapse of some years. The classic upright posture allows long days in the saddle and the seat, unlike some we've sat in, was designed to be sat in rather than for style. The police bikes are usually carefully maintained and can be bargains. *Courtesy Harley-Davidson Archives*

Not least, alas, were the troubles H-D went through in the late 1960s and 1970s. The machines used oil, didn't handle the electrical demands as well as they should have, didn't carry the added weight well, and the factory lost business.

It made sense, therefore, that when H-D had the V2 engine, the FXR frame, the alternator, and so forth, they revived the police package. Nor was it all that difficult. The basic combination was the FXRT, with the full fairing but with a solo seat, radio, and other gear replacing the saddlebags and dual seat.

The campaign and the FXRP worked well. In the years of the Great Depression the actual sales kept many a dealership alive. In better times, it's not so much the money as the endorsement; if the bikes didn't work the cops wouldn't use them. Nor does it hurt for the public to see the brand name. (For some reason we don't resent the horse the officer rode us down with.)

Model year 1986 featured common sense for the product, confusion with the names and letters.

The entry-level Big Twin was the FXR, now named Super Glide. Then came the FXRS Low Rider, with options. One third of the buyers the previous year went for the handling kit (the Performance Suspension Option), so for 1986 there was the FXRS Sport Edition, with taller suspension and dual front disc brakes. The FXRT plain touring model was joined by the FXRD, *D* presumably for Deluxe, with a sound system, top box, and dual exhausts—yup, still another shot at the baby FLH market.

The limited-edition model in 1986 was the Liberty Edition, with paint and graphics, as mentioned, celebrating the anniversary of the statue of that name.

The models also got a switch so the turn signals could be set to blink until turned off, which was how all the other makes did it. Or they'd go off if you lifted your thumb, which is how old-time Harley guys like to do it.

A minor downside for the year was new regulations required intake and exhaust systems that were more restrictive.

There was a subtle but significant shift in emphasis for 1987. In terms of function the standard FXRs were the best, while the factory and homemade choppers, the Customs as they came to be known, were the hits of the street.

The new FXR for 1987 was the FXLR, the Low Rider Custom. It had the V2 engine, isolation mounts, five speeds, and belt drive, like all the FXRs that year, but the front wheel was a 21-incher, as first seen on a stock Harley on the 1980 Wide Glide. The rear wheel was solid, as per the earlier Disc Glide. The expectation, which proved right, was that buyers would like the chopper look and enjoy the advantages of the isolation mounts and the belt drive.

The FXRD was dropped because it didn't sell; but to compensate, the FXRT, the one without the top box, got a better sound system. The FXRT kept the valanced (as in wrap-around) front fender, and the other Rubber Glides got the smaller version borrowed from the XR-1000.

All these additions, subtractions, and minor changes must have worked. Either that, or the factory had things to do elsewhere, because in 1988, there was no news in the FXR department.

The Basic FXRS was called the Low Rider, one suspects because Low had sales appeal, like New and Free. And the suspension was shortened, adding to style but subtracting from handling. *Courtesy Harley-Davidson Archives*

Adaptability has long been a Harley-Davidson strong point. This is the FXRS Convertible, and as a glance at this and the previous photo illustrates, what they did was put a windshield, saddlebags, and a backrest on the Low Rider. All the gear works, and it all comes off quickly and easily for rides that don't need touring equipment. *Courtesy Harley-Davidson Archives*

What they'd been up to was revealed in 1989, and it was a neat idea.

The full name was Low Rider Convertible. It was the basic FXR, as seen before, except that it came with a Lexan windshield and leather pouches to fling across the rear fender. Both the shield and bags had quick-detach fastenings, so the owner could be a sport in town or the mountains, and could easily fit the touring extras for summer vacations on the road. The system worked in practice and gave the buyer another way to look forward to doing things, and the Convertible has been popular ever since. Nor did the highway foot pegs, the sissy bar, or the choice of paint schemes hurt.

The FXRs Diverge

This is complicated. The FXRs carried over in 1990 except that they got some shared improvements like a new carburetor, the diaphragm clutch, the normal sorts of changes in the electrics, and the dreaded base gaskets.

In 1991 H-D brought out a new and very different version of the FXR. It was called an FXR at first, but because it was different in many and major ways, and because the ideas embodied in the new version worked so well, the new model became a model line in itself.

The name that first year was Sturgis, and the model with that name, lettered FXDB for 1991, went on to become the Dyna Glides, as seen in chapter 11.

Along the way the FXR line, the original new version of the Superglides, were all named Low Riders. In 1991 the line included the versions listed already: the

In the same theme but the other direction, the touring FXR came with a top-line option, a top box and sound system. Exhaust was two-into-one rather than staggered duals, the seat had more padding, and the passenger got floorboards like the operator's. Good value, weak sales appeal. *Courtesy Harley-Davidson Archives*

plain, the sport, the touring, and the convertible, this year with self-canceling turn signals, upgraded, tires, and some added color options.

For 1992 the FXRs got recalibrated carburetors—the rules got tighter every year, which is why the carbs had to be changed again and again—along with new oil lines and a new cover for the pump. There was better material for the brake discs, and the factory was fitting a retainer to "ensure that the drive sprocket nut stays tight for the life of the vehicle." If that doesn't make you stroll out to the barn and check the nut on your pre-1992, nothing will.

Here's an odd, perhaps even significant note for 1993: This was the 90th anniversary of H-D production. To observe that, in 1993 there were six anniversary models, as in paint, graphics, and limited production.

None of the six were from the FXR line. Instead, the Rubber Glide models were the FXR Super Glide, the basic; the Convertible, which in effect replaced the FXRT, which was dropped; the FXRS-SP, the Low Rider Sport Edition with low bars, raised suspension, and dual front brakes; and the FXLR, the Low Rider Custom with solid rear wheel, a 21-inch front, and a one-piece combo of dog-bone risers and flat bars, on which rode the speedo.

All four models had the V2 engine, five-speed gearbox, and belt drive. They also got a revised breather system for the gear case to air

The modest introduction of the laid-back theme was the FXRC Custom, with wire wheels and orange-and-root beer paint, plus chrome. The front fender came from the XR-1000. This was supposed to be a limited edition, but it sold less than the limit, evidently, and examples turned up for sale after the model was out of the catalog. (This is also a good look at the efficient frame, rumored to have offended the faithful.)

119

The R series' true custom was the FXLR, with disc rear wheel and a 21-inch wire wheel in front. The model had highway pegs and extra chrome and sold well, much better than the touring models. *Courtesy Harley-Davidson Archives*

box, reprofiled levers, and sight glasses for the brake master cylinders.

Remember the song about how you needn't have a degree in meteorology to know enough to come in out of the rain? Same for 1994.

The 1994 FXR series—proclaimed by the factory as "Harley-Davidson's group of sport machines . . . (combining) custom styling with contemporary levels of function"—was comprised of two models. There was the FXR Super Glide, just as it had been the previous year, and there was the FXLR Low Rider, with solid disc rear wheel and 21-inch laced front wheel; again pretty much as seen before.

Speaking of folk clichés, H-D made use of one. It raised the Convertible's windshield, bags, and badges, and ran a new machine underneath it.

True. The 1994 Convertible, same neat idea and hardware, was simply transferred to the Dyna series.

Presenting the case for the defense, these were interesting times for Harley-Davidson. Demand was driving supply, as they say in business school. Harleys were so popular that enthusiasts from overseas were coming to the United States and buying bikes they couldn't get at home because H-D was limiting exports! Yes, and try that one, Ford and Chevrolet.

But, as seen with the FLT series, the lines that didn't sell instantly had to defer to the ones that did. The FXRs weren't moving as fast as the Dyna Glides, the Softails, and the Sportsters. Thus, for 1995, there were no more FXRs. Instead, the basic Big Twin and the Convertible package were transformed into Dyna Glides.

The move made sense, in that the factory did what the buying public wanted. At the same time, the FXR series was the lightest, most agile, and efficient of the Harley Big Twins, and the most sporting and responsive to performance modification. In touring trim, it was as good a cross-country motorcycle as was ever made, and it's a shame the line couldn't have been kept on line.

What to Look For

Because by this time all the F-series Harleys wore common components—the same version of the 80-cubic-inch engine, the five-speed gearbox, and, for most of this period, the belt final drive—all the cautions for the FXRs are shared with those for the FLs (and the Dyna Glides and Softails to follow).

So for the record, do the standard checks for mechanical condition and paperwork. Ask if the bike went in for any recalls. Locate the alternator/regulator plug so when—or we should now say *if*—the plug comes loose, you can find it in the dark.

Starting for the Ages

This is a truly universal hint for all Harleys and all motorcycles. It's positioned here because it's convenient and logical, but the wisdom doesn't apply only to FXRs or V2 engines.

Begin taking notes here:

Seems as if every time I read a test about some new model, especially those with fuel injection, the tester remarks on how you can fire it right up and hit the road, no hanging about for the engine to warm up.

Folks, don't do that. It's the very worst thing you can do to an engine.

The Right Way came indirectly. When I was researching the base gasket problem, which occurs on all V2s and not just the FLTs, I remarked to my source that I hate reading about abuse of cold engines.

Me too, he said. Not only is that dumb, it aggravates the seeping gasket syndrome. A remarkable share of the V2s that seep have been fired up and driven away cold. There's something about the character of the alloys or the proximity of different metals near the oil passage that makes V2 engines susceptible to that particular abuse.

Hmm, I said. Once years ago I was talking with the engineers at Husqvarna—for more on those bikes, ask the black sheep of your family who rode off road—and they said they did a test with two identical bikes. One they rode hard soon as it fired up, the other they started and ran at

Buyer mix and match. This is a Disc Glide, to which the owner has fitted chrome covers, leather saddlebags, straight pipes, and forward controls.

This FXLR is equipped with windshield and quick-dismount saddlebags, witness the frames still in place. The pipes are H-D accessories, and the controls are central, as the factory fitted them. Again, this is the type and style of modification you'll find in your search for the used Harley that fits you.

a fast idle until the fins on the head were too hot to touch.

The second engine, the warmed one, lasted exactly twice as long as the abused one.

Hmm, my source said. His advice has been to not ride away until the rocker box was too warm to touch. Same thing, seems to me. Which makes this a universal rule: Don't ride the bike until the engine is warmed up. Even if you can do it, don't. Your V2 won't seep oil and it will last twice as long, and that's a promise.

End of universal advice.

One hint of what comes next is that when you look, the FXRs are difficult to find, especially the ones with the Sport option. It could mean not all that many were sold new, which is part of the case; but it also means the people who have them don't want to sell them. That, in turn, could mean the buyers aren't much moved by fashion; they don't need this year's model every year.

The worst part here is that because the FXRTs weren't all that popular at first, they were the cheapest to rebuild as show or custom specials. Probably more of a factor was that there weren't that many FXRs sold new, which makes them more rare used.

But what those of us who like the FXRs prefer to think is that there aren't many on the market because the people who already have them wanted them, enjoy them, and simply don't want to sell.

Models	Utility	Saddletime	Collectibility	Style	Accommodations
1984–94 FXRS Sport	★★★★★	★★★★☆	★★★★★	★★★☆☆	★★★★☆
1984–93 FXRS Convertible	★★★★★	★★★★★	★★★★★	★★★☆☆	★★★★☆
1982–92 FXRT (includes P/pack)	★★★★★	★★★★★	★★★★☆	★★★☆☆	★★★★☆
1984–94 Other FXRs	★★★★☆	★★★★☆	★★★☆☆	★★★☆☆	★★★☆☆

About Those Stars

Merit is only part of what drives the collector and secondhand markets. But merit counts, at least for you and me.

The V2-powered FXR series are excellent motorcycles. They don't give trouble and they delivered what the buyer was supposed to want, as in speed, power, comfort, and reliability. Dealer Bill Bartels says one reason the rough and tough bikers don't mind being seen on the Evo FXRs is because the V2 versions are much better on the road, period. Not only that, the FXRs proved, along with the Evo FLTs, that H-D could make modern and competitive motorcycles.

At this writing the FXRs occupy a peak in the Big Twin line. Considered as motorcycles, an FXR rated at three stars is a better machine than a three-star XLH, FLH, or FLST. They were the most efficient, lightest, best handling, and most comfortable of the V2 Harleys to date. They lend themselves to improvements, and they are the best suited, again in the F-engined line, to extra power.

Then comes the fashion factor.

When I was new to motorsports the fad was for cars that had their gearshifts four on the floor, right out of the box, not like your dad's old slug with three on a tree. Then I became a historian and learned, to my delight, that in the previous generation, when dad's dull sedan had the gearshift on the floor there were kits to convert to the column shift. In other words, form beats function, and we don't want what the old folks had, no matter what it was.

Which is why this chapter begins with the claim that the FXRs are the best bikes in the world.

This matters because at this point in time the Harley-buying public is keen for models styled to mimic the past, models that are less functional because of that styling. This means, or such is my prediction, that the cleaner, faster, less cluttered, and better-handling FXRs will be in demand when the cruisers become—and they will become—motorcycles everybody else already has.

This incoming tide will raise them all, which is why I mention that the average here is higher than it is elsewhere.

But because function will become important, the best machines as machines—the sports and convertibles, the ones that are the best to ride and the best on the road all day—will become better investments than the others, the non-sports and the Customs. That is, the best machines will beat the market, led, speaking of guesswork, by the Disc Glide.

Just don't ride away until the engine is warm, okay?

Chapter 9

1984–98 Softails

Not least among Harley-Davidson's several virtues is the willingness of the people in charge to take chances.

Sometimes, as the French phrase it, The Bear Eats You. H-D's history includes the chapters with the Italian subsidiary and the entry-level two-strokes. There was the Cafe Racer, and later we'll meet the XR-1000. They were projects and products that didn't work, where the only credit goes for at least giving it a shot.

And there are chapters in which You Eat The Bear. It happened with the Knucklehead, the Electra Glide, the Sportster, the Superglide, and the Tour Glide.

And it surely did happen with the Softail.

This bear-into-lunch properly starts with another virtue, the ability of H-D's people to not insist on inventing everything themselves. As the story goes, some H-D execs saw a bike modified by an outside engineer. He'd revised the frame, relocated the rear springs, and made a new swingarm, and the result looked like the old Hydra-Glides, the ones with rigidly mounted rear wheels, "hardtails," as the chopper crowd says.

The Juneau Avenue guys liked the idea so much they bought the rights to it and engineered a new model based on the rigid look. Why? Because they expected that the look of the past was the look of the future.

The name was Softail, an obvious play on words, and the letters were FXST, *F* for the V2 engine, *X* because the Softail was considered a Superglide at that time, and *ST* because H-D adopted the practice of abbreviation: Earlier the letters had simply been random, as in *L* for the second version of an engine and *H* for the third. Then came *XLS* and *XLT* for sport, touring, and so forth.

The Softail appeared for 1984. It was mostly a Wide Glide fitted with the V2 engine, a 21-inch front wheel, and the rear of the Superglide frame massively revised.

Just as important were the features that weren't there. The FXST offered kick start as well as electric, but kept the four speeds of the earlier FX models instead of the newer five-speed gearbox. And the V2 engine was mounted solidly in the frame, compared with the FLTs or the FXRs introduced in this time frame.

Some of this could have been to save money and time, but the factory guys said then, and since, that they expected the buyers of the nostalgia-based Softails to prefer the vibrations of the rigid engine: That's what motorcycles were supposed to feel like.

Same for the suspension. There wasn't any engineering reason for having less wheel travel and thus a harsher ride and less comfort, but one feature of the old rigids was that they were low and carried the fender

close to the tire. So the Softail was given a limited suspension; it rode low and the fender was snug on the tire. And if that meant the Softail wasn't as good on the highway as the conventionally suspended Harleys—which is exactly what it meant—that didn't hurt sales one bit.

The passenger seat was more like a perch and the foot controls were set forward to provide the classic, as seen in biker-exploitation flicks, outlaw slouch. Which again is what the forward mounts did. They also made it slower and more clumsy to get your foot on the brake pedal.

The Softail was longer (66.3-inch wheelbase) and lower (25-inch static seat height, by one measure) and of course wider than anything else in class. Claimed dry weight was 618 pounds, and the magazines reported 650 pounds with fuel in the tanks.

Oh yeah, the tanks. It may have slipped the author's notice, but has it been mentioned that since the days of the E and F the Big Twin has had tanks, plural? This dates way back to when they were called saddle tanks, two half tanks bolted together across the frame backbone. Mostly they were covered by a panel, strap, or the instruments, and they looked so like one big tank it's always a surprise to see the two halves hanging on the shop or showroom wall. (Sportster and Superglide tanks look like one tank, because they usually are.)

This is mentioned because the Softail's tanks, like those on the FLH and so forth, are linked by hoses concealed beneath the paneling. The Softail came with a cap on the left and a cap on the right.

At fuel stops, if you remove both caps and begin pumping gas into the right tank, slooosh, out gushes gas from the left tank. It's the sort of mistake that teaches so strong a lesson one only has to be taught once.

The Softail was newer and older than it looked, with a much modified FX frame using shocks and springs mounted below the engine and with a swingarm that looked like the solid-mount rear sections of the past. There was kick start along with electric and the rear fender's kick mimics the chopper crowd's use of the front fender in back. *Courtesy Harley-Davidson Archives*

Next move was the Heritage Softail. The letters are FLST, the *L* signaling that the rear fender is low and flipless, the way the FLH used to do it, and the front wheel is a 16-incher on massive downtubes; there are no Sportster parts here, so it's no longer an FX. *Courtesy Harley-Davidson Archives*

But that mistake was mentioned in the magazines, I suspect now because the press, which tends to be hard-core, purist, and gear-headed, didn't understand the Softail or the customs from other makers that hit the market at the same time, because they (the press) had trouble accepting a motorcycle that wasn't as good a machine as it could have been if it hadn't been such a fashion statement.

The public had no such trouble.

The Softail sold like beer in the bleachers, so for the 1986 model year the Softail was joined by an upmarket model, the Softail Custom. Readers of the previous chapter will recall that the FXR's Convertible was moved to the Dyna Glide series. Same thing here, as the Softail Custom was a Disc Glide, as in the solid rear wheel and extra chrome and trim.

Speaking of form and function, the Softails were converted to the new clutch, the five-speed gearbox, and belt final drive, while the Custom had touches like a black-accented engine with chromed covers, red and burgundy paint, and burgundy accents on the black frame. Knockout stuff, and if anybody ever needed a reason to spend Saturday morning washing and polishing the bike, here was a good one.

This—the trim and paint, that is—was a trend that became a rule.

There was a new—and different—Softail for 1987. The name was Heritage Softail Special, and the letters were FLST.

Spot the change? Yup, the *F* was for the original engine, and the *L* was because the Heritage Special used the FL-style forks and front wheel, not the Sportster derived, as in *X*, front end. The FLST engine was black and chrome, and the body panels were blue and cream. The Special had a windshield, leather saddlebags with studs and conchos (those silver things), and a seat with a backrest.

On purpose and by design, style department head Willie G. Davidson hit the perfect chord. The Heritage Special was exactly what guys did to their motorcycles back in the 1940s and 1950s. There was a wonderful cover on the *Saturday Evening Post* back then, with the three kids stopped in their tracks by a Harley that could have—and may have?—served as the model of the Heritage Special.

So 35 or 40 years later those kids and all the other kids worldwide bought the motorcycle that made them come home from school late all that time ago. And anybody to whom that didn't happen missed out, and we who were there are sorry for them.

Willie G's next smart and successful move, for 1988, was to revise and improve the leading-link front suspension designed by William Harley in his engineering student days and used from 1907 until 1949, when the telescopic forks were adopted. The Springer, formally lettered FXSTS, as in Soft Tail Springer, was a stripped FXST in other ways, but the front suspension looked like the old style. It wasn't identical, however, in that the new leading links were stronger and more durable and provided more control than the old ones.

The FXSTC was the Custom Softail, with extra trim, padding, and chrome. The kick start was deleted while the Softails kept the old-style oil tank. *Courtesy Harley-Davidson Archives*

The Springer used the leading-link front suspension first seen in 1907 on the FX-style (i.e., flipped rear fender and small headlight) frame and body. The V2 engine, five forward speeds, and belt final drive were used for all the F-series models by 1990. This example is highly modified, with extra lights, straight pipes, windshield, and mounts for saddlebags. Best guess here has to be he rode to Daytona Beach, took off the bags, and went cruising.

They also gave less wheel travel and were therefore stiffer and less comfortable and didn't handle as well as the telescopic forks did. (Which is, after all, why H-D and all the other makes worldwide went telescopic in the first place.)

As noted with the original Softail, all this retro style, as the art people call it, was accompanied by sound, careful, and thorough engineering. There are limits to the FXST models, but that's not the same as flaws.

And they sold.

So for 1990, 1989 having been a year during which the factory simply made all the bikes it could make and sold all the bikes it could make, the new model was the Fat Boy.

This was good marketing wrapped around an inside joke. In the early days of the big twins, they came with tall 18-inch wheels and narrow tires. In 1940 the factory switched to 16-inch wheels and fatter tires. They gave a softer ride, at the expense of handling, but were in fashion. When they were trimmed for sport, they were known as Fat Bobs, bob being short for bob job.

The Fat Boy was something of a pun and was used because the wheels were solid disc, which contributed to a hefty profile, and they were 16 inches in front and rear. The letters, FLSTF, were logical: *FL* meant the big twin front end, as contrasted with the FX that designated the XL's skinnier forks and taller tire. *ST* was for Softail, and the second *F* was, of course, for Fat. (The Softails, lettered FX by this time, used an even taller and skinnier 21-inch front wheel and tire.)

The front fender was wrapped around the wheel, the exhaust pipes were one high and one low (shotgun style in the vernacular), the handlebars were low and wide, and the paint was a silver sort of gray. The result was a machine that looked solid and hefty, all one piece. Once again, the new-this-year model was in limited production that first year, and it sold out.

Then came something of a hold for model years 1991 and 1992. Late in that second calendar year the factory unveiled the Heritage Nostalgia, which was a variation on a variation, sort of, because it was a Heritage with special two-tone paint, special bags and seat, wide whitewall tires, and the shotgun exhaust first seen on the Fat Boy, all as Retro as could be.

The Softail series for 1994 included five versions: Custom, Springer, Heritage Classic, Heritage Special, and Fat Boy. Those with the 21-inch front wheel were contemporary, the factory said, while those with the 16-inch fronts were styled to look like motorcycles from the past. They all had the V2 engine, five speeds, and belt drives; and the nostalgia did not extend to adding oil leaks or inadequate electrics. Some history wasn't fun.

There was another addition for 1995, and it was a mix of the early limited equipment.

The engineers put in many hours revising the Springer's basic design so it could deliver modern predictability and control while looking like that 1907 design. (In 1907, for example, there were no front brakes at all, never mind disc brakes.) *Cycle*

The name was Bad Boy and the letters were FXSTSB. All this is coming naturally now, so surely we know that the initials translate to a Softail, 21-inch front, Springer forks, right? Right. But the paint was black for frame, suspension, and body panels, set off with two-tone blue scallops and extra chrome, with slotted disc rear wheel and spoked front, staggered dual pipes, black risers for the low bars, and a bullet headlight, not one from the early Sportster. It was another knockout.

H-D caught up, presumably, in 1996. All six models got electronic speedometers, and the factory said quality control of the gearbox was

The work paid off. Even the crew at *Cycle*, much more inclined toward sport than cruising, said that the front wheel was controlled, the handling secure and reliable, and the only loss was in wheel travel, which required the springs to be stiffer than optimum handling would have required. *Cycle*

improved, and the gears were more closely matched, so they ran quieter. The Softails got a one-piece instrument console and round keys, and the Fat Boy and Heritage Custom got different decorations for their tanks.

The 1997 new model was something of a personal note. Willie G introduced the Heritage Springer Softail, lettered FLSTS, and said it was based on the 1948 Panhead and that the idea for the Heritage Springer came to him while on the road.

Then, clearly, he went back to the studio and did a lot of hard work. As the name and letters suggest, the FLSTS was a Springer with the 16-inch front wheel. To make that work, the factory had to get the geometry of the closely mounted fender to follow the path taken by the revised suspension, while at the other end the classic tombstone-look taillight had to be shaped and sized so it both looked like the original light and met federal requirements for size and brightness.

With this came fishtail mufflers and a powder-coated engine with chrome-plated gearbox cover and oil tank, plus a tractor-style seat, leather extras, bags, and trim. Paint was Birch White, with either red or blue scallops. That paint combo dates back to the twenties, hard though that is to believe.

Does this sound as if the actual machine had gone as far as technology and budget could take it? That's just about what it was. That is, once the factory had the engine and the mechanical parts working as well as any machine could, all it could do was vary the style, which it did with critical and commercial success.

One Step Back

There was some negative proof of this for the 1998 Softails. The Bad Boy was dropped from the model line. No reason was given, but it's not tough to guess that the variations on the theme began to be seen as just that.

And anyway, the 1998 Softail line, the Softail Custom, Springer Softail, Fat Boy, Softail Classic, and the Heritage Springer should have been plenty. If not, there were 95th anniversary treatments offered for the Fat Boy and the Heritage Springer.

What to Look For

Begin with the easy part. The Softails were designed to appeal to a specific market, enthusiasts who like motorcycles but aren't terribly hard core, as in riding every day or accumulating high annual mileage.

This is good because the Softails aren't that good at slogging through bad weather or leaping great stretches of interstate. They will do it, in the mechanical sense of trouble-free riding, but the occupants will be tired long before the engines are.

The Fat Boy was a logical and effective extension of the FL-style Softail, with solid disc wheels (a popular accessory 40 or 50 years ago), silver paint, and staggered pipes: plenty of bulk, no fat. *Cycle*

And that's good, for the buyer of a used motorcycle at least, because the odds are you'll find a motorcycle that's been garaged, maintained, and not ridden a whole lot. There will likely be extras, and the owner won't have fixed the carb or installed an overdone camshaft or otherwise messed up a good engine.

Thus, given the earlier remarks about the charging system, the seeping base gaskets on certain early V2 engines, and the recalls involving some of the electrics, there's not much to be worried about.

Assuming that the prospective buyer appreciates that these are fun bikes, not workhorses.

A Question of Philosophy

Ever notice that there seldom seems to be a good time to bring up unpleasant subjects? This is at best a delicate subject, and it's introduced here because this is as good a place as any.

The subject is restorations of the future, and don't get too upset. This has little to do with what you or I will need to worry about in our personal futures deep into the next century. It's a question of philosophy, and it's here mostly because it's something all Harley-Davidson fans should know about, personal or not.

The Heritage Softail Classic, lettered FLSTC, could be bought with bags, backrest, silver dots and conchos, and a windshield, just like the dressers of the 1950s. *Courtesy Harley-Davidson Archives*

To begin, step back to the joke about Abe Lincoln's axe. His axe could still be with us despite its two new heads and three new handles, because back when the industrial age began, people valued their work and their possessions. A person needed one axe, or one rifle or revolver, for his or her lifetime. The means through which this end was achieved was interchangeable parts and replaceable parts every place there would be wear and tear.

Harley and the Davidsons were heirs to this philosophy. They came from starched blue-collar families, skilled mechanics and craftsmen. They worked on the railroads where good work was literally a matter of life or death.

When they designed and built those early motorcycles, they followed the examples of Colt and Whitney and took care that every part that could wear or break could be replaced. The first result was that the first H-D sold to a private owner delivered 60,000 miles to its owners, this on the roads and conditions of 1903. The second result was that Harley-Davidson quickly (and accurately) became known for quality of material and design.

The third result was that nobody's ever thrown away a Harley-Davidson. If it wears, that part can be replaced. If it breaks, ditto. If it's crashed or burned, the parts that are still sound can be saved, and when

you have enough sound parts, you assemble a Harley-Davidson the factory didn't build (I have one like that in my barn as we speak).

Why this matters to us begins with how it works, as in those replaceable parts. The cams in my Harleys rotate in bearings and bushings. The cam in my Honda rotates in holes cast into the cylinder head. If the Harley bearings wear, I can pop them out and replace them. If the Honda loses oil delivery and the surfaces wear, I need a new cam or a new cylinder head.

Why would an excellent company, a company known for its engineering skill, do such a thing? Because saving money on all those parts and the extra processes means you can deliver a good product to the first owner, who won't keep the machine long enough for anything major to go wrong.

At one time a man bought a hat, checked it out in the mirror, and wore it when he needed protection from the weather or when there was an occasion for which a hat was needed. Now we buy hats that look goofy, we pretend we are so dumb we don't know how to put one on, and we wear them when they are totally inappropriate, perhaps even offensively rude.

In such an age it will come as no surprise that making a product to last forever will get you flunked out of business school.

The point? When H-D's evergreen Big Twin, the ancestor of the V2, appeared as the Knucklehead in 1936, the engine used alloy cases with steel housings in the centers, put there permanently when the cases were cast. The main bearings rode in the steel housings, so the bearings could be replaced easily. This continued through the Panhead, the Shovelhead, and the early Blockhead.

The Heritage Nostalgia was introduced in March 1992 but was billed as a 1993 model because you couldn't get one right away. Shotgun pipes had little fishtails on them, and the flaps for the bags and seat were finished, or perhaps decorated, in trim that mimicked cowhide, as in black and white. *Courtesy Harley-Davidson Archives*

The basic Softail, as in the 1991 version here, remains a solid seller, and thus a likely model to find on the market. The front disc brakes have always been single, by the way, as a signal that the factory doesn't think this is a sports machine. (They are correct about that.) *Courtesy Harley-Davidson Archives*

And then, in the late 1980s, the factory changed the method of fixing the inserts in the cases; the coarse spines became finer. The inserts began coming loose in the cases. It happened infrequently, but it happened.

In 1991, that was cured by leaving out the inserts. The primary side main bearing is simply pressed into the aluminum case half.

Each time you press the steel bearing into the aluminum case, it will wear. There will come a time when the fit won't be tight.

Which means the cases can't be rebuilt anymore, and just to be fair about this, at the same time, H-D switched from steel inserts for the XL engine's tappet guides, to running the lifters directly in the alloy case half. Again, when the moving parts wear, the part they move in may have to be replaced.

So? So the later V2 and XL engines won't, in theory here, hold up for as many rebuilds. Sixty years from now the percentage of sound engines will therefore be reduced.

Will this matter? In hard fact, that is? The good news here is that the engines go ever so much longer and farther between rebuilds. And there are 10 times as many late V2s as there ever were Knuckleheads, and you can still find Knuckleheads for less than a new Road King.

In sum, we purists may, and do, deplore the practical shift in values, and we Harley fans need to know all we can. But in plain fact, the odds are there will be enough V2s to go around, so to speak, in 2066.

Back in the real world, potential buyers would probably be better served by checking to make sure the Softail in question, 1989 through

1992, has had its rear brake line assembly and positive battery cable checked, as per the recalls for those items.

Year and model	1995 FLHTCUI Ultra Classic Electra Glide
Engine	ohv 45-degree V-twin
Bore and stroke	3.50 x 4.25 inches
Displacement	80 cubic inches
Brake horsepower	60 (est.)
Gearbox	five speeds
Wheelbase	16F/16R
Suspension	telescopic forks, swingarm rear
Weight	785 pounds (tank full)
Seat height	28.2 inches
Fuel economy	38 miles per gallon
Top speed	91 miles per hour

For model year 1997 the engineering and styling departments put the FL-style big front tire on the Springer front end with Heritage trim and accessories. They called it, as we could have predicted by now, the FLSTS Heritage Springer, a fond recall of the 1940s instead of the 1950s. *Courtesy Harley-Davidson Archives*

Evolution Solidglides

Not to carry the evolution theme too far, but the final versions of the original Superglides, the 1984 through 1986 FXs with conventional rear suspension, rigid engine mounts, four-speed gearbox, and V2 engine, could be known as the Dead End Kids.

This wasn't tragic. Instead, it was H-D's way of keeping one foot on solid ground. Nobody really knew how the public would accept the Softail, for one thing, and there was a segment of the public that didn't trust the isolation mounts.

This is a rare one. In 1995 the radical Softail was the Bad Boy, an FX-style Springer except much of the part that ordinarily was chrome-plated—the fork linkage, tubes, and the oil tank, for instance—were plated black. To the sales department's presumed surprise, the Bad Boy didn't sell and it was withdrawn after just two years, so while it wasn't popular, it will be rare. *Courtesy Harley-Davidson Archives*

Playing it safe, H-D continued building the old-style FX line during the switch from Shovelhead to V2, and while the Softail expanded from one model into its own series, and as the Softail line (the FXSTs) expanded, the FX line shrank.

In model year 1985, the first full year of the V2 engine, there were four solid-mount 'Glides: FXEF Fat Bob, FXWG Wide Glide, FXSB Low Rider, and FXST Softail.

For 1986, as mentioned earlier, there were the Softail and Softail Custom, with five-speed gearbox and belt final drive. The Custom had the solid rear wheel first seen on the Disc Glide, which was discontinued, and the Wide Glide was the only Harley with kick start and the only Big Twin with four speeds and chain final drive.

This can be tremendously confusing. Harley-Davidson puts lots of value in and on its various model names, so the habit is to use the same name, Wide Glide, Sturgis, Custom, or whatever, on motorcycles that are usefully different. Thus we've had two versions of the Sturgis, the Convertible, the Wide Glide, and so forth.

What this means here is that the original Superglide, the one with the FL frame and engine and the XL front end, came to, well, a dead end.

They were good machines. A V2-powered Wide Glide, especially with the flames that had to be special ordered toward the last, is a better machine than the first one was. But nobody will know it. They likely won't know what the bike is, or they'll think you put the wrong engine in the frame.

In sum, it's a good buy on merit, but a lackluster buy as an investment; three stars for the lot.

Going against predictions, this is a 1991 Heritage Softail that's had the extras taken off and replaced with stuff like the straight pipes and the hop-up carburetor. Oh, and the plated cover on the front hub is there to balance the disc on the left, and because the older FLHs had covers like that.

Models	Utility	Saddletime	Collectibility	Style	Accommodations
1984 Softail	★★★★☆	★★★☆☆	★★★☆☆	★★★★☆	★★★☆☆
1988 Springer	★★★★☆	★★★☆☆	★★★☆☆	★★★★☆	★★★☆☆
1990 Fat Boy	★★★☆☆	★★★☆☆	★★★☆☆	★★★★★	★★★☆☆
1992 Heritage Nostalgia	★★★★☆	★★★☆☆	★★★☆☆	★★★★★	★★★☆☆
1985–98 V2 FXEF, FXWG, FXB, and other FLSTs	★★★★☆	★★★☆☆	★★☆☆☆	★★★☆☆	★★★☆☆

About Those Stars

If it's accurate to predict that because the FXRs will be more popular later because they aren't appreciated now, the same goes for expecting the Softails, which were the sales success of their time, to gradually lose value—nothing major, mind you!—as they get older. More of them are for sale, and the novelty moves elsewhere.

This has little to do with their actual merits. The Softails are sound and strong and able to run for years with only minor attention. But they are not workhorses. They weren't built to go cross country. They'll do it, but they weren't built to keep their occupants relaxed and comfortable coast to coast.

Exception is made here, with some trepidation, for the first years of the limited edition Softails, the first Springer, the first Fat Boy, the original Heritage Springer, and so forth. They made news when new, and they were distinguished enough to be identified on the street and thus will likely be appreciated later.

And the paint schemes alone, the special ones in good condition, are worth the time and attention it takes to keep them original, making them some of the few Harley-Davidson limited editions that will be looked for, and looked after, when the newness has worn off.

Evolution Era

1991–98 Dyna Glides

Give some attention first to the motorcycle shown here. Look carefully at what can be seen, and see if you can think of something that can't be seen.

Now flip back in the book to the photos of the original (or subsequent, since they all have the component in question) FXR Rubber Glide. Is there something visible there that's not seen on the Dyna Glide? The answer is yes, and the component about which we are concerned here is the frame.

Yes, the frame. In particular, the rear frame rails, the ones you can see on the FXR and can't see on the FXD.

This is as intriguing as it is subtle. When the FXD was introduced in 1991, the factory information referred to the "internal frame," and those of us who plodded that deeply into the factory's literature wondered, what on earth is an internal frame? The frame is what keeps the wheels from hitting each other and the engine from dragging on the ground, right? What's internal or external about that?

What H-D meant but didn't spell out was that surveys focusing on the FXR series showed that some people didn't like seeing those rear tubes. Older Harleys didn't have such things because the frame didn't extend much past the seat. Imported motorcycles had frame tubes extending from the seat back to the shocks or the fender, so rear frame tubes didn't look Harley. And because of that, the people surveyed said they wouldn't buy an FXR.

Sounds silly, albeit logical in its own way, but that little quirk was one of several factors fed into the data processor for the next generation of Harley-Davidsons.

Which is exactly what the model shown here proved to be.

The name was Sturgis, to celebrate the anniversary of that South Dakota get-together, and to also observe the 10th anniversary of the first H-D Sturgis, the Superglide with the drive belts. The initials were FXDB; the *D* representing Dyna Glide, the factory's name for the new chassis, and *B* to remind us of the original Sturgis, which was lettered *B* for belts, and yes, one often does need to take notes.

The really important news was that the Dyna Glides, as they came to be known, were using an improved version of the isolation mounts. They needed fewer attachment points to isolate the engine and drivetrain from the frame and people. Because of that the engine, gearbox,

and swingarm needed less space inside the frame.

Because of that, the engine could be slightly relocated. It was also rotated and tilted four degrees forward from vertical. That, in turn, meant the oil tank could be situated lower in the frame, just above the gearbox, with shorter and less obtrusive oil lines and with the frame rails tucked tighter, as in out of sight.

There could be some quibbling here, in that the freedom to relocate the engine could have allowed the factory to put the engine where it would provide optimum front/rear weight distribution. The wheelbase could have been shorter, and the Dyna Glide could have been more sporting than the FXR Sport.

But it wasn't. The Sturgis Two, which nobody ever called it, was longer and lower than the FXR.

The Dyna Glide used the V2 engine, five-speed gearbox, cast wheels, belt drive, and so forth, since there was no need, as *Cycle* said in its test, to reinvent the wheel. The engine, suspension, and controls were located and positioned for style, and *Cycle* also noted that the custom look—which was the reason for putting the engine and controls where they were—propped the rider up against the wind and made highway travel more tiring than it needed to be.

But that was nearly the only shortcoming. Most of the press felt, to our discomfort, like the factory PR guys when they have to admit to last year's failings when they speak of this year's fixes. Yes, the magazines said collectively, we did tell you the FXR is so smooth you can't feel any vibration, and yes, now we tell you the FXDB is even smoother than that.

Still, in the interests of The Look (which translates outside Milwaukee to mild chopper styling), the Dyna Glide was given longer forks

The first Dyna Glide was the FXDB Sturgis, named for the Rally (and the second time H-D used the name). Also repeating, the Sturgis II was a limited edition and heavily black. *Courtesy Harley-Davidson Archives*

The second Dyna Glide was named Daytona, after that event. The letters were FXDB, *D* for Dyna and *B* for belt, rather than for Daytona Beach. The Daytona was a new paint treatment, which lets us see that the Dyna's frame isn't visible aft of the engine, and also how the profile strongly resembles the old FLH from the Shovelhead era. This was no accident. *Courtesy Harley-Davidson Archives*

with more rake, and a longer swingarm, which stretched the wheelbase to a full 65 inches, longer than even the FLT.

The result of all this, at the top of the page, was H-D's designation of the FXDB as a new model, which it didn't seem to be until all the new parts and changes were reviewed.

The second stage was that the new Sturgis was new *and* improved, in many ways. The new mounting system did in fact do a better job keeping the V2's inherent vibrations away from the occupants, all up and down the rev and speed range.

Nor did performance suffer. *Cycle* and *Cycle World* both tested an FXDB, although not in the same model year, and both came up with quarter-miles times in the high 13s (13.58 seconds for *Cycle*, 13.70 for *CW*). Miles per gallon were 38 for *Cycle* and 50 for *CW*, hinting that the former test crew ran on the throttle stop all the time.

There were some quibbles. The FXDB was longer and heavier, and the stretched-out forks gave a harsher ride. The Dyna Glide's controls were forward, so air pressure at highway (read high) speed was tiring. The Dyna Glide was slick, smooth, and a step forward technically, the magazines said. It simply wasn't as sporting as the FXRs were.

The Dyna Series

Following a now-predictable pattern, H-D began the 1992 model year by converting the special this-year-only model into a series.

The Sturgis name and paint were dropped, and instead there was a limited edition, the FXDB Daytona. And no, I don't know why they kept the letters and changed the name.

The Daytona commemorated the 50th time there had been races at Daytona Beach. (It doesn't work out in years because the first race was in 1937, on the beach, and there was a gap during World War II.) The FXDB got a second front disc brake, buckhorn bars, and extra chrome trim, with the paint scheme blending two-tone dark blue with kind of a metalflake pearl.

The unlimited edition, the Dyna Glide everybody could order, was the FXDC, the Dyna Glide Custom. The unpredictable thing here was that in the other series, Custom had come to mean the 21-inch front wheel. But the Dyna Glide Custom had the 19-incher, the same wheel and dual brakes and every mechanical fact of the Daytona, right down to the 598-pound claimed weight and 26.6-inch seat height.

The Custom's paint was silver and black, with the aluminum covers and other parts either unpainted or chrome-plated.

The only differences were that the Daytona was limited by fiat, while the Custom was limited by how many the factory could make. The final difference was price: The Daytona listed at $12,120, while the Custom was $11,599.

Model Year 1993

Tradition of a sort returned in 1993, as the Daytona and the Custom were dropped. This year's model was the FXDWG, the Dyna Wide Glide, and like the earlier WGs, the Dyna version came with wide triple clamps, a 21-inch front wheel ("spoked, not cast," as James Bond would say), and one front disc brake. It also came with a bobtail rear fender, the one that mimics the old days when the sharp guys threw away the rear fender and put the front one in its place.

The top of that new model, the series' special edition for 1993, was the 90th Anniversary Dyna Wide Glide. It was like the other FXDWG except for its paint, which was silver and charcoal, where the standard Wide Glide was either two-tone red or aqua and silver. As one might expect, the Anniversary Wide Glide, one of six special editions made that year to celebrate the 90th year of H-D production, was limited to 1993 examples.

The other in the series was the FXDL, the Dyna Low Rider. And for still another note on nomenclature, the factory began to call the FXRs Low Riders; but now they gave that name to the basic Dyna Glide. (Oops—they weren't calling it the Dyna Glide yet.)

The Dyna Low Rider was the basic FXD, with the standard Super Glide front end—the Sportster headlight and 19-inch cast front wheel, lower bars, and dual front brakes. The only concession to The Look this year was a set of highway pegs (footrests in front of the frame tubes),

The Dyna series' frame was tucked away, but it was there. The square backbone resembles that of the FLT, while the shock mounts are well forward, not as twist-resistant as the old FXR's frame, but more in keeping with the styling theme. *Cycle World*

Dyna Glide's oil tank was placed just above the gearbox because moving the frame rails inboard took up space beneath the seat, while moving the engine forward in the wheelbase opened space behind the engine. By this time all the F-series Harleys came with five speeds and belt drive, and the *B* for belt had been dropped. *Cycle World*

offering an optional place to rest one's boots.

All the Dyna models had revised engine mounts with a changed compound for the semirubber biscuits and new support plates. All the Dynas shared with the other models some revised levers for the clutch and brake, which put the lever closer to the rider's hand. And it should be said for the record that all the Dynas of course used the V2 engine, the five-speed gearbox, and the belt final drive.

The Convertible

The 1994 news was major: The Dyna chassis got a new look, by pulling the fork rake back from 32 to 28 degrees. That speeded up the steering, putting the FXD into the sports arena. At the same time and on the same model, the front and rear suspension was raised, as was done earlier with the FXR and for the same reason, to give more control and cornering clearance.

This came with just the one Dyna Glide that year, the FXDS-CONV.

Yep, the Convertible. The concept, and the easily removable saddlebags and windscreen, were moved from the FXR series to the FXD in 1994. The idea, obvious now that it's been done, was to give the Dyna series a sports model, as in *S* for sport, because the original FXR series was being phased out.

And in 1994, the design that began as the second Sturgis became the Dyna Glide, officially that is.

The other FXDs, the DL Low Rider and WG Wide Glide, kept the earlier frame and suspension, with a 65.5-inch wheelbase compared with 63.88 inches, for the FXDS. The DL had the cast 19-inch front wheel, the WG had the 21-inch spoked wheel, and so it went, pretty much the same as the previous year.

Dynas also got the improved engine cushions, and the frame now used forgings and investment castings in place of stampings for the major junctions. The Dyna Glide frame was the first for which Harley-Davidson used computer-assisted design in all the major dimensions and decisions. The factory said, with no disputes from outside, that the Dyna Glide frame was the best in terms of quality control and predictability that they'd ever made.

Year and model	1995 FXD Dyna Super Glide
Engine	ohv 45-degree V-twin
Bore and stroke	3.50 x 4.25 inches
Displacement	80 cubic inches
Brake horsepower	55 (net)
Gearbox	5 speeds
Wheelbase	62.6 inches
Wheels	19F/16R
Suspension	telescopic forks, swingarm rear
Weight	621 pounds with full tank
Seat height	32.5 inches
Fuel Economy	50 miles per gallon
Top speed	108 miles per hour

The Super Glide Returns

Still more logic was used for the—wait for it—Super Glide.

The Dyna Super Glide, lettered FXD, was the Convertible minus bags and windshield. That is, it had the same suspension and so forth. It was the basic Dyna model, and it had become the entry machine for the Big Twins, as the FXR series was gone from the lineup in 1995. Not for the first time, H-D jacked up the name and ran a whole new motorcycle in beneath it, while shifting the market niche (the entry level) from the old series to the new and better series.

How good was it? *Cycle World* compared the Dyna Super Glide with the Honda Shadow ACE, an 1,100-cc V-twin with lots and lots of, um, custom and cruiser touches, as seen on Harleys first.

Honda went so far in the cruiser direction, in the magazine crew's opinion, that in terms of function and performance and daily riding, the attributes for which we all at least pretend to judge motorcycles, the Dyna Glide was the better motorcycle.

After years of talking about character and tradition, in other words, the magazines could honestly say Harley-Davidson had returned to par, which probably meant more to the execs in Milwaukee than the black ink had done. (Oh yeah. *CW* said there were some who believed the Honda had more of a cruiser style. If that's not faint praise, I never heard it.)

The other three Dyna models, the Wide Glide, Convertible, and Low Rider, carried on mostly as in the previous year.

There were differences in detail, with the WG, DL, and CONV offered in choices of solid, candy, or two-tone paint, and not always the same shades as the other models, while the basic Super Glide was offered in either candy or solid paint, no two-tone. (Obscure note: The factory offers a service where you can have an outside painter, authorized by the factory, do your body panels in any color or scheme on the planet, through the dealership. It's possible therefore to find a stock bike painted in ways that were never in the catalog.)

Speaking of details, the most secure job on Juneau Avenue has to belong to the guy who wields the tape measure. Due to incremental differences in suspension, tire size, or even because the saddlebags extend fractionally behind the taillight, the four Dynas have four different wheelbases, overall lengths, seat heights, and so forth. And the Wide Glide has a different fuel tank and three different front wheel options.

The second way to have a job for life is to be the parts clerk who can remember all this.

As the Dyna Glide line grew, there were moves in several directions, as in the highway pegs in custom style and the tapered ends with noise-making tips for the peg-dragging sports riders. What doesn't show right away is that the touring Dyna and Softail families used variations in the length of the primary case and the angle of the engine's placement, so you can't always buy one drivetrain and bolt it into another frame. *Cycle World*

As the FXRs were phased out, the Dyna Glide family grew. This is the 1993 FXDWG, meaning Dyna Wide Glide, with 21-inch front wheel, headlight modeled on accessory lights of the past, forward-mount controls, and ducktail rear fender. *Courtesy Harley-Davidson Archives*

Model Year 1996

The factory's headline for the 1996 model year told the story indirectly: "Featuring enhancements across entire model line." What they meant, of course, was that there were no major changes across the entire model line.

In the Dyna Glide series, the major change had a medium impact. The center of the frame was revised. It looked the same, with the rear tubes out of view and so forth, but the section that carried the seat was lower and so was the seat and the ride height (by 0.88 inch, speaking of tape measures). And the boxes for the battery and electrical components were moved and reshaped.

Cast wheels were standard for the four models, at both ends, with the exception of the Wide Glide's laced 21-inch front wheel. Laced wheels, meanwhile, were optional for the other three models, and there were also new decorations for the fuel tanks. (Inside note: When the motojournal crews get restive at new model press viewings, we do the Wave and chant Bold New Graphics to express our reaction to the same old stuff.)

Model Year 1997

Such sarcasm must be wasted because for 1997 the same four Dyna Glides were offered, again with minor changes to the electrics. That is, smaller batteries were used because the rest of the system was more efficient. Beyond that, there were some nifty paint schemes, and for $320 you could have laced wheels.

The new line adopted the older names, as in the 1993 FXDL, the Dyna Low Rider: The Glide tag was dropped from some of the names. The Low Rider had sporting features, as in the dual front discs and the cast wheels. *Courtesy Harley-Davidson Archives*

But that was about it. The Dyna Glides had been established. The Motor Company set out when the new frame and mounting system was ready for production to replace the first versions, the FXRs, and they did just that. It was done in increments, and it was done well.

The reservations here are more theoretical than practical.

The Dyna Sport could have been more compact, and thus lighter and more sporting, than the original R-sports were. The designers used the new system for sales rather than speed. One may find that less than perfect. It doesn't mean the Dyna Glide Sport isn't sporting, because it is.

Model Year 1998

Consolidation was the theme for 1998, as the Dyna Glide line retained the same four models: Super Glide, Low Rider, Convertible, and Wide Glide.

All the Dynas—in fact, all the Big Twin models—got a revised clutch with a total of nine pairs of plates. The more plates, the more contact area, and that means the same grip with springs that aren't as hard to compress, and that means a lighter pull on the clutch. You could get laced wheels for your Dyna Glide in the Americas only. One assumes this was because the European Union demands acres of paperwork for options, and the export division didn't figure the sales would be worth the hassle.

What to Look For

A benefit easily overlooked here is that the Dyna Glides are a complete family in themselves. There's the sporting FXDS, the stylish FXWG and FXLR, and even the touring CONV. The Sportster, Softail, and

The 1997 Super Glide, the FXD, was the entry level Big Twin, replacing the FXR and retaining the original Super Glide's Sportster headlight and front end. *Courtesy Harley-Davidson Archives*

FLHT bases are therefore covered. If the Dyna family was a company in itself, it would have a sports, cruiser, and touring division. They simply wouldn't go as far in the three directions as the other H-D series do.

What does this mean? It means that when you go looking, you can find pretty much most of what you want in the Dyna Glide line.

There are no special warnings here. The Dyna Glides are the newest members of the Harley-Davidson family and even high mileage examples won't have been through as much as, say, an early Sportster or Superglide. If a Dyna Glide has been abused or neglected, it will be obvious, so just keep on looking.

The across-the-board warnings apply in that the V2 engine is just as likely to seep from its base gaskets or have the wires fall out of the black boxes in a Dyna Glide as an FLHT. The proper warm-up sequence and the caution about nonrebuildable components apply here as much as they do for the FXRs or the FLTs or the Softails.

The market may be skewed in the near future by the supply of used Dyna Glides: They are now the basic Big Twin and may be in shorter supply than some of the other models. The factory's official reports lag behind the model years, but the sales figures that have been made public have had the FXRs and later the FXDs about equal in volume to the Softails.

But a scan of the classifieds shows more Softails for sale than either the first- or second-generation Rubber Glides. The author's guess is simply that showing off becomes less fun, while riding motorcycles never gets boring, so those who bought to show off sell first.

But that's just a guess. More useful here is the fact that if there are fewer examples of a given model for sale, it will be more difficult to find the one you want.

Same idea and new frame, the FXDS-CONV was the FXD Super Glide fitted with windshield, bags, backrest, second front brake disc, and backrest. As with the original convertible, all the touring equipment comes off in seconds. *Courtesy Harley-Davidson Archives*

Models	Utility	Saddletime	Collectibility	Style	Accommodations
1991 FXB Sturgis	★★★☆☆	★★★☆☆	★★★★☆	★★★★☆	★★★☆☆
1991–98 Dyna Glides	★★★☆☆	★★★★☆	★★★☆☆	★★★☆☆	★★★☆☆

About Those Stars

Although the supply of Dyna Glides is limited, the ratings are relatively low. Shouldn't rare bikes sell for more than common ones?

Ordinarily yes, but not this time. Some of this comes from the rating system and remember, when we rate, say, an XLH higher than an FLHTC, we don't mean the Sportster sells for more than the Tour Glide does. We're rating in class.

On that basis the original Dyna Glide, the 1991 FXDB, the second Sturgis, is a truly limited production model, along with being really new, so it rates as a model that will appreciate. This doesn't mean the other Dynas aren't excellent motorcycles. They do have improvements and they do their jobs, plural here because the Dyna line has expanded into a family as in the convertibles, Wide Glides, and so forth.

They will all do what they are intended to do. That there aren't a bunch of them up for sale proves that.

What keeps the stars at an average level is that the Dyna Glides are new, still in production, and getting better all the time, so the used Wide Glide competes with the new Wide Glide for the enthusiast's money. Ditto the sports models and the touring options.

The ratings of average aren't the slurs they appear to be. Instead, if the past does predict the future, those who buy Dyna Glides now, new or used, won't even notice (much less care) if the bikes are worth more in the next few years. The selling price won't matter simply because the owners won't want to sell.

Chapter 11

1972–98 Racers

Ever hear the little nugget of folk wisdom that says there's never enough time to do it right, but there's always enough time to do it over?

It's all too true for most of us, but what the wise folk left out is that sometimes, when you do it over, you get to do it right.

And sometimes you don't.

And sometimes you keep on trying.

And that, in so many sentences, is a tidy summation of Harley-Davidson in competition during the Evolution Era, including the present day.

The XR-750, Part Two

The epigram with which this chapter opened will ring true for those who read the earlier chapter, in which the H-D racing team had to bring out a new machine without the time or the budget to do it right. The name was XR-750, the actual machine was a reworked XLR engine in a revised racing frame, and the project was the lowest point in Harley's racing history. As mentioned, things were so bad they even parted out half the unsold production run for tax purposes (and perhaps secretly to get the wretched things out of their collective sights).

However, pause for dramatic impact, while the iron-top XR-750 melted in the heat of battle and the team used up its older KRs to keep something on the track, the team engineers were given the time and money to do it right.

As they did, in spades, in 1972.

The official name for the new production racer was still XR-750, because it was based to some degree on the X-series Sportster engine. It was a four-speed, unit-construction, air-cooled, 45-degree V-twin, and some of the parts, notably the clutch and primary drive, were shared with the earlier XLs.

But the new XR had a larger bore and shorter stroke than the first one had. Plus, the heads, porting, and oil systems benefited mightily from work done with the old version, and most important of all, the new engine used high-tech aluminum alloy for the heads and cylinders. No more waffle iron.

The new XR used the same basic design for the dirt-track frame and for the frames used by the factory team for the road-racing bikes built for the team's use. Unlike the dirt-track frames, the road-racing frames were only available to you if you were the right person, knew the right people, and asked at the right time.

This isn't exactly the best place for a warning, but as mentioned in the earlier chapter on competition, this material is complicated and arcane and sometimes the facts aren't in the book, so learn before you

leap. (Speaking of the book, your energetic author wrote a history of the XR-750. It's available by phone or in stores, and sales pitch or no, if you are going to own or restore an XR-750, you need this book.)

Blush. That said, the next fact is that the new XR-750 on its first day was as powerful as the first XR-750 was on its best day. The new XR, with its trademark twin trailing carbs on the right and dual pipes high on the left, became the best in class, on the dirt at least. It matched and then defeated the Triumphs, BSAs, Nortons, and Yamahas and even the occasional Honda Four, which the rules allowed then.

As kind of a subsection, there was an XRTT, a road racer, but it wasn't nearly as public. The factory built the 200 examples of the dirt racer; they were brakeless in the catalog (although any 1972 XR you find will almost surely be wearing a rear disc brake; Airheart's best). And then came 50 XRTT frames, with a 51st made as sort of a prototype. The dirt frames were based on improved versions of the original XR-750, while the road-race frames were based on the new design but with relocations of various components and dimensions favored by Cal Rayborn, the best road racer on the team, and arguably in the world, in 1972.

The dirt XR bodywork was virtually the same as seen in 1970, with the fiberglass tail, seatbase, and fuel tank (2 gallons in the catalog, but it will hold 2.25 if you push). The oil tank, that triangular shape beneath the seat, is alloy and holds 3 quarts.

The road racer, called the XR-TT as mentioned—never mind that the TT class in 1972 was contested on 900-cc twins—used the earlier big tank and streamlined seat, also fiberglass, and often wore a larger oil tank as well.

The first really race-based XR-750 appeared in 1972. This is the production model and was sold with no brakes, as it would be raced in half-mile and short track events. The heads and cylinders are alloy, and there are two Mikuni carburetors. This model was much newer than it looked. Just as one subtle change, compare the height of the steering head in this frame with the steering head's location in the 1970 model. *Courtesy Harley-Davidson Archives*

There was another rule change, dropping the requirement from 200 motorcycles to 25 engines. Following that, the 750 two-stroke fours and triples simply overpowered the four-stroke twins, XR included, and Harley-Davidson dropped out of the road races, not to return (with an occasional exception) until the VR1000 in 1994. We'll get to that.

The supply of XRs has always been based on demand, so in 1975 there was another production run of the dirt version, 100 examples. They used a revised frame, still with the trademark castings for the rear engine mount and swingarm pivot. The nickname for the castings is twin tomahawks, by the way, because if you have a vivid imagination, that's what they look like. To some people, anyway.

The XR engine was tuned, tested, and gradually boosted, from 70 brake horsepower when it was first run, then to 90 brake horsepower where it held through the late 1970s, then 100 brake horsepower, and now, in the late 1990s, there are XR-750s producing 110 brake horsepower. And when they're done right, they'll hold together for a 25-mile national.

The frames have varied. Illustrating a trend here, in 1978 there was another run of XR-750s, to order. The frames were done to the factory specifications, subcontracted through Mert Lawwill, who'd been a team rider, then national champion, and then a designer, builder, and supplier of XR parts. The actual production of the frames was by Terry Knight, whose Washington shop was a long way from Milwaukee. Production totaled 83.

Why'd they do it like that? Because Milwaukee had other things to do and guys like Knight made a profit on projects that would only eat the factory's time and money.

In 1980 there was another production run, the last one for the XR-750. These bikes—well make that these frames because the engines changed year to year and stayed stock maybe 20 minutes after the buyer took delivery—were known as the TT bikes.

The 1972 XR-750 used Ceriani forks and Girling shocks, as did the first version, but the cases, heads, cylinders, exhaust and intake systems, and engine internals were new. Great care was taken to keep the profile and exterior as close to the first XR and to the XL series as was practical. *Courtesy Harley-Davidson Archives*

This had nothing to do with road racing, not by 1980. Instead, as the XR (and rival) engines gained power, the dirt and the tires were as they'd been, and traction became a problem. You gain traction by putting weight on the rear tire, and you do that by raising the machine, so the 1980 frames used longer shocks and pulled the forks—Marzocchis instead of the Cerianis fitted from 1970 until 1980—closer to the frame, to quicken the steering. And the mounts were reworked so the front of the engine, yes, just the front, sat lower in its cradle.

The factory records show 160 of the 1980 TT XR-750s were made. They weren't all made and delivered at once, by the way, but when they left, they were considered 1980s.

Aside from some minor flaps, the rules have remained firm and fixed since then. (In one such flap, Honda bought an XR-750, made a new and improved version, and won the national title with it, leading to restrictor plates for anything more powerful than a Harley-Davidson.)

Harley-Davidson has been fielding a team and winning since then; and more to the Motor Company's credit, it has been careful to ensure that any racer can go into a store and get all the parts needed to build a competitive XR-750.

Thus, in 1990, after an outside tuner demonstrated an improved cylinder head design, the factory made another batch of engines. The racing department took this opportunity to make some changes to the cases and other parts, to the extent that although the name and identification system were the same, the factory had to recertify the engine with the AMA. Not only are there different parts in the 1990 XR engine, there are seven fewer parts.

The official number given out was 115 sets of cases, with heads and cylinders; the D-port engines, so called because the intake ports are shaped like a D laid on its flat side, were assembled by a trained team inside the racing shop and sold ready to go. This was in sharp contrast to the old days when the first thing you did with a new XR engine was take it apart, check it out, and correct the flaws you (always) found.

Thus, by the official record, there have been no XR-750s produced since 1980, and no engines since 1990.

The record isn't the whole story. If we add up that first 200, and assume the 50 XRTT frames got engines (from the parts bins) plus the 83 machines from 1978 and the 160 done in 1980, we have about 500 alloy XR-750s. Add to that figure another 50 or so machines built with D-port engines and new frames, some with a single rear shock, as in motocross, and we have enough XRs, new and used, club racer or money maker, to establish a market. And have some fun, as we'll see.

The road-racing XR-750, labeled XRTT for historical if confusing reasons, was a more limited model, in that the frame, tank, seat, and fairing were different. The rear brake is disc, surely because it's light. Only a handful of XRTTs were built and sold, although the model was listed in the catalog. *Courtesy Harley-Davidson Archives*

The XRTT used a huge, drum front brake: Discs were not yet proven and Daytona is no place to take chances. The bodywork was derived from the earlier XR and the KRTT before that, mostly because the shape worked. *Courtesy Harley-Davidson Archives*

The XR-1000

One of the more obvious ways to have fun with an XR-750 has to be riding one on the street: People have been doing that since the days of production-class racing, at least.

In the mid-1970s, when the XR first ruled the roost, the guys at H-D R&D realized the public would like such a project. So the company put together some prototypes, mounting the starter and alternator and lights, muffler, horn, mirrors, fenders, a steel fuel tank, and so forth, and tuned the engine to pass the federal emissions levels.

It didn't work. Well, it did work, in that it ran and could be ridden but it gained weight and lost power, and management decided the sporting public wouldn't settle for the performance they'd get at the price they'd have to pay. The project was abandoned. (By the factory, as we'll see.)

Several years later, when the managers bought the firm and needed something to stir the enthusiast's blood, portions of the street XR idea were merged and blanded—and yes that's blanded and not blended; I invented the verb for this purpose—into sort of an XR-750 for the street.

The name was XR-1000.

The XR-1000 was a mitigated disaster.

The most obvious flaw was that instead of converting an XR-750 for the street, the company converted an XLX into a semi-XR, kind of like throwing a wolf's pelt onto a sheep.

That's harsh. Fairness dictates the admission that the company did what it could to come as close as the laws of government and economics allowed.

The frame, running gear, body, chassis parts, and even the paint were XLX, the basic price-leader Sportster. Same bore and stroke, same 61-cid displacement. (Note: The engine used was the iron-top Shovelhead version of the XL, not the later Evo. This model is in this section because it follows the chronological pattern.)

The engine got improved iron cylinders with XR heads and XR-style carbs and exhaust, as in two carbs trailing high on the right, twin megaphones high on the left. The XR-1000 was the fastest stock Harley-Davidson tested by a magazine up to that time, with a drag strip time of 12.88 seconds. The engine gained 10 brake horsepower on the

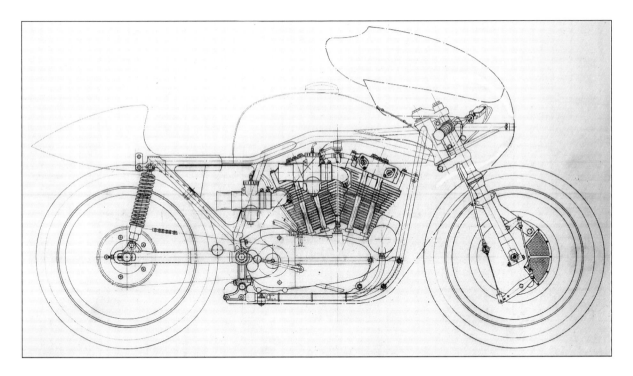

Plans from H-D's racing department show how the low-boy frame wrapped around the engine. Most factory-supplied frames came from outside vendors but used the forged iron twin tomahawks for the rear engine mount and swingarm pivot. *Courtesy Harley-Davidson Archives*

stock iron XL, and of course it passed the federal requirements.

But the XR-1000 wasn't the fastest bike on the road. Next, and to me this is the worst flaw, the XR-1000 didn't look different. Unless you knew what you were looking at, you couldn't tell the gray XR from the gray XL.

Because this model came when the factory hardly had enough pennies to count, it had to pay its own way, meaning the extra 10 horses added $2,000 to the retail price.

Adding to that, the enthusiasts most likely to buy such a factory hot rod probably knew they could pack 10 more horses into (or out of) the iron XL engine with cams, carb, and exhaust, for a fraction of the two grand. As a result of these shortcomings, the XR-1000 didn't sell. According to Rick Conner, who did the most recent accounting of the factory's figures, H-D built 1,018 XR-1000s in 1983 and 759 in 1984. Built ain't sold, and I know for a fact there were XR-1000s on showroom floors deep into 1985.

That may have been a good thing. Due to some engineering problems, the XR engine needed a special run of cases and other major parts. (The XR heads were taller than the XL heads and the XR engine had to fit unmodified into a stock XL frame, meaning the rest of the XR-1000 engine had to be shorter than an XL engine.)

In short, they weren't done right. They had to be redone and the design had to be changed.

The XR-1000 naturally was dropped from the catalog at the end of 1984, to be eclipsed later by the Evo XL engine. If there were bright spots in this chapter, they'd have to be that the factory did make a modest profit on the deal. That is, each XR cost less to make than it sold for,

XR-750s are modified almost instantly. There are several catalogs of outside XR parts. This example has a gear case cover and distributor from former national champion Mert Lawwill, the frame is kicked out to clear the oil pump, the front of the gear case is fitted with an expansion chamber, and the back of the case has an added breather, the sprocket cover is new . . . it takes years to learn all this, but it's worth it if you collect racing gear.

and in 1983, an XR-1000 that was as like an XR-1000 as Jeff Gordon's Daytona 500 winner is like a Chevrolet Monte Carlo, won the Battle of the Twins at Daytona. Jay Springsteen was the rider, the bike was really an XR-750, enlarged and fitted into a frame from the XRTT days, and it was a glorious day. But such a heritage is scant comfort when your flywheels fly apart at 5,000 miles.

Year and Model	1994 VR1000
Engine	ohc 60-degree V-twin
Bore and stroke	3.858 x 2.60 inches
Displacement	61 cubic inches
Brake horsepower	150 (claimed)
Gearbox	five speeds
Shift	left foot
Wheelbase	55.5 inches
Wheels	five-spoke alloy, 17F/17R
Suspension	upside-down forks/single shock
Weight	390 pounds (claimed)
Seat height	NA
Fuel economy	NA
Top speed	180 miles per hour (est.)

The VR1000

When it comes to tenacity and courage in the face of adversity, Rudyard Kipling and Teddy Roosevelt *both* could take lessons from Harley-Davidson.

And speaking of faith in the future, everything in this section will have to be taken on faith, and with the proverbial grain of salt,

Winners. The man is Bill Werner, who's tuned 3 national champions (Gary Scott, Jay Springsteen, and Scotty Parker) to 12 national titles and 130-plus national race wins. The bike is Parker's 1986 XR-750, one of a truckload the factory provided its team. It's a production XR-750 just like the 1972 model was, except the frame is different, the gas tank is aluminum not fiberglass, the seat's changed, the forks are larger, the exhaust is a boom-box, so called because it's big and lets the engine meet noise limits. Again, we can go on and on but the point is, no two XRs are alike.

because what has to happen to earn the VR1000 a place in a buyer's guide hasn't happened yet. That's because in 1994, Harley-Davidson revealed another Superbike project.

Why, it never actually explained, but it must be that the top of the Motor Company knows nostalgia won't last forever, that new models

What you see is what you can build. This is a factory-framed XR-750, with early glass and frame, but it's been fitted with lights and mufflers as well as brakes, and it's registered for the street. There are probably a couple dozen such XRs in this trim by now. They are as much fun as you think. *Nick Cedar*

The XR-1000 was a notion that didn't quite come off. As it looks, the XR-1000 was a tuned-down mixture of XR-750 and XL-1000, with two carbs and high dual exhaust in XLX frame and trim. *Courtesy Harley-Davidson Archives*

will be needed, and that H-D has to keep reminding people that the thinking behind the FLT, Dyna Glide, and V2 still matters.

Road racing is the fashion. Well okay, it's not as big as motocross, but H-D tried motocross and it didn't pay off. Anyway, Harley-Davidson hasn't been in the two-stroke single business for 20 years. Running parallel to that, racing has always been part of motorcycling, and it may simply be that H-D's managers know racing is a good place to be.

Whatever, H-D created what amounts to a new racing department with the specific task of creating, testing, and winning with a Superbike-class machine. As indicated, the name is VR1000, and it's about as different a Harley-Davidson as has been seen in Milwaukee since the opposed-twin, fore-and-aft W-series Sport of 1919.

About the only traditional thing about the VR is that it's a V-twin, but the vee is 60 degrees, not 45, which makes it in better primary balance, albeit it's longer fore-and-aft than a 45-degree engine (and less balanced and shorter than the other classic, the 90-degree V-twin).

The VR is water-cooled, with twin overhead camshafts for each cylinder and with the cylinders cast as part of the crankcase: There are no barrels as such. The connecting rods are side by side, not fork and blade, and they bolt onto the crankpin and have solid bearings, while conventional Harley engines use roller bearings and built-up flywheels and crankpin. The VR has fuel injection and electronic ignition and four valves per cylinder. In sum, it's got all the modern racing features, as it should.

The engine bolts into a twin-spar frame fabricated in aluminum, with upside-down forks and single rear shock; again just as the competition from East and West do it. (If there's room here for a flight of fancy, to the romantic eye, the spars of the frame look like oversized versions of the castings used for the engine mounts and swingarm pivot in the original and early alloy XR-750s. As noted earlier, those castings were known as twin tomahawks. Take a gander at the VR frame and see if you don't agree.)

Perhaps as romantic, the tank and seat of the VR1000 bear at least a family resemblance to the XRTT of 20 years earlier, albeit the shape of the fairings must have been dictated by the radiator and the readings from the wind tunnel.

As we'd expect, the VR came with triple disc brakes, a five-speed gearbox, and all the electronics one could imagine. During the VR's appearances to date, from Daytona 1994 through the 1997 Superbike season, the VR hasn't won a race, despite riders like Miguel Duhamel, Doug Chandler, and Chris Carr, world and national champions in other classes and on other bikes.

Why no wins? That's too complicated and detailed to examine here even if this writer had the answer, which he does not.

For those of us who are really optimistic, the lack of wins may turn out to be a blessing thoroughly disguised.

The XR-1000's only glory came in the AMA's Battle of the Twins series, when Jay Springsteen and later Gene Church, shown here, vanquished the Italian and English twins with this very special version of an XR-1000: It was mostly an XRTT powered by an XR-750 engine enlarged to XR-1000 bore, stroke, and displacement, as the rules allowed. *Courtesy Harley-Davidson Archives*

What H-D really did to help the sport is shown here; dollies loaded with production XR-750 engines. These are the 1990 D-port engines, a special run at the foundry followed by careful assembly and testing by professional racing mechanics: The privateer or dealer who bought one of these engines got guaranteed, reliable horsepower out of the box. *Courtesy Harley-Davidson Archives*

The VR1000 has Harley-Davidson genes, in that it's a new engine, frame, suspension, and bodywork, but the latter is done so it looks as much like the XRTT as science allows. This example, parked at the team's tent at Laguna Seca in 1997, has mirrors, lights, signals, and mufflers, but it's not certified for street use in the United States.

The AMA requires all Superbikes to be production based; that is, the race model is supposed to have been built from a road model. In almost all cases, from Japan, Italy, or England, what the builders have done is make the competition bike and then hang some street stuff on it.

Same here. With an audacious twist. The rules don't say the road model has to be actually sold, nor need the sales be in the country of origin.

So what Harley-Davidson has done is get the VR1000 certified in a country of convenience, which is a diplomatic way to say if you pay the fee, you can do what you want. The country of convenience for this project is Poland, which means that country's motor vehicle department has recognized the VR1000 as a street-certified motorcycle. H-D has released photos of a VR1000 with headlight, turn signals, muffler, and license plate. The AMA rules don't say you have to actually sell 50 examples, nor must you offer them where you make them.

At the best unofficial, don't-quote-me estimate, there have been 38 VR1000s actually built. The road-racing team has several, obviously, and there are a couple in favored private hands being raced. The official word is, you the ordinary person can order one and it will be delivered if and only if you swear a federally approved oath to never take your VR1000 on a public road.

What to Look For

Everything is this section brings to mind the quote from Winston Churchill: "Anyone who claims to understand the situation cannot be in possession of all the facts."

Begin with the alloy XR-750. (The hyphen is used here because when the XR-750 was new, that's how it was in the catalog and parts book, but the official literature for the VR1000 is like that, no hyphen. Odd language, Harleyspeak.)

But as one begins to look, one must learn. Check out the books and the facts and be ready to tell the difference between a factory frame and an early Lawwill frame. Hint: The Lawwill has a humped backbone.

There have been, oh, half a dozen small outfits making frames for the XR engine. Knight, Lawwill, Champion, and C&J made good ones. I've seen a couple that didn't look as good, nor did they have brand names, and they surely don't work as well.

The original frames had twin tomahawks; the outside-made frames didn't. The most recent have a single rear shock absorber, sometimes centered, other times offset. The early and midlife frames have two shocks, upright or canted, forward or above the rear axle.

This is the same VR1000 as shown in the previous picture but it looks different because the stock paint scheme is black on the left, orange on the right, with a white stripe down the middle. The stock exhaust looks a powerful lot like the optional muffler on the 1998 XL1200S, don't you think?

There are different heads, pipes, ignitions, and oiling systems. Each tuner has his or her favorite configuration, and the configurations change from track to track. Suffice it to say here that you'd set up the XR differently for a mile track that's long and thin than you would for a mile track that's short and wide.

In short, there's more to be learned here than can be packed into this chapter. Buy the books, go to the races, and learn to tell what you're looking at before you buy it.

The XRTT

Take the above and multiply it by a 2.2 difficulty factor. There were several dozen XRTTs made, compared with several hundred XR-750s in dirt trim. Nobody knows where the XRTTs went.

And right this minute there are people making more, as in there has been a production run, outside the factory to be sure, of XRTT frames and glass and alloy. There's even been a reproduction run of those neat, huge, front drum brakes.

This is neither a crime nor a sin. This is the free market. One can even argue that an XRTT made new in 1998 is just as genuine as one made in 1972; that is, they both have frames and brakes from outside the factory. It's a genuine H-D engine, why worry?

The problem comes from the

The engineering, sales, and racing people take VRs with them for public show and test, and the machine is a usable, viable street motorcycle in preproduction form. What the actual production form will be, isn't known at this writing. But examples have been sold, they will be offered for sale again, and they will be valuable when that happens.

free market. New old stuff is more valuable than new stuff. Thus, while there's nothing wrong with buying a never-raced XRTT, especially if you plan to race it yourself, you need to be really sure how old, new, or authentically factory it is. Rephrasing the carpentry rule, read the book twice and make the offer once.

XR-1000

The important part with the XR-1000 is going to be service history.

The XR-1000 had its own cases, heads, and barrels. The parts manual will have photos and the code, explaining the numbers and letters that should be on the engine and the frame. Make sure they match.

There was a second run of cases from the foundry, because the first ones were flawed, and it will be an advantage to have that version, if all else is equal. Nor should one shy from a high-mileage bike, simply because if it's been ridden a lot it's almost sure to have been treated to the fixes.

Against that, kind of like the turbocharged cars of 10 years ago, if it's low mileage and hasn't blown up, bet that it will. This sounds contradictory, but if an XR-1000 doesn't blow up, it's easy to ride. None of the modifications made it more demanding (well, the two carbs mean a stiffer throttle, but that's all).

The final warning here is, be sure it's stock. A normal XL, as is the standard street Sportster, will have benefited from a larger fuel tank or more comfortable seat, but an XR-1000 changed that way will simply be less special than it was.

VR1000

Asked just how many VR1000s have been sold to date in Poland, Willie G. Davidson looks you right in the eye and asks, "Have you been there?"

"Um, no."

"Well if you went, you'd see VR1000s streaming past on every street corner of every town in Poland."

And then of course, to his credit, he can't keep a straight face any longer and grins his trademark grin.

He and the reporter both know perfectly well that VR1000 sales in Poland match those in the United States. That is, there haven't truly been any. At this writing at least.

But it will happen. If you were the owner of a racing team and you had a good track record and the budget to field a team with top rider and parts and so forth, you could buy a VR1000 from the factory, and they'd help with parts and access to code and chips for the injectors and ignition.

The major collector will have more difficulty, the ordinary collector will have still more, and the regular folks, you and I, will have to work really hard to get a VR.

But they will be available, a prediction made simply because that's always been the way it worked, works, and will work. The factory made a handful of eight-valve racers in the 1910s and 1920s, kept them for the team, didn't sell any, and took them back to the plant when the team suspended operations—and 70 years later there's a handful of eight-valve racers in museums and collections. It will happen again.

What to look for? Parts. A VR is bound to be stock. It can't be anything else, and no part from any other motorcycle will swap.

Models	Utility	Saddletime	Collectibility	Style	Accommodations
1972–80 XR-750	★★★★★	★★★★☆	★★★★☆	★★★★☆	NA
1972 XRTT	★★★★★	★★★★☆	★★★★☆	★★★★☆	NA
1982–83 XR-1000	★★★☆☆	★★☆☆☆	★★☆☆☆	★★★☆☆	★★★☆☆
1994–98 VR1000	★★★★☆	★★★☆☆	★★★★★	★★★★☆	★★★★☆

About Those Stars

Nutball collector speaking here, okay? The production-line XR-750, the one set for dirt and sold to the public, is the most successful Harley-Davidson made, if you combine race wins, titles, critical acclaim, and happy owners. It's a work of art.

The XR is also tremendous fun. A guy I know, collector with a barn full of exotic and impressive machines, had his staff build an XR for fun. The collection sits in the barn. He can't resist the XR. Rides it all the time, neighbors be darned, and this is a portly gentleman of late middle age.

XRs do that. They are great fun, as in 90 brake horsepower and 350 pounds. They can be converted for street or raced for money or sport, and most maintenance can be done by the practiced owner. So, if the XR-750 is all that great and practical, why does it rate only four stars for collectibility?

Because the cat has escaped from the bag. At this writing the alloy XR is a known value; people are hunting down tired examples and tucking spare parts beneath their workbenches. The price of a good example has doubled. A few years ago, you could scoop up a tired XR for a couple of grand. Not anymore.

This doesn't mean the price will keep on doubling. It won't. Instead, there will be a gradual increase every year from now on.

That's the push. The shove is that there's been a proposal to change the rules for Grand National racing. H-D, Honda, Suzuki, and Ducati now make 1,000-cc V-twins. The notion is, if the GNC rules required such machines, the four factories would take part, instead of just Harley, and there'd be more competition, interest, and involvement.

Maybe so, maybe no. In 1981, Harley, Honda, and Yamaha all entered 750-cc, production-based, V-twins in the national series. Yamaha lost and quit losers, Honda lost, rebuilt, won, and quit winners, and H-D lost, lobbied, worked, and hung in there. But the factory wars were over.

The big makes can't do this in motocross. The stakes (and the crowds) are too big, and the customers are too numerous. Motocross is for marketing; Grand National is public relations. So if it doesn't pay off, it's dropped. History says the proposal that is supposed to get four brands on the track won't work.

But even so, suppose the new rules do come in and the VR1000 replaces the XR-750 as Harley's dirt racer. What then?

Still the same. The XR-750 will still be art, they'll still be fun, and there will still be more buyers than sellers, just as the fuel-injection Corvette and 427 Cobra retained their value after new rules made them obsolete for racing.

The XRTT

The road-racing alloy XR-750, the XRTT in the book, was made in more limited numbers, and it's got as much appeal, utility, and so forth as the XR-750. So why the same ratings? Because the road racer has already appreciated, to the extent that there are new ones being assembled from old, or even reproduction, parts. The bottom line is higher, so to speak, in that right this minute you can buy a complete dirt XR for the same price you'll pay for an XRTT rolling chassis (complete except with no engine).

Vintage racing is getting bigger all the time. Dirt track requires some skill and practice just to take part, never mind doing well, while road racing offers more events and you can look good even if you aren't all that fast, which means here that an XRTT is easier to have fun on, and that adds to its value.

Um, do be sure it's a genuine old one if you find an XRTT for sale, or offer less money if it's not. A reproduction is fine for the track and for fun, but they aren't worth more than they cost to assemble, and an ex-factory XRTT is.

The XR-1000

Here's the bad news. This is the tough part, where the author knows he's gonna hurt some feelings. Call me your Dutch uncle.

The XR-1000 has peaked.

The model has a bleak history. It didn't sell well. There were and will be serious problems with reliability, and the XR-1000 never attained the King-Hell status the original XLCH held the patent on.

The XR-1000 had one brief, shining moment: that day at the Daytona speedway when the replica XR-1000 named *Lucifer's Hammer* grabbed the Italians by their pride and ground them into so much sausage.

For reasons of reverse appeal (there are always those who figure something must be terrific if the public didn't like it), most XR-1000s were bought by collectors years ago. They think their examples are valuable and set the price accordingly, which means if you want one—and I'm not saying you shouldn't, okay?—you'll have to pay for it.

You won't make any money, it's not all that special to ride, and you'll ride with one ear open all the time. Meanwhile the rest of the world is busy with other interests. The XR-1000 will become just another small, sad chapter in H-D history.

The VR1000: Tomorrow's Legend

Here's the five-star investment, and yes, all this is pure guesswork.

There is precedent. As cited earlier, machines made by the factory for team or favored-friend use only have always managed to find their way into public hands.

True, the VR racing program has been a failure. After four years of effort, untold millions in R&D, and the services of riders who have won world and national titles on other models and makes, the VR is still off pace. It's improved, but the competition has improved ahead of it, so to speak.

What's coming next?

The VR project could be abandoned, in which case the ones built so far become treasures, like the sword your great-great-great grandfather wore in the war between the states.

Or the factory abandons politics and lets the dirt track team, guys who are not now allowed to help the road race effort despite their track records, into the camp. The VR wins and each example becomes a trophy, like the cloak your even earlier ancestor wore at Valley Forge.

Or the VR becomes the basis for the new Grand National series, in which case the team that keeps the XR-750 in front puts the VR in front (see previous paragraph).

Or the VR becomes a full production model, a true replacement for the FXR or the XLCH, a real sports bike. In that case, the early ones equal, say, the Lotus designed by Colin Chapman and not the committee that replaced him, or the Ferrari made before Sr. Ferrari sold to Fiat.

Can't lose, is the phrase we're after here.

There won't be many VR1000s on the market, but if you find one don't let it get away.

Chapter 12

1986–98 Buell

Eric Buell tests the dictum that timing is everything. Timing is important, no doubt about that, in motorcycling as much as in love or war. But while Buell's timing has been nearly perfect, he's also added talent and tenacity to the mix.

By the record, it's all part of Buell's character. He's an engineer and racer, again by the record better at the former than the latter, and he worked at the Motor Company until he decided he'd rather be on his own. In 1983 he tackled a tremendous project, producing his own 750-cc racer, a two-stroke four, and got the first one finished just as the AMA changed the rules and decided the national championship would be decided not with racing 750s but with production-based Superbikes.

Yes, the timing couldn't have been worse.

Except that Big Twins were part of the new class, and this took place just as H-D had a surplus of XR-1000 engines, spares to fix bikes that didn't need to be fixed because they were still on the showroom floor.

The RR1000

Buell and H-D did a deal. Buell designed a frame for the XR-1000 engine. It was as advanced as could be, with round chromoly tubing and with isolation mounts for the engine and drivetrain.

This was an advance on the earlier FXR and FLT designs, in that first, the X-series engines are unitized, with the crankcases, primary drive, and gearbox all in one unit (and by the way, they're more rigid and compact because of that). The swingarm was pivoted from the back of the unit, and the single shock absorber went beneath the cases with linkage that worked the spring/shock in extension rather than compression. The frame, which weighed half as much as the factory's version, was a trellis, with the engine suspended from the frame and lending rigidity at the same time.

The 1986 RR1000, logically named because there was some talk of road racing in the Battle of the Twins class, got full bodywork. The fairing was based on research done years earlier by H-D, so it was efficient and it was, well, bulbous. The blunt front had science on its side, but style wasn't part of the equation.

Wheels were 16-inch castings, the fashion of the day, and there were massive forks and triple disc brakes. Wheelbase was 53 inches, claimed dry weight was 395 pounds, and the steering head was raked to 25 degrees, a racing setting.

Again as good timing, Buell had the backing of Vetter/Bell, at the time that accessory firm was looking to expand. Buell offered Harley-

Davidson an outlet for those engines, as well as a chance to make a splash in the enthusiast magazines, and thereby have some claim that it was paying attention to the future.

In the events, so to speak, Buell made enough RR1000s to use up the 50 spare engines, which qualified the RR1000 for racing. But the stakes had been raised, and the Buells never did all that well on the track.

Elsewhere, the RR1000 was quickly seen to be exactly what it was, a race bike with lights, horn, and muffler. Almost all the examples therefore went straight into collections: actually riding a road race bike on the street, with narrow bars, no steering lock, and a posture the Inquisitors surely invented for those of insufficient faith, didn't appeal to the average motorcycle nut. Never has.

The bodywork came off as bodywork, rather than racy or stream-lined. The RR1000 looked like an enclosed motorcycle, which history tells us has failed the market test for at least 70 years.

What the RR1000 did mostly was get Erik Buell into business.

The RR1200

Timing again. There was a market for limited-edition sports bikes and Harley-Davidson appreciated that interest, but for other reasons had instead introduced the Evolution XL engine. By 1988, the supply of XR engines had dried up and the Evolution XL engine had grown to 1,200 cc. Buell simply reworked the frame and other components to accept the XL1200 engine.

The RR1000 was the first production Buell, and it looked like what it was, a road racer with the legal minimum of street stuff. The bodywork was more efficient (or so we must assume) than attractive, the seat was a place from which to work, and the RR1000 wasn't much fun to ride. *Cycle World*

Beneath the RR1000's enveloping body panels was an XR-1000 engine in the best home it ever had. Buell's frame was light and stiff with the engine mounts designed to isolate vibrations from the rider. The RR1000 was well engineered but found no place in the market. *Cycle World*

The new model was still fully enclosed except for odd cutouts for the oil cooler and various controls, and the front fender was still shaped like a shroud, but it worked to direct cooling air to the engine. Still unusual, in sum.

The XL1200 engine wasn't a racing engine and couldn't be used for class competition, but it was a more practical and reliable engine and could easily be tuned to outdo the XR engine for power. Buell produced 65 RR1200s during 1988 and 1989. (A note of thanks here for figures like that. Engineers are good at keeping records, but companies aren't always good at sharing them.)

The RS1200

Buell seems to have a knack for coming up with catchy names. The first Buell was named the Battletwin, a tag retained even after the 1000 engine was replaced with the 1200, which wasn't eligible for racing.

Better, Buell is no fool. In 1989 the company introduced the RS1200, named Westwind.

The model retained the unique and efficient frame, suspension, and the XL1200 engine. But first, the full bodywork was replaced with what the trade calls a half fairing, as in the top half, and with a tank that blended into the rear seat and fender.

Next, and probably as vital to the sales effort, the RS1200's bodywork allowed for a passenger seat. There was a concealed hinge in the panel behind the operator's seat, which when released allowed the panel to lift and lock upright, uncovering the pillion seat and providing a back seat/seat brace for the second occupant.

The significant difference between the RR1200 and the RR1000 was the new Evo XL1200 engine. Note the indents for the rider's feet and scoop for the brake disc in the fairing-like fender which encloses the front wheel. *Cycle World*

Nobody at Buell has ever talked about this, but surely the less inclusive bodywork meant less streamlining, and knocked a couple of miles per hour off the top speed. That is, the new style was less efficient.

What it did, though, was turn science into art. All the unique features, as in the shock/spring tucked beneath the cases, the skewed hamcan air cleaner, the two-in-one exhaust system that joined on the right and swept around to the left, the cast wheels and tremendous front discs—all this went public.

One of the reasons people keep re-inventing the enclosed motorcycle is that the bike doesn't sell. The public didn't want full bodywork in 1915, and it didn't in 1985. It's safe to predict it won't in 2005.

Stripped, the RS1200 reveals the trellis frame with the engine hung from the tubes and vibrations isolated by the flexible mounts. Witness the tubes and linkage from the steering head to the front of the cases. Note also the belt drive, the smaller front fender, and the low-slung shock/spring next to the muffler. *Cycle World*

The RS1200 was a much more useable motorcycle. You could hop on and off and make tight turns, take ladies for rides, and it still went like stink; and if there was some who thought it looked funny, okay, it handled and went better than anything H-D was making.

Acting like sort of a junior Motor Company, Buell kept the frame, suspension, and bodywork and changed the engine, then kept the new engine and changed the bodywork. In 1991 the Buell—make notes here, there was one model in the catalog—became the RS1200/5 with the five-speed gearbox now offered in H-D's Sportsters.

With that change came new forks, inverted and carrying a front wheel with braided steel lines and a six-piston caliper, three upgrades which Buell's history lists as production firsts.

A second model was added, the RSS1200, which was like the single-S machine except it had the provision for a passenger seat.

We are not dealing here with overnight success. Buell sold 102 of the first version RS1200, 100 of the five-speed model, and 75 of the two-seaters.

David Outvotes Goliath

When Charles Darwin articulated the theory of evolution—one can't say he invented it, evolution was there all the time—he came under fierce and immediate attack, and he attracted some defenders who were even more keen on the theory and energetic in their enthusiasm than Darwin himself. One chap did such a good job manning the barricades he became known as "Darwin's Bulldog."

Friends like that are good to have.

Eric Buell had that kind of friend, in the incorporated person of Harley-Davidson.

Moving from track to road, the 1991 RS has much less bodywork, a smaller if less efficient muffler, and semi-soft boxes for touring. The backrest rachets up, clearing space for a passenger. *Gess Photography*

The semi-streamliner RS series proved several points, as in the frame and suspension worked, and the models could fill a niche in the market. But Buell was working on his own dime and there were things he couldn't do, a point beyond which he couldn't expand.

Harley and Davidson had a different set of needs. The Motor Company was selling all the nostalgia it could make. What H-D lacked, in effect, was a cutting edge, a way to explore and do smaller (and potentially more risky) projects than the full corporation could do. Kind of like why the Navy has carriers and destroyers in the same fleet.

What H-D did was pipe Buell aboard.

Early in 1993, after protracted negotiations, Harley-Davidson became a minority—yes, a 49 percent holder—in the new Buell Motorcycle Company. What this meant was that H-D would provide money for product development and production expansion, while Erik himself was still working for himself. Hard to imagine a better situation for a bootstrap guy like Buell, nor can one not be impressed by such a show of faith on the part of the Motor Company.

The New Buells

The results of this partnership first appeared late in 1993, billed as 1994 models. The new name was Thunderbolt, lettered S2—presumably this stands for second series—and it was once again a mix of new and well-proved.

Best part of the S2 had to be the improved accommodations. The S2 got 17-inch wheels and the wheelbase was extended to 55 inches against 53 for the RR series. The added space allowed more room between seat and bars and higher everything, so there's less racer crouch and less back strain.

The extra money available for the S2 meant WP shock and forks, and allowed projects like the hamcan replica air cleaner: It looks like the circa-1966 H-D unit, but it's made of carbon-fiber, no less, and lacks all the internal baffles that choke down the other, as it were, XL1200 engine. How'd they do that? This is a wry comment on human nature.

The story starts with the size of the muffler, actually. First of all, a big muffler will allow more airflow with less noise and less restriction. Two, the average motorcycle nut hates big mufflers, thinks they're ugly. Three, a major manufacturer, for instance Harley-Davidson, therefore can't offer big and efficient mufflers; and four, guys like Buell, who are dealing out of the mainstream anyway, can. The S2 got a big muffler, looks be damned, and it worked so well the air cleaner could be freed up.

That, in turn, meant the XL1200 engine in the S2 could crank out more power, 76 brake horsepower on the engine dyno, than either the Sportster's XL1200 or the F-series 1340 engine. No kidding.

The Thunderbolt really filled a niche. Presumably times and fashion had changed, something that happens every day, and the term "Sporting Harley" was no longer a contradiction. Some 1,500 examples of the Thunderbolt went out the door.

But there was some demand for more accommodation, so for 1995 Buell introduced additions, in the form of the S2T Thunderbolt. Note here that Buell takes

Rear seating is better finished on the 1992 RSS. The hamcan-style air cleaner is skewed to improve clearance between it and the rider's knee. Power was a basically stock XL1200. *Gess Photography*

the H-D confusion even further, in that while you can work out the reasons for X, XL, and XLH, and while you can figure out why WG stands for Wide Glide and so forth, there's nothing even close to that logic in the Buell nomenclature.

Except here, where the *T* added to the S2 meant touring, with (obviously) room for two people and with saddlebags, lowers to shield the legs from the weather, and with the pegs lowered and the bars raised, for a more reasonable all-day posture.

Because it had the most equipment, the S2T sold for the highest price and was, logically again, the flagship of the growing fleet. Factory figures show 429 of the touring models went out the door.

Lightning and Cyclone

But sport was still the major part of the appeal, and late in 1995 Buell showed just how well it was using H-D's investment. Keeping with the stormy weather theme, the new models were named Lightning and Cyclone.

The Lightning was the barest Buell yet, with fuel tank and abbreviated seat perched atop the sketchy frame, with the frame rails, mounts, and components out there in the open, with wind protection limited to a small deflector (in the style the English used to call a flyscreen), and with the pointed end of the seat so high that it wasn't the fender, that purpose being served by a matte-black panel molded around and moving with the rear wheel. The license plate rode on the back of the fender.

If one wished to avoid controversy, one would say the Lightning's looks are controversial. If one was willing to speak out, one would say the Lightning looks odd.

Make that ugly.

Make that a motorcycle that looks like it's standing still when it's going 100 miles per hour.

The 1995 S2 Thunderbolt used the seat and tank as the bodywork rather than have bodywork to cover the parts. The passenger seat was permanent, the fairing cut back, and the front fender was even more so. *Gess Photography*

And note that lots of people don't care. They don't even wonder why the Buell ID system went from RS to S2 and then filled the gap (or stepped backwards) by designating the Lightning the S1.

They don't care because the Lightning is a classic hot rod. It gets special cylinder heads and camshafts, a rejetted carb, and that tremendous muffler and an air cleaner that's just as big and oddly shaped. The flywheels are trimmed by 4 pounds so the engine will rev quicker, and it's got 91 brake horsepower.

The Lightning was the new H-D performance champion, being the lightest Buell with the most power from the XL1200 engine. Sticking with money and logic, the Buell Motorcycle Company's owner sponsored and the AMA accepted a road-race series, for virtually stock Lightnings, presumably ridden by their owners or at least by semi-pros.

The series is regulated by putting the winners on a chassis dynamometer and testing the engine to be sure it doesn't exceed stock output. (That's not as simple as it sounds. The better tuners rearrange things so the maximum power comes on early, with the fatter delivery curve that gets you out of the corners better.)

Simply because the Lightning was and is the fastest, lightest, and most sporting, it's sold right along with the Thunderbolt. It's fair to say the Lightning is a better version of parent H-D's XR-1000. Except with the Buell version, it worked.

One can stretch just a bit and say Buell's M2 Cyclone, the low-price leader, is the smaller firm's version of Harley's XLX; that is, the Cyclone comes with most of what counts, priced to sell.

The M2 Cyclone is also like a Lightning, minus. The *M*—no, there's no hint as to why it's an *M* not an *S*—has the Lightning's heads,

but the milder camshafts and the smaller air cleaner. Meanwhile, the XL1200 engine is rated at 83 brake horsepower, rather than 91 for the full-sport version.

By the 1997 model year the Buell line-up had grown to what the factory calls four models: M2 Cyclone, S1 Lightning, S3 Thunderbolt, and S3T Thunderbolt Sport Touring. (We won't worry about whether the upgrades for the Thunderbolt justified moving up one number, or why the S3T is a separate model when you can get all the T stuff on an S3.)

Turning Up the Wick

For 1998 Buell upped the ante yet again. H-D's own line for the model year included the Super Sport 1200, an XL1200 with speed stuff.

Buell's version was the White Lightning.

The name makes sense. The paint is white, a glittery pearl sort of white for the bodywork, monochromatic white for the wheels, and just plain white for the frame. The White Lightning is an S1 with the chopped rear upper fender and the elaborate rear lower fender, but the tank is the big one, the 5.5-gallon job from the Thunderbolt.

The engine is the special part. Buell now offers reworked XL heads, with revised and larger ports and valves. These and other modifications boosted the White Lightning engine to 101 brake horsepower.

Oh, um, that's at the flywheels. But there were race options that let the private buyer easily hit the 90-brake horsepower rear wheel limit imposed by the road-race series.

The 1998 S1 Lightning minus the white got a blue frame with orange bodywork, a combo that looked (to the author if not Erik Buell himself) as odd as it sounds. And there was a dual-seat option

Buell's Cyclone was a new model, pushed back in the sport direction. The fashionably high and pointy rear fender was so high and pointy that the real-fender mounts cover and move with the wheel. This is the second series of H-D-backed Buells, quickly identified by the giant air cleaner. *Buell Motorcycle Co.*

Buell's designers had no trouble using older parts, like the H-D ignition switch and choke knob, along with the Cyclone's monstrous muffler and road-race-like rear-set gearshift linkage. The H-D-backed models are nicely finished and don't give bothers the way the earlier Buells did. *Cycle World*

for the Lightning and revised brakes for all and lots of extras. Clearly, H-D is investing in Buell and the future.

By what can't be an accident, Buell prices are right in there with Honda, Suzuki, and Ducati, outfits that also offer versions of V-twins with technical advances and character. (We'll talk more about character later.)

Marketing, meanwhile, has been extensive. Harley-Davidson is the minority shareholder but manages to weave the Buell dealer network into the upperscale H-D network. And there's a club for Buell owners, the Buell Riders Adventure Group. (BRAG, get it?) They have outings, meetings, and rides, all part of the fun.

What Next?

Predictions often go wrong, in no small degree because people don't always do the logical thing.

As in? Let's say that on the one hand, you have the VR1000 racing program, which is restricted to racing what's supposed to be and is pretending to be a road-legal production motorcycle. On the other hand, you have the Buell Lightning, as stripped a road machine as one can sell to the public, a bike that went almost instantly into its own road-racing series. If one looks at both of these phenomena, one can't help wondering, what's next?

No, this guide isn't for buyers of new motorcycles, but what will come next does influence what will happen after that, which is where we come in.

There are two sides to this coin. First, is the sporting Buell project giving H-D the progressive image the company will need in the near future? Does this take some pressure off the VR1000 project? That is, why must the VR become a real sporting road burner for sale to the public, if the Buells are doing that job?

On the other side, H-D, The Corporation, is doing an unusual thing, running the racing program in-house. (Sure, they say they don't get leaned on or get pressured in a friendly way. Right. Sure. And you don't play different ball when your dad's the coach.)

When the others aren't watching, Harley employees will say off the record that there is sure—underline that sure—to be some production, or productive, use made of the VR1000 engine.

Sorry to twist the metaphor here, but what if there was a blend of cutting edges? What if there was a prestige Buell with the proven Buell features like isolated mounts, light and effective suspension, striking bodywork, and a VR engine?

The Lightning is the newest Buell model, with the rear fender cut so high and short that the taillight and license plate mount on the wheel cover. The Lightning also has suspension upgrades, as in the upside-down forks and a tuned engine. In common with partner H-D, Buell uses a mix of parts and tuning options and standards to tailor its basic engine/frame product into a set of choices for the customer.

What to Look For

We do another 180 here, looking to Buell's past with an eye on the future.

For the early models. what to look for is simply going to be, an example. There was only a handful of RR1000s and RR1200s made, and most of them, make that virtually all of them, went to collectors.

Not into collections, not incidentally, but to collectors. The early Buells found their most favor with people who liked to park the unusual in their barns. It's almost a sure bet that an example of an early Buell will be completely stock, have low mileage, and be in the hands of somebody who knows what he or she has got.

The same applies to the RS series, except that they are more numerous and less, sorry, ponderous. They have more steering lock and can be ridden more often, for longer distances, in more comfort.

Buell's White Lightning uses an XL1200 engine tuned to 101 brake horsepower. The bike features the same fuel tank as the Thunderbolt, pearl/white paint, has no provision for passengers, and has its own race series, which says all that needs to be said. *Buell Motorcycle Co.*

This is one of those facts one likes to skip over, but the plain fact here is, Buell was learning how to make motorcycles. The RS models and the plain S Thunderbolts that were the first truly production Buells, have a history of needing more attention that your average Honda step-through.

That means things break. And fall off.

So, while an XL-powered Buell won't have the inbuilt fragility and short fuse of the XR-1000-engined examples, they will be a bother. And they probably will have been a bother to the previous owner. First step here is to ask for a complete history. Don't

ask if anything went wrong, ask what. And look really carefully at the exhaust mounts and the front portions of the frame.

This isn't quite as predictable as the alternator plug on late Shovelheads, or the weak camshaft bearing in Evolution FLs, or the oil breather bothers with later XLs, but things do fall off Buells.

Research is the key here: Asking somebody with something to sell how good it's been is kind of like asking the barber if you need a haircut.

One technique might be to find Buell owners whose machines aren't for sale and ask them for a quick review. Then, when you find one on the market, you can start with a look at the left front fairing mount tubes, for instance.

Because this is gloomy, it's fair to counter with a comparison. Jaguars used to be famous for being wonderful cars when working right, and for not working right lots of the time. Then they got serious. Ford stepped in with money and professional help, and Jaguars now work well and are fun to drive, at the same time.

The same is happening with Buell, as it spends money to improve the product. Meanwhile, by all accounts, Buell personnel are good at backing up the product when things go wrong.

Year and model	1996 Buell S1 Lightning
Engine	ohv 45-degree V-twin
Bore and stroke	3.50 x 3.81 inches
Displacement	74 cubic inches
Brake horsepower	75.5 (at the rear wheel)
Gearbox	five speeds
Wheelbase	54.5 inches
Wheels	17F/17R
Suspension	telescopic forks, swingarm rear
Weight	470 pounds (tank full)
Seat height	30.9 inches
Fuel economy	43 miles per gallon
Top speed	129 miles per hour

Models	Utility	Saddletime	Collectibility	Style	Accommodations
1987–88 RR1000	★★☆☆	★★★☆	★★☆☆	★★★☆	★★☆☆
1988–89 RR1200					
1989–90 RS/RSS1200	★★★☆	★★★☆	★★★☆	★★★☆	★★☆☆
1994–95 S2/S2T Thunderbolt	★★☆☆	★★★★	★★☆☆	★★★☆	★★★☆
1995–98 S3/S3T Thunderbolt	★★★★	★★★★	★★★☆	★★★☆	★★★☆
1996–98 Cyclone	★★★★	★★★★	★★★★	★★★☆	★★★☆
1997–98 Lightning	★★★★★	★★★★	★★★★	★★☆☆	★★☆☆

About Those Stars

This is a success story wrapped inside a note of severe caution.

As noted in the chapter, Erik Buell's bikes have changed, make that improved, since he went into business, even more so since he accepted Harley-Davidson as funding partner.

There isn't something about which it would be fair to complain. We are all better off for Buell's success. What the improvements do, though, is make the earlier Buells look not at all good.

Check the ratings again. Yes, they are harsh. The very first Buells, the RR series, were simply not suited for life on the road or the track, which is why they don't look good in terms of enjoyment, investment, or usefulness.

Things get a bit better when the XR-1000 engine is abandoned for the Evo 1200 Sportster engine: The engine and driveline are at least useable, so the owner is much less likely to push the scooter home, and the 1200s can be souped up safely. But the RS and RSS are demanding to ride, and they don't return as much for the effort as you'd get from, oh, a new Buell or even a Ducati or Moto Guzzi for the same price and condition. Nor will the RS series appreciate much; like the first Buells, the RS was collected early in its life.

All this is fairly obvious. What isn't as clear at a glance—and this is the serious warning—is that the S2 and S3 models are a whole lot more different than they appear to be, or than they are in the catalog.

The S2 and S2T Thunderbolts, made in 1994 and 1995, when H-D was involved but hadn't yet had the chance to do some useful teaching in the manufacturing and quality-control departments, were troublesome. Not in the same way as the XR-1000-powered Buells. The trouble was more along the lines of the cycle parts not being quite right here, or quite tight there.

Sure, a lot of this comes from disgruntled owners. There hasn't been a survey, but as demographer Ben Wattenburg wrote, you collect enough anecdotes and you have data.

Or, as *Cycle World* said about its long-term S2, "one of the sorriest buckets of bolts ever to set tread on tarmac."

Why the numbers work this way, nobody has explained, but what Buell did, with help, was first, make the glitches as right as they could be made, and second, design the S1 Lightning, which is a much-improved machine.

The intention is the same; that is, the S2 and S3 Thunderbolts, with or without the T, are the sport/touring Buells, with full gear and the best brake suspension.

The differences are major and important. The S3 Buells are better than the S2 Buells in just about every important way (well okay, the S2 has a more comfy seat). The difference is reflected in the ratings, as it should be.

The Cyclone follows routine, in that because it's the newer frame and normal engine minus some of the S3's fancy parts, it costs less new and will hold value about the same. The Lightnings are, of course, the fastest, lightest, and most sporting and Spartan, while their newness will keep their price high, again following market logic.

There is one factor working against the Buells as investments, and once again, it's not a complaint. Quoting *Cycle World* again, "Erik Buell's best bikes are still ahead of him."

Chapter 13

Twin-Cam 88 Era

1999 Twin-Cam 88

Early in June 1998, just as this book was going to press, the publishing company that produces *Cycle World* and *Big Twin* magazines came out with a special magazine celebrating Harley-Davidson's 95th year.

In the magazine there was an interview with The Motor Company's chief engineer, Earl Werner. He was asked about the future and he used most of his time talking about what H-D did *not* plan to do.

Sure, he said, there have been multi-cylinder projects. In the past, Harley built and sold (admittedly, by the handful only) racing engines with 60-degree V-twins with overhead cams, four-valve heads and water cooling.

But in the main and in the future, Werner emphasized, HD would focus on the classic, air-cooled, two-valves-per-cylinder, pushrod, 45-degree twin.

Why, readers wondered for a couple of weeks, did he spend so much time saying that?

Because, as was revealed by *Cycle World* in July, the long-rumored new Big Twin was a fact, due for the 1999 model year and it came as scant surprise that the new engine rumbles straight down Werner's outline.

With some major differences.

For our purposes here, the timing is both perfect and terrible.

Perfect because we just barely managed to get the facts and photos in time for this book's publication.

Terrible because we have no field experience with this engine or how it works in the models using the two-cam engine for 1999.

The engineering teams anticipates no problems. They point out that Harley-Davidson now has an up-to-date research center, and got some help from outside experts and has the funding for engineering and testing, which is to say, it's much better now that it was when the Model E Knucklehead was introduced in 1936, the E and F Panheads—we'll deal with the letter and code not far down the road—in 1948, the Shovelhead in 1966 or the Evo in 1984.

The engineers calculate that the Two Cam engine has been tested for 2.5 million miles, has run 14,000 hours on the dynamometer, has passed the 250-hour-at-full-power street test and in the factory's mules have done 100,000 road miles, all with no problem.

Against that, no product build by the human hand has ever behaved in daily use the way the tests and testers expected it to. All we can predict from now is that there will be some things that don't work as expected, and that they will be fixed.

Technical Data

There are two major, make that Major, facts about this new engine:

One, it does follow The Motor Company's tradition in that it can be fairly proclaimed a direct descendent of the Evo, which came from the Shovel, which came from the Pan, which came from the Knuckle.

Two, the new engine is different. Really different. The best illustration of that is the designer's calculation that the Two Cam and the Evo share a total of 18 parts.

Okay, make that three major differences.

The Two Cam has more displacement. The new flywheels and larger crankpin shorten the stroke to 4.0 inches from 4.25. The new cylinders have more finning and are larger on the inside as well, with

The first glance at the Two Cam is deceptive, as it closely resembles the Evo. The tip-offs are the flatter cam cover, the added space and new angles for the pushrods, and the extra finning for heads and cylinders. *Courtesy Harley-Davidson Archives*

abore of 3.75 inches. The Evo's bore is 3.5 inches, so the Two Cam, while not being oversquare in the modern manner, has grown from 80 cubic inches to 88, while the shorter stroke allows it to make useful power at 6,000 rpm, while the stock Evo runs out of steam at 5,000.

Oh, the power? The factory is a bit coy about this, but with slightly longer camshaft timing and a moderate compression ratio of 9:1, the official estimate is 62 horsepower at the rear wheel, up 10 or so from the Evo.

And we'd better add one major advance to the list, because the Two Cam has, as you will have guessed, two camshafts rather than the one used in Harley Big Twins since 1936.

To understand the how, we must begin with the why.

The customer did it. As is well known, Harley-Davidson had done wonderfully well in the market for 10 or 15 years and the other motorcycles makers (yes there are some, but don't tell who told you) have gone as far with the Harley look as it's possible to get away with.

The rivals, both foreign and domestic, have offered larger V-twins and more powerful V-twins. At the same time the government has demanded lower emissions and less noise and the models have become larger and heavier . . . the big Harleys needed more power.

The Two Cam project began with the Evo being tested in a higher state of tune.

This required a larger and stronger crankpin for the fork-and-blade connecting rods, but when the crankpin held up under the added power, it stressed the engine cases until they cracked.

The Dyna glide with the Two Cam engine looks nearly identical to the Evo-powered version, as in shared running gear and cycle parts. This the basic verison, with the carburetor. Fuel injection will also be available. *Courtesy Harley-Davidson Archives*

This required larger and better-supported main bearings, especially on the timing (right) side, but that's where the camshaft lived, at the lower center of the vee, and if the camshaft was raised it did even worse things to the valve train geometry.

This is a coincidence, sort of, in that the speed tuners have been building cases that use four one-lobes camshafts, just like the Harley XL engines do, because you can get a straighter and less flexible shot from cam lobe to rocker arm if the cam is directly below the rocker. The valve train follows directions, you could say, and is more accurate, another factor in raising the effective rpm limit.

The Two Cam's new cases allowed some other improvement, notably at the rear where the surface that aligns with the primary drive and the gearbox could be made larger and stronger.

This is an odd situation, in that when the Big Twin was new, the engine bolted to the frame and the gearbox bolted to the frame and they were bridged by the primary drive, with the primary chain adjusted by sliding the gearbox back and forth on its mounts.

This required maintenance and caused trouble. Motorcycles converted, in the main, to unit construction decades ago and there has been criticism of Harley's Big Twins because they've been bolt-up components all these years.

In fact, with the Two Cam the system is probably as rigid and inflexible as a pure unit could be, while critics can be deflected by the fact that separate construction doesn't bother Ferrari or Mercedes-Benz, why should it bother H-D?

The new cases could handle more power, so the cylinder heads' ports were improved and the combustion chambers revised. The heads and barrels are new, while the rocker arms are four of those few carry-over parts.

From the left, the Two Cam is very much like the Evo—or the Knuckle, for that matter—except for the wider fins, which nearly fill the vee, and the new and stronger mounting face, at lower right, for the primary drive and gearbox. *Courtesy Harley-Davidson Archives*

The Dynas get the Two Cam conventional carburetor, while the top-of-the-line FL models have the fuel injection from the Evo.

The extra displacement, more efficient valve gear, and better intake and exhaust flow added up to more power, which meant more heat, so the heads and barrels got extra finning.

This is probably on e of the most noticeable of the Two Cam's features and, in the author's opinion, makes this an attractive and impressive engine, while at the same time, it's so obviously a Harley-Davidson that the non-believers probably won't notice anything different unless old and new are side by side.

What doesn't show is another radical step, the elimination of the timed breather.

This begins with physics. Those two pistons gallumping up and down in sequence create tremendous pressure variations inside the cases. Since the Year Dot, H-D engines have used this pressure to clear oil from the engine and push it back to the tank.

Not any more. The R&D team rigged all manner of test systems and measured where the pressure and oil were and how they influenced

The betting, inside and out, is that only the educated few will spot the Two Cam engine in the 1999 Dyna Glides, which is just what The Motor Company wants. *Courtesy Harley-Davidson Archives*

each other and shaped the internal passages so that now, with the oil pump sized to collect two-point-five times as much oil as it delivers, over-scavenging in other words, there's no need to stop and start the air flow in the engine.

Meanwhile, and for a second aid to cooling, there are passages to spray oil on the bottoms of the piston crowns.

Where The Two Cam Goes

Half this is classic Motor Company. As has been done since the days of the first Two Cam (about which more later) Harley-Davidson has been careful to not do all things new at once. The first isolation engine mounts were used with the older Shovelhead engine Then the Evo went into the proven chassis, for instance.

Same here, with the second half being classic marketing. The Two Cam for the 1999 model year will power the Dyna and FL lines, while the Evo will be used in the Softtails, for now at least. Putting the new engine in the flagship means it's important, and that the buyers of the Two Cam models will have bragging rights.

At the same literal time, the new engine uses the existing gearbox, chain primary drive, belt final drive, frame, brakes, wheels, suspension and so forth. The new cases are lighter and stronger, while the heads and cylinders simply fill what used to be space, and the warranty office need only be concerned with the new engine.

The Name Game

This is classic Man Bites Dog, in that at this writing The Motor Company hasn't taken advantage of its own history, surely the first time the current management has failed to do so.

How so? For H-D's first five or six decades, the engine code letters were changed with displacement. The inlet-over-exhaust 61 V-Twin was the J, for instance, while the 74-cubic inch version was the JD. When the Knucklehead was a 61, it was the E or EL. When it was enlarged to 74 cubic inches, it became the F or FL. The 45-cubic inch K model was given a longer stroke, grew to 54 cubic inches and became the KH.

But twenty years ago, the letters had become the models, as in FLT, FLH, FXST, and the engine remained the F when it grew from 74 to 80 cubic inches.

Too bad. Back in the days of the J, the basic engine came with one, central camshaft. They needed more power and control, so the engine got two cams, speaking of uncanny coincidence, and the two-cam Harley was the JH, the 61, or the JDH, the 74.

If ever there was a chance to cash in on history, this has to be it. The Two Cam 88 was born to be labeled the JD, and then when they soup it up with fuel injection, it should be the JDG. Or so it seems from here.

Meanwhile, the classic usage the fans can use, beginning this instant, is to call it the Two Cam, as has been done here and was done back in 1928: The official names were Two Cam 61 and Two Cam 74.

(Not twin cams, okay? That's term used only by tweed-caps guys in imported sports cars.)

About Those (Future) Stars

As mentioned earlier, the Two Cam 88 is so new all we have at press time is riding impressions and predictions.

Both are good news, mostly. The guys who have ridden the 1999s with the Two Cam engine say they are crisper, cleaner and stronger, with no more noise or vibration.

It's safe to say that the Two Cam will be a better engine period.

It's just as safe to say Harley-Davidson has raised the ceiling. The new engine will be an improvement, people will want to have the newest thing and while H-D has ramped up its production capacity to keep supply in tune with demand, there may well be a waiting list for the Two Cam.

Let's not overstate this, but the added demand for the new engine will have an effect on demand for the 1999s with the Evo engine and for the older models, the used Evos.

What this will mean for individual bikes can't be put into numbers, nor should we revise the ratings elsewhere in this book.

If this could be graphed, the gap would be at the top. That is, those in search of a clean 1968 FLH or a 1971 FX with the red, white, and blue paint, won't need to look more diligently nor pay extra because the Two Cam is on the market.

But the Two Cam may well ease some Evos off the waiting list, easing demand for used Evos of later vintage.

Don't disregard the ratings, in sum, but be prepared to enjoy the Two Cam, or to gaining bargaining power if you're still looking for a Shovelhead or an Evo.

Appendix

People and Places

The late Charley Thompson had the best training any president of the Harley-Davidson Motor Company ever had.

He was a schoolteacher in Louisville, Kentucky, and he got interested in motorcycles. He got so interested he bought the local dealership. He was so good at being a dealer he became H-D's national sales manager. He was so good at being sales manager that he became H-D's president.

Charley Thompson knew his stuff.

The most important thing a dealer can have for his customers, Thompson used to say, is something to do with their motorcycles. He was right, as he usually was, which is why we'll deal here with how to find fun on your motorcycle.

But first, we need to find the machine.

The Used Bike Market

Thanks in no small part to the popularity and increased production of Harleys during the past 10 or so years, a used late-model example is as close as your local newspaper.

This is a fairly recent development. When Harleys got hot, when they suddenly were In, there was a great rush to buy, and the demand was so strong the dealers ran out. Take a number, they said, and there were used bikes selling above list, simply because you had to wait for a new one and the open road was calling.

By now, in most parts of the country and the world, this is no longer so. There are enough Evo Sportsters, FLTs, Softails, and the like on the market that the sellers are in competition, and you can get a sound, low-mileage example at a fair price or better.

There's also a chance for strokes of luck. If, underline the *if,* you find the unappreciated classic, the local paper is one of the best places to find it.

Why? Because the bike is unappreciated in that the seller doesn't know that, for instance, the 1971 Superglide is as rare as it is. It's old, the paint's faded, it won't start, therefore the price is low.

In the middle, so to speak, with a larger mix of models and years than the local paper usually gets, are the dealerships.

H-D is big business now, and the motorcycle stores are more like car dealerships where the best way to move the new out is to take the used in. Your local Harley store—and by now surely there's one near you—will probably have at least a modest supply of used scoots.

Adding to that, most dealerships have bulletin boards. Owners of bikes for sale are allowed—encouraged if the dealer knows his or her stuff—to post ads and photos. You probably won't stumble across a really rare bike this way, but the board is worth checking.

Sort of in the middle here are the various traders, those publications seen at the convenience stores, the ones with the editions for cars, trucks, boats, RVs, and motorcycles. The traders are something of a culture in themselves, and I don't recall I've ever seen anything I wanted in one. Nor are they published in all areas. But, one never knows, so as Joe Bob would say, check it out.

We are working back in time, if not up in price. The more rare Harleys are offered in publications that are more difficult to find than the local papers or traders are.

Yup, that's why it's called a field meet. This is 1939 and out of our time frame, but it sets the stage. One of the ways motorcyclists combated the hooligan image in the 1930s was to ride sedately to a place, an open field for instance, and engage in low-speed, low-risk fun. *Courtesy Harley-Davidson Archives*

The Publications

We have an overlap here, in that the publications with ads for collectible motorcycles also have, to one degree or another, articles of interest to those collecting the bikes offered in the ads.

Leaning most heavily in the ad direction is

Walneck's Classic Cycle Trader
P.O. Box 9059
Clearwater, FL 34623

The magazine has lots of ads, jumbled together. You find later models and antiques, machines and parts, road and racing one after the other, plus reprints of old tests. You learn more than you wanted to know, which is fun.

Old Bike Journal
P.O. Box 391
Mount Morris, IL 74107

This one has the same format, ads and articles, except that often the articles are new but about older machines. (Worth noting here that neither of the above deals only in Harley-Davidsons, but heck, there's nothing wrong with liking old motorcycles for themselves, eh?)

The Rest of the Press

This has to be progress, I think. When the original buyer's guide was done, 12 or 13 years ago, a lot of time and effort were devoted to being sure the new Harley nut could find facts and reading material. Since then, the supply has (at least) caught up with demand.

There are several monthly magazines dealing with Harleys. There's *American Iron*, *Big Twin*, *American Rider*, and *Iron Horse*, just off the top of my desk.

183

This young lady on a Harley-Davidson Hummer, the two-stroke single with which H-D lured the young after World War II , is dropping Ping-Pong balls into a cup while weaving between a line of cups. Standard field meet stuff. *Dave Gooley*

They are a lot alike while at the same time each has its own focus. Because of the H-D boom the newsstands have found space for these and maybe some others, which means those who are interested can learn more firsthand.

With two exceptions.

One is a monthly newspaper called *Thunder Press*. It's all Harley, really all H-D with the sole exception being a department in the back devoted to Buell.

The founder, Reg Kitrelle, began as a bike nut and went into business on that basis. He seems to know Charley Thompson's rule. First, *Thunder Press* has the biggest and best schedule of coming events: races, rallies, runs, shows, campouts, the works. They are listed month by month and by region, as in southern and northern California, the Northwest and the Southwest (meaning Oregon, Washington state, and Arizona), and the Rockies.

This is neat stuff. The paper covers mostly events and parts, with a tech column and gossip. Beyond that, they are working to expand. There's an East Coast edition in the works, and clearly the plan is to go national, with sections for each, well, section.

There are good classified ads, from private parties and the giant dealerships, and lots of new parts and good sources for stuff like ramps, stands, and used parts: I have bought from several of the advertisers, paying cash just like any other reader, and got what I paid for.

Further, Kitrelle creates events. Events? As in?

The Playing Fields

Motorcycling has been a social sport ever since the first enthusiasts got together for Sunday rides, picnics, and such.

When speeds were sedate and power was limited, there used to be hill climbs and endurance runs for everybody. Then it got so you really didn't dare open 'er up on the public highway, not as part of a club meeting.

Races and hill climbs went their own way and the social contests became more like pranks, as in tossing inner tubes into barrels, or trying to bite a hot dog dangling from a string, or seeing if you could ride your bike up a plank and pause to tip said plank and ride down it, like a teeter-totter.

Perhaps the most popular contest was the slow race, where contestants see who can be the last rider to cross a line without putting down a foot.

All this went into a decline several years ago. But *Thunder Press* has brought it back with a national slow race series. Since then, working with Buell and H-D, *Thunder Press* has invented a solo event, one rider at a time speeding around a tight, paved course, as in parking lot, against the clock.

It's proven safer than it sounds.

And that's only part of the action. There are road runs where everybody meets and rides slowly to someplace else for food, drink, and often music. There are events with food and music but also with contests and games. Everybody rides there and home at their own pace, in their own groups.

There are camp-outs, to which you ride and meet, or sometimes meet and ride there. There are shows and concerts, which need no explanation.

There are toy runs, almost always before Christmas, where the price of admission to the party is a toy. There are charity runs on the same theme. There are poker runs, with stops to pick up cards and the best hand gets a prize and then, there's food and drink.

There are real runs, by which I mean the riders gather and head for the hills and the curves and the open road, which are still there if you know where to look. (This is written Monday morning. Yesterday I was on a real ride, with the local chapter of the Antique Motorcycle Club of America. There were Pans and Knucks and early Shovels, along with Triumph twins, Kawasaki triples, Ducati 916s, and Honda Blackbirds. Glorious sunshine, challenging, empty roads. Suffice it to say here that I got lost and realized that if I had to get lost, I couldn't have done it at a better place or in a better time. I returned to the route in time for lunch, my XR working like a champ. Clearly I am in this to go riding, but I digress.)

What we have at this writing is the sort of problem we should all have all the time: an oversupply of good clean fun.

You can't do it all. What you can do—should do—is go to the various events and learn firsthand what happens there and what's the most fun for you. Ignore opinion. (Spousal opinion excepted, of course.) Restore and show it, fine. Restore and ride it, just as fine. Ditto for racing and rebuilding. No matter what you do, though, you'll need to find where it can be done.

Which circles us back to *Thunder Press*. If you live in the West, check the H-D store or the shop that's not allowed to use the logo while they repair the product. If they don't have the paper, or if you're out of the area, write to *Thunder Press*, 12 Camp Evers Lane, Scotts Valley, CA 95066 and ask where and how you can get a copy.

What, When, and Where

The other publication is *Cycle News*, which has been in business for 30 years. Their business is racing. *CN* has tests, products, industry news, and gossip, but nearly everybody reads it for the race reports, which include world and national dirt track, road racing, motocross, and so forth.

Plus, *CN* has an excellent calendar and the coming events there aren't the same ones you'll find in *Thunder Press*. *Cycle News* has pages of small ads and classifieds, with a special section for collectors; the emphasis is on competition, not road machines.

CN is seldom found on newsstands and is mostly handled by motorcycle dealerships, as in the Big Four. If there's no such shop near you, you can write to:

Cycle News
P.O. Box 5084
Costa Mesa, CA 92628
Or take the easy way and call the free number: (800) 831-2220.

Joining the Clubs

This is quite a circle, eh? Still another source for coming events is *American Motorcyclist*, the magazine of the American Motorcyclist

Nowadays we're more likely to see scenes like this: the line of motorcycles waiting to take off for Blue Groove Two, the second get-together for Buells, Sportsters, and modified racing bikes.

Sporting group rides are generally open to bikes by class, not make. This is the motel parking lot before Blue Groove Two, with Cyclones, Thunderbolts, a rare RSS1200 second from the back on the left and up front on the right, a fearsome special, homemade frame powered by a big-block V2.

Association, which means you get the magazine when (and not until) you join the club.

If you wish to. It's possible to be, in the title used by A. Conan Doyle, a solitary cyclist. Or you can ride with friends and not go through the bother of a club or clubs.

Except, working from the top, joining a club isn't just doing something for yourself. The AMA sponsors and organizes lots of road events. The club has its own museum and its own annual festivals. The AMA sanctions the national and regional professional and amateur races for flat track, road racing, enduros, hill climbs, motocross, name it.

The AMA is also a political organization. This may come as a shock, but motorcyclists are a special interest group, right along with environmentalists, old folks, and everybody else to whom the laws apply.

We, which I say here because I am a member of the AMA, have lobbyists and specialists. And we represent motorcycles, as a sport and as a hobby, never mind the useful part (and don't think for a moment that we got in the car-pool lane without the AMA's expertise).

There are millions of motorcyclists. There are a couple of hundred thousand AMA members, which is to say literally millions of bikers benefit from the AMA's work, which is to say freeloaders, okay? Join.

American Motorcyclist Association
33 Collegeview Road
Westerville, OH 43081

Probably the next most important club for the Harley rider/owner is the Harley Owner's Group, always shortened to HOG. (Oh dear, historical marker coming up. For reasons now lost in time, the big Harley twins are sometimes known as Hogs. Newspaper and television reporters usually call all Harleys by the nickname, but strictly speaking the inside FL crowd takes offense at that.)

The Motor Company clearly picked the club name to reflect the historical nickname. And don't worry, you're welcome in HOG even if you have a Sportster or maybe even a Sprint or Topper.

HOG is a national club at the top and sponsors events, but most of the actual job activity is done at the local level, which means the locals get backing from a dealership. Naturally, how well the club runs and how much it offers the members varies with the dealer and the helpers the dealer provides, at least as much as with the members themselves.

My suggestion here is to check and see if your nearest dealership has a HOG chapter, and if so, go to a meeting or on the next ride, to learn if you're going to have a good time if you join. If you have a good time, join. If they go too fast or too slow or you don't like the atmosphere for whatever reason, don't join.

Beyond that, there are other specialties, for instance the two national vintage racing clubs:

American Historic Racing Motorcycle Association
P.O. Box 882
Wausau, WI 54402

AHRMA began as a road-racing club, closely linked with the AMA. It's the largest and the most national, and there are now divisions for road racing, dirt track, motocross, and trials.

Vintage Dirt Track Racers Association
26750 County Road 122
Ramah, CO 80832

VDTRA is, as the name implies, a dirt track club. It began in the Midwest when AHRMA had no dirt track races. VDTRA is still mostly Midwest; it does the annual races at Sturgis, for instance. VDTRA is comprised of people who raced when young and still enjoy it. VDTRA is lower key, as in less emphasis on winning, fewer fights over rules, than I've found in AHRMA.

The two clubs are sort of rivals; in 1997 both had races at or near Daytona Beach. I belong to both clubs and raced both series, using the same bike, my XR-750, but I had to swap white number plates in AHRMA for yellow plates in VDTRA.

(Still another bit of history and human quirks. Way back when, the AMA had green, red, yellow, and white number plates, with white reserved for the experts, the professionals. You had to work your way up and guys who earned that white plate were justifiably proud. The Sturgis rally grew out of a club of such riders, the White Plate Association, and now you know where that odd name came from.)

What that meant was that when vintage racing began, a lot of chaps like myself, riders who've earned the T-shirt that says, "The Older I Get, The Faster I Was," didn't mind at all being allowed to run white plates.

Not surprisingly, the retired racers who'd earned those plates were a bit put out that those who hadn't earned them acted as if they had. It's probably simplistic to say this all proves AHRMA is run by guys who didn't earn white plates and VDTRA is run by guys who did, but I suspect there's a lot of that involved.

Next, local clubs. We, people I mean, are social beings. We like being with people like us and there have been motorcycle clubs for nearly a century. At this date, there are clubs within clubs, and clubs that cross the usual lines; clubs for one make, clubs for one purpose, as in touring or racing, and clubs for an area, say a city or county.

There are too many to list, as they say in the ads. But the AMA, *Thunder Press*, and a couple of other publications carry long and complete lists of clubs. Or, check the bulletin board at the dealership.

Sources and Parts

Mention was made earlier of the Great Divide between the Shovelhead models, XL and FL, and the Evolution models. The change was major, a

Other events are back in parade mode. This is Daytona, with a large and mixed-brand crowd waiting to ride from the town to the track, while thousands wave and the police let the bikers run the lights (no kidding). It's all fun, which is what motorcycling is supposed to be about.

milestone in Harley-Davidson history. The division also extends to parts, which is to say there are H-D dealerships and shops where they don't have much interest in the older bikes.

The good news here is that there has arisen a whole other set of people who care a lot, and who work at it.

In general, the dealers fall into two categories. The first category includes dealers like the one nearest me (I'm glad to say), where they don't stock the older parts or even the more rare items from the current line but will happily order them for you. Yes, it takes a week or so and you pay now, take delivery later.

The other type has already sold all the older stuff. They will refer you to the shop to whom they sold it. This system works, sort of, except that it can lead to some inconvenience for riders. For example, that's what happened at the dealership second-closest to me, and the independent shop that bought all the old XL parts is on the other side of the county.

The good news in general is that there have been farsighted enthusiasts who've preserved the old parts by buying them before they were pitched. What's more, the Harley-Davidson business has become so big there are huge national companies making and selling just about any part you can imagine.

Everything is out there. As the genius mechanic who was my boyhood hero had on his shop wall, All You Need Is the Money.

And some more advice. A lot of these reproduced parts aren't quite as good as the originals, and some are better.

Who are these good guys?

Arlen Ness, for one. Most of his work is done in the chopper or custom mode, for outrageous Big Twins, but he does supply some normal bits, and they are top grade. Here is his address:

Arlen Ness
16520 E. 14th St.
San Leandro, CA 94578

The best of the mail order places is J&P Cycles. I came to this conclusion firsthand, when I realized it was faster for me to call in the order to the warehouse in Iowa and have them ship the box UPS, right to my house, than it was to order the parts from the dealership. J&P has just about all the old parts you could need for your older FLH and pages of extras for your Dyna Glide. You can reach J&P at

J&P Cycles
P.O. Box 138
Anamosa, IA 52205

Or you can call the toll-free number, (800) 397-4844, and you'll get the sprocket overnight.

Racing and sports fans will find it useful to join a club, except it's not the usual club. The Competition Network for Harleys is really a network, made up of people who own XRs, CRs, KRs, and Buells. There's an occasional newsletter with ads, but more useful still is the list of members and what they have, so when your CR blows up you can call all the CR guys and shop for a new connecting rod. The Network's address is

Competition Network
P.O. Box 95881
Hoffman Estates, IL 60194

For the really rare stuff, the court of last resort is

Finder's Service
454-458 West Lincoln Highway
Chicago Heights, IL 60411

The finder's service is an offshoot of an old-line H-D agency. It can be a bother because it requires the factory parts numbers, details, and occasionally a deposit, if the part in question is expensive.

But they say they've found 98 percent of the parts they've been asked to find. When your first-year FX needs only the final three pieces to be perfect, the bother is worth it.

And Now . . . Over to You

When I first began the original H-D buyer's guide 14 years ago, it was the proverbial "They thought the project was a waste of time." Nobody would care, they said, and the market's not big enough to justify the work.

Well. I guess we showed them. Harley-Davidson has gone from the edge of disaster to a worldwide symbol of success. The cliché has gone from the Harley owner as beer-guzzling outlaw to the Harley owner as Gucci-shod chief executive officer. There are both now, just as there were both then.

What's changed is the numbers. There are literally more than a million Harley owners now. It's easier to find the model that you choose, and easier to restore it, repair it, or find a place to enjoy it.

What hasn't changed is the slogan I used the first time: Get on your bike and do what you like!

Letters from Home

According to legend there are only two men who fully understand Harley-Davidson's system of identifying models with letters. One man has retired, folklore goes on, and the other has forgotten the details.

History's version is almost as much fun. When Harley and the Davidsons first went into production they used numbers, as in the Model 5 was made in the fifth year the firm made motorcycles. Letters were for engines or options: The 9A was the belt-drive single, circa 1913; the 9B was the 1913 single with chain drive, and the 9C was the V-twin. In 1916 they switched to numbers for the calendar year.

The system used now traces back to the mainstay intake-over-exhaust V-twin, whose basic designation in 1921 was Model J. The J displaced 61 cubic inches. When the factory offered a 74-cid version, that was called the JD. The original J engine had one camshaft for the four valves. When the later version arrived it had two camshafts and was offered as a 61 or a 74, respectively designated JH or JDH. The JDH had different wheels and a higher state of tune, but you could order the fancy parts with the plain engine, and when you did that, the model was the JL.

Note here that the letters seem to have been piled on a table in the drafting department and when a designer needed to distinguish one model from another, he picked up a letter and applied it.

(Yeah, sure you could claim *D* stood for displacement, but what about *H* for two cams or *L* for sport? The best guess for those early years has to be random chance.)

Letters that did stand for something first appeared in the catalog, if not daily use, in 1952. The 74 was offered with hand clutch and foot shift, as opposed to the other way round. To distinguish between the new and the old, which could still be ordered, the new style was the FLF, the second *F* meaning foot, and the old one was the FL. In 1973, when electric start became an option for the Superglide, the optioned model was the FXE, *E* for electric and so on until the *B* for belt, *WG* for Wide Glide, and so forth.

Parallel to all this have been the exceptions. The J series used *D* for displacement and *H* for added cams, but when the K series grew from 45 to 54 cid, the new engine was the KH, not the KD. We can probably guess why: When the E series grew from 61 to 74 cid it wasn't called the EH, eh? But if 61 to 74 meant *E* to *F*, why not recycle *J* for when it went from 74 to 80? (*G* was the servi-car and *H* was already in use.)

And so it's gone for 75 years. We can look it up. We can see or deduce the reasons for the exceptions. What we can't do is crack the code because there doesn't seem to be one.

With all that out of the way, and ignoring minor options like reverse gear or hand shift, here are the letters and models for which they stand in our time frame:

Touring Models

Designation	Year	Model
FL	1966	Fleet 74
FLH	1966	Customer 74
FLHB*	1966	Electra Glide (B dropped in 1970)
FLP/FLHP	1966	74 with Police Package
FLT	1980	Tour Glide
FLHT	1983	FLT frame, old-style fairing
FLHX/S	1984	Final FLH frame, Shovelhead engine
FLHTC/FLTC	1984	First V-2 engine, with extras
FLHS	1987	FLT with windshield
FLHTCI	1995	Fuel injection added
FLHR	1994	Road King
FLTRI	1998	Road Glide (frame-mount fairing)

*Note: The *B* for battery and the *F* for foot shift were part of the model designation. They don't appear on the cases. The *P* for police package was stamped on the cases during the years when the VIN began with the model code.

Super Glides

Designation	Year	Model
FX	1971	Original Super Glide
FXE	1973	Electric start becomes an option